Silken Threads Lacquer Thrones

BIRMINGHAM CITY
UNIVERSITY
DISCARDED

Susan Conway

SILKEN THREADS LACQUER THRONES

Lan Na Court Textiles

BIRMINGHAM CITY LIBRARY UNIVERSITY

Delicated to Constance Howard and Marianne Straub.

This book would not have been possible without the generous assistance of many people and organizations to whom the publisher is deeply grateful. We would like to thank the following:

The Bank of Thailand Museum Textile Collections, Chiang Mai; The James H. W. Thompson Foundation, The Siam Society under Royal Patronage, Darabhirom Museum, Chiang Mai; National Museum, Bangkok; National Museum, Chiang Mai; Hariphunchai National Museum, Lamphun; The Oriental and India Collections, The British Library, London; The Asian Collections, National Museums and Galleries on Merseyside, Liverpool;

Barbie Campbell-Cole, Khun Chaba Suwatmekin, Khun Chutinart Songwattana, Chao Dararatana Na Lamphun, Khun Duangchit Taweesri, Khun Paothong Thongchua,

Payap University Archive, Chiang Mai; National Archives, Bangkok; Presbyterian Historical Society, Philadelphia; The Pitt Rivers Museum, Oxford; The Green Centre for Non-Western Art at the Royal Pavilion Art Gallery and Museums, Brighton; Public Records Office, Kew, London; White Lotus and River Books Archive.

First published and distributed in Thailand in 2002 by
River Books Co., Ltd
396 Maharaj Road, Tatien,
Bangkok 10200, Thailand
Tel: (66) 2 225 4963, 2 225 0139, 2 6221900
Fax: (66) 2 225 3861
Email: orders@ksc.th.com
Website: www.riverbooksbk.com

Distributed in the rest of the world
(excluding North America) by
Thames & Hudson Ltd.
181A High Holborn, London WC1V 7QX

A River Books Production.
Copyright text and collective work © River Books 2002
Copyright photographs © River Books
and Susan Conway 2002,
except where indicated otherwise.

All rights reserved. No part of this publication may be reproduced or transmitted in any form or by any means, electronic or mechanical, including photocopy, recording or any other information storage and retrieval system, without prior permission in writing from the publisher.

British Library Cataloguing-in-Publication Data.
A catalogue record for this book is available from the British Library.

Special Editor Henry Ginsburg
Editor Narisa Chakrabongse
Design Supadee Ruangsakvichit and NaHaPa
Production Paisarn Piemmettawat
Additional photography Pattana Decha

ISBN 974 8225 65 8

Printed and bound in Thailand by Amarin Printing and Publishing.

Contents

Introduction:
A Hidden Culture   6

Chapter One
The People of this Muang   16

Chapter Two
Princes and Politics   34

Chapter Three
Culture and Design   54

Chapter Four
Status, Protection, Ethnicity:
Lan Na Court Dress 1781–1871   76

Chapter Five
Power Dressing 1871–1919   132

Chapter Six
Textile Design   178

Chapter Seven
Nineteenth Century Trade   222

Chapter Eight
Craft Workers at the Court   240

Appendices
The Royal Families of Lan Na   262
Acknowledgements   266
Bibliography & Archives   267
Glossary   276
Index   278

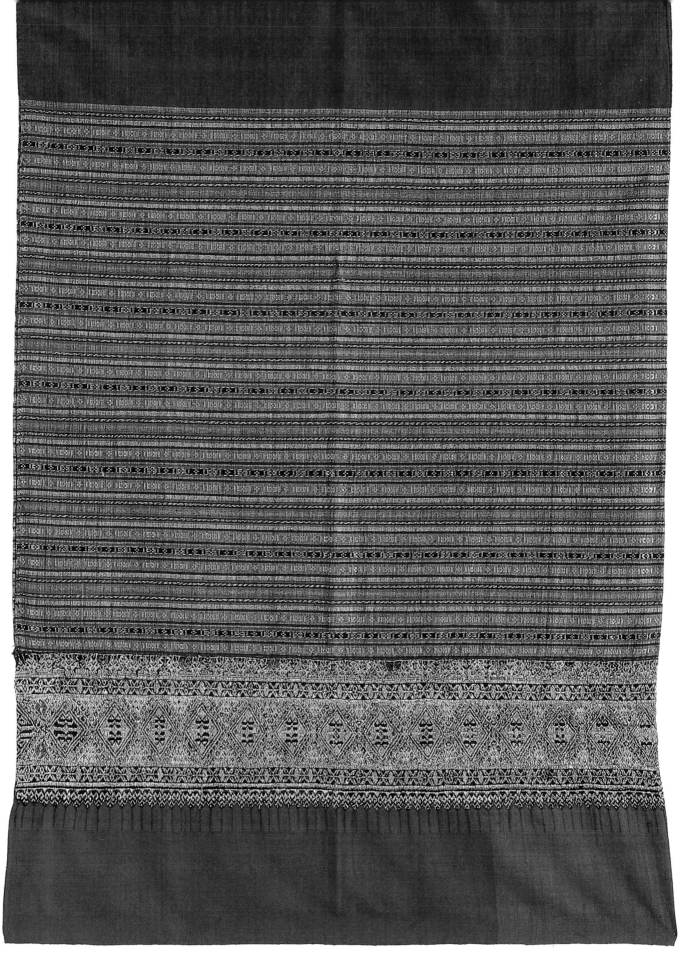

6

A Hidden Culture

Inland Southeast Asia has not attracted the kind of attention devoted to coastal Southeast Asia where throughout history foreigners arrived in droves to trade and make conquests. The inland states were isolated by mountains and primary forest that presented formidable physical barriers. The rivers were only navigable in the rainy season and even then rapids, rock pools and eddies meant journeys were fraught with danger. If you survived the rivers, there was danger of disease and attack by wild animals in the forest. Before the nineteenth century most of the knowledge acquired by Europeans was hearsay. Yet behind the physical barriers there existed a fascinating and unique culture ruled by princes whose power radiated outwards from valley settlements into the distant hills, becoming weaker or even not recognised at all, in the outer reaches of the territory.

The court dress of Lan Na that formed part of inland Southeast Asia, is a fascinating subject for study. The way the royal families were clothed and how they decorated their bodies reflected their view of themselves and the way they wanted to display themselves to others. Through dress they exhibited their Buddhist and spirit religion beliefs, their politics, ethnic identity and their wealth and authority, and this in turn defined them as belonging to a particular time in history. As times changed, so did dress and interestingly this affected men more than women.

Portraits of royalty at the Lan Na courts can be found in scenes from mural paintings in Buddhist temples and in the text of the Buddhist chronicles. The princes exerted some authority over the artists who painted the murals and over the monk scribes who wrote the chronicles. However, in the nineteenth century, outsiders from Europe and America produced written accounts, portraits and photographs that complimented, or in some cases challenged indigenous versions of local history and court life.

Lan Na *phasin* woven in silk with silver and gold metal thread. (Bank of Thailand Museum, Chiang Mai)

A Lan Na prince as portrayed by a temple mural artist, Wat Wiang Ta, Phrae.

At the beginning of the nineteenth century Lan Na was made up of the major principalities of Chiang Mai, Lamphun, Lampang, Phrae and Nan. Smaller political centres existed in the hinterland, ruled by dependent princes and chiefs who reproduced their own versions of the royal courts of Lan Na (*see map*). Under these secondary polities there were yet smaller dependencies. Areas of influence between principalities were fluid and large areas of primary forest remained uninhabited or formed a habitat for migratory groups in the hills. However, the division between hill and valley people was subject to change and migratory hill people sometimes settled and intermarried with valley farmers. Meanwhile, leading families formed marital alliances with the rulers of surrounding inland principalities with whom they traded and at times waged war. A complex history involving conquests, movements of people and intermarriage has further contributed to this unique and diverse culture.

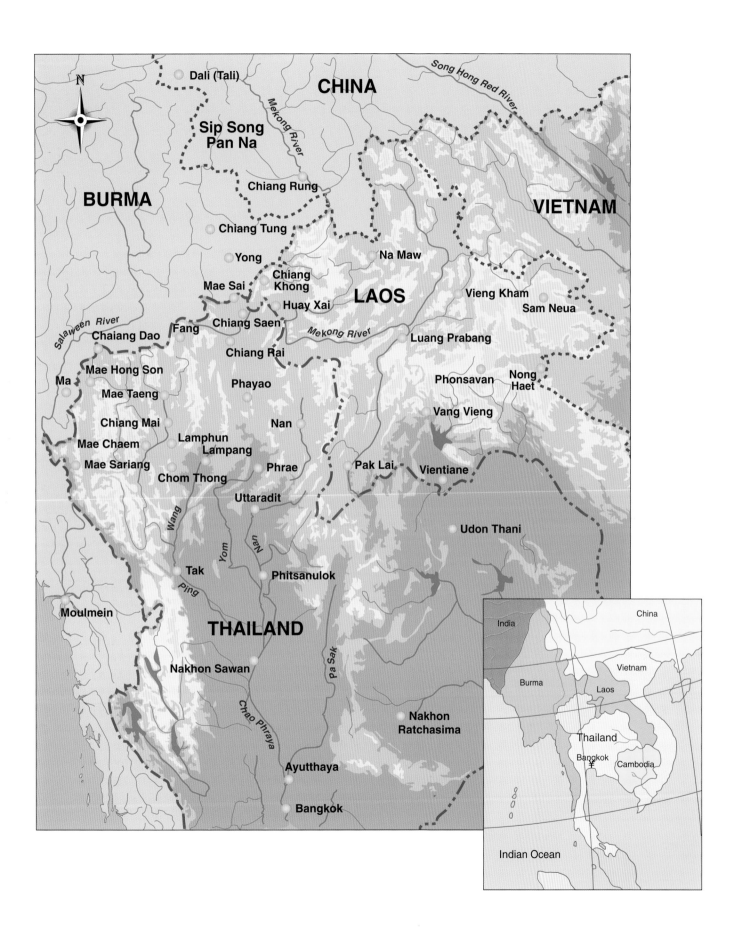

Wat Pong Yang Kok in Lan Na
architectural style.

Right: The *stupa* at Wat Chamdevi,
Lamphun, which was restored in the
early 13th century.

From the time of King Mengrai (1259-1317) founder of Lan Na, diplomatic, economic and cultural ties were secured with surrounding kingdoms and principalities, particularly Sipsong Pan Na (Xishuangbanna Autonomous Prefecture), eastern Shan States (Burma) and Luang Prabang (western Laos). Lan Na was independent until the 16th century when the Burmese invaded and remained for over two hundred years although at times they appointed indigenous rulers as governors under Burmese authority. The Burmese were finally expelled in 1774, by the combined forces of the Lan Na Tai, their allies in the surrounding principalities and the Siamese. In the nineteenth century Lan Na was tributary to Siam and by the third quarter of the century the Siamese were eroding the authority of the princes. In 1892 Lan Na was integrated with the kingdom of Siam. In 1939 the kingdom was renamed the Kingdom of Thailand and from then on the people of Thailand are referred to as Thai.

From the time of its establishment in the 13th century, Lan Na and the surrounding inland principalities had developed a culture markedly different from India, China, Burma and Siam. This fact has been overlooked by those who relied on nineteenth century European concepts of the region, framed perfectly in the British expression 'Lesser India'. Colonial India was not culturally compatible with the nations to her east, particularly the inland states, a fact that was not understood by the British who, because of the way the Empire was administered, mentally grafted them together. Officers of the Indian administrative service were transferred to Burma where they interpreted local culture and customs through the traditions of India. Items of dress and textiles from the inland states sent to Britain in the colonial era, or later bequeathed to museums by relatives, often ended up in collections under the umbrella of India or Burma and were catalogued accordingly. Textiles and items of dress from Lan Na and the surrounding inland states were also identified as coming from Siam because foreign residents, who had no knowledge of their provenance, purchased them in Bangkok. It was the middle of the twentieth century before Lan Na dress and textiles, collected by or donated to museums, were correctly documented.

The attitude to inland Southeast Asia that the colonial era fostered is found in many texts that focus on Indian art. Goetz (1959: 24) who wrote in the immediate post-colonial era, is a typical example. In describing the art of Nepal, Burma, Malaya, Sumatra, Java, Bali, Siam, Cambodia and Annam (Vietnam) he wrote:

seen from the angle of any civilisation, all the diversity is reduced to a fundamental unity, to what we can only call Indian art.

From today's perspective this is a gross simplification. Although Southeast Asian coastal states traded with India and were profoundly affected by Indian culture and religion, they developed their own artistic style and iconography. As to the inland states, the Indian impact was considerably less significant as these regions were isolated from direct contact and their links with India were tenuous. Buddhism in Lan Na can be linked to Sri Lanka and ultimately to India but while fulfilling certain religious requirements, the iconography has a distinctive Lan Na form.

Cultural connections with China have sometimes been overplayed because tribute was paid to China in the 15th century and Chinese textiles were worn at some inland courts. However, accounts by American Presbyterian missionaries stress a lack of Han Chinese presence in southwest China. Interestingly, they describe that particular region as having cultural similarities with Lan Na, forming part of the network of states whose subjects intermarried and traded. Certainly there are similarities in the textiles and dress of southwest China and Lan Na particularly shared weaving techniques and iconography. Weavers in north Thailand today recognise these similarities and as a result view the weavers of southwest China as distant relatives.

When Lan Na was unified with Siam in 1892 the issue of cultural difference was not addressed although the people of Lan Na were distanced from Siam by culture and by political and social traditions. However their traditional links with the surrounding inland states were significantly weakened when France annexed western Laos in 1893, including territory that was part of Nan. Meanwhile by 1895 the British had established effective control over the Shan States. After World War II borders were closed between China, Laos, Burma, the Shan States and

The Lord Buddha and monks, temple mural painting, Wat Luang Rat Santan, Phayao. This wall painting on dry fresco was damaged when the temple collapsed a few years ago.

Women at a temple ceremony in
Chiang Mai, 1981.

Right: Musicians taking part in a
procession as part of a temple ceremony
in Chiang Mai, 1981.

north Thailand.[1] Their re-opening in recent times has enabled academics
to explore the cultural similarities that exist in the area.[2]

The Lan Na people practiced spirit religion and from the twelfth
century, were champions of Theravada Buddhism. In the 14th century the
Venerable Sumana of Sukhothai established a Sinhalese Theravada order
in Lamphun and then in Chiang Mai. This Buddhist sect became the
leading intellectual and cultural force in the kingdom for over two
centuries. From the 15th century, monks, particularly from forest
dwelling communities, and sponsored envoys, travelled to Sri Lanka to
study and bring back to Lan Na what was considered to be an
uncorrupted form of Sinhalese Theravada Buddhism. This relatively
egalitarian form of Buddhism affected the structure of Lan Na society and
the way the princes governed. In contrast, neighbouring Siam was
receptive to Indian and Khmer concepts of royalty, and a more
hierarchical form of religion and society developed there.

Sinhalese Theravada Buddhism remains relatively faithful to what is
considered to be the original teaching of the Buddha. This involves the
concept of human life in a process of continuous change. The aim of
religious practice is to be without ego, freeing the self from the
materialism of the world, a goal expressed in the rules that govern the life
of Buddhist monks. The ultimate goal is to reach nirvana, the extinction
of suffering embodied in the cycle of birth and rebirth. Lay members,
including royalty, accept a number of precepts that include attending
temple ceremonies and feeding and clothing the monks. In this way the
lay community make 'merit'. The concept of merit involves reaching a
happy and virtuous state of mind in this life, and gaining spiritual grace
for the next life. Members of the royal family and the wealthy made merit
by building temples and monuments and maintaining religious
communities. Women, including female royalty made merit by
presenting robes, bed sheets and pillow covers to the monks, and

Modern temple decorations (*tung yai*) made from plastic and coloured wool.

Left: Buddha images covered in gold leaf.

banners, coffin covers and other woven textiles for use in temple ceremonies. Some princesses were excellent weavers and produced these items themselves while others relied on their attendants and slaves. Women at all levels of society presented textiles to the temple at special gift ceremonies *(kathin)* held during Buddhist Lent. It is an indication of the value placed on weaving that families often gave finely woven pieces of cloth to the temple, in memory of a deceased weaver.

The Lan Na princes and their subjects also practised spirit religion that deals in the world of the supernatural. The religion focussed on mystical symbolic diagrams *(yantra)* and rituals passed down from one generation of spirit doctors to the next. In Lan Na, as in other societies, the basic formula was adapted to suit local beliefs. Women played a major role in rites associated with malevolent spirits and possession. However when particularly powerful forces were at stake, such as appeasing the spirits of a city or of the state, it was a prince who performed the rites.

The book begins by defining the people of Lan Na *(khon muang)* and the immigrants who in the 19th century contributed to this rich and diverse culture. It then identifies the princes who ruled the country and the myths and legends surrounding them. Their relationship with the neighbouring inland states and with Siam deeply affected the way they governed and ultimately led to the end of the Lan Na dynasty. Chapter three analyses textile production and the roots of design. The following chapters examine dress, textiles and regalia worn by royalty living at the Lan Na courts. These chapters also record the dramatic change in male court dress, in contrast to the conservatism of female dress, that occurred towards the end of the 19th century. Dress and textiles were made at the Lan Na courts and indigenous materials and imported yarn, fabrics and ideas were used in their production. Foreign princesses marrying into the Lan Na royal family brought their own distinctive forms of dress to add to the diversity of court dress at that time.

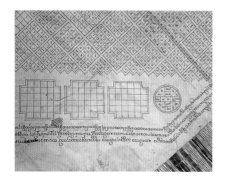

Above: A cotton spirit cloth with symbolic diagrams *(yantra)* of circles, squares and triangles filled with numbers, letters and symbols, read or recited as magical incantations *(gatha)*.

Top: Carved and painted fish suspended from a bamboo pole as part of temple decorations for the Buddhist Festival *bun phrawes*.

Above right: Buddhist nuns in a temple compound.

Right: An ancient *bodhi* tree in the grounds of Wat Phra That Lampang Luang, Lampang.

14

A woven temple banner *(pha tung)* hanging inside a temple.

Left: A prince of Nan, temple mural painting, Wat Phumin, Nan. The portrait may be of Noi Indra, described in the Nan Chronicle as Governor in 1716 AD.

[1] The name of the nation of Burma was changed to Myanmar in 1989.

[2] Zhu Liangwen 1992, Nathalang 1997.

Chapter One

People of this *Muang*

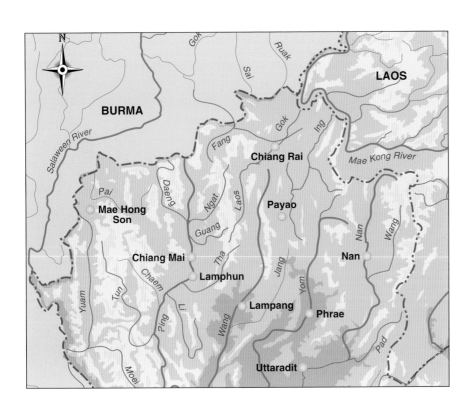

Lan Na was established as an independent kingdom in the thirteenth century and comprised what is now north Thailand and western Laos. In 1892 Lan Na was unified with Siam to form the kingdom of Thailand and from that time the Tai of Lan Na are referred to as Thai. Slightly larger than Ireland, Lan Na has a seasonal monsoon climate that supports an agrarian society based on wet rice cultivation in the valleys and swidden (slash and burn) agriculture in the hills. In traditional farming communities, the production of cotton and silk fitted into the annual cycle of rice production and weaving was an indigenous skill associated almost exclusively with women.

Lan Na village women prepare a meal. Temple mural painting,
Wat Buak Khok Luang, Chiang Mai.

The Chiang Mai valley showing the Ping River and rice fields.

Right: A valley in the Lan Na hills close to the border with the Shan States.

Rice seedings tied in bunches waiting to be transplanted to the rice fields.

Origins of the People

The inhabitants of Lan Na in the 19th century have been identified as primarily Tai although they had not always been the majority population. The classification of the Tai as a people with a common identity is primarily based on linguistic evidence, as charted in maps and written classifications.[1] They are described as belonging, linguistically, to the Thai Kadai group. Penth (1994) describes the Tai as settling in Lanna from circa 800-1050 AD, in small numbers, probably with the approval of existing inhabitants, and he bases this claim on evidence from the fields of philology, ethnology, pre-history and physical anthropology. One hypothesis places their origins in south China, from where, it is argued, they migrated south into Assam, the Shan States, Lan Na, Laos and northern Vietnam.[2] Buddhist chronicles, such as the *Jinakalamali-pakarana*, the Chiang Mai Chronicle and the Nan Chronicle record that the Tai became the dominant group at the beginning of the 13th century.[3]

The way the Tai settled in Lan Na is open to debate. A possibility proposed by Leach (1954), based on his contemporary studies of the valley-occupying Tai and the hill-residing Kachin in the Shan States, is that the Tai should not be thought of as the descendants of an immigrant alien people. They should be considered as mixed Tai and hill people who settled in the valleys and adopted wet rice cultivation. He also comments on the time span for assimilation stating that there is historical evidence that hill tribe people, by adopting the manners, dress and language of lowlanders, tended to merge with them completely over the passage of only a few generations. Of course, cultural assimilation was not a one-way process and ancient hill tribe customs were fused with traditions associated with valley dwellers.

When the Tai came to live in Lan Na, the majority population among whom they settled are described as Lawa, who in contrast to the Tai are

Sons of the governor of Muang Lai with other two officers.
(River Books Collection)

placed linguistically in the Austro-Asiatic, Mon-Khmer group. They had established a powerful state in the Chiang Mai region in the 8th century. The integration of Tai and Lawa appears to have been one of gradual assimilation, involving intermarriage. Seidenfaden (1963) argued that as a result, a more accurate term to describe the Tai who inhabit Lan Na would be Tai-Lawa. This view is supported by Tai legends, such as those recorded in the Chiang Mai chronicles.[4] One legend tells the story of a Tai prince who while out hunting for a golden stag reaches the Ping River (on whose banks the city of Chiang Mai is now situated). Under the direction of a local hermit he builds a city named Wiang Lan Na and takes as his consorts two Lawa women.

The Tai chronicles tell us that by the 12th-13th century the Tai had become the most powerful group in Lan Na and they portray the Lawa as savages who they claim to have civilised by converting them to Buddhism. Nimmanhaeminda (1966, 1967) has described Tai ceremonies that involve placating savage Lawa spirits. The Tai ritually slaughtered buffalo to solicit their ancestor spirits to provide monsoon rain. In a Buddhist ceremony, held at the same time as this spirit religion rite, a cotton banner bearing an image of the Buddha was raised from a tree. The movement of the image as it swung in the wind was intended to deceive

A spirit house in a garden, Chiang Mai.

Right: The entrance to Wat Lai Hin, Lampang.

the Lawa spirits, considered to be cannibalistic, into believing that the Lord Buddha was alive and wished them to reject the custom of devouring human flesh. The Tai preoccupation with placating Lawa spirits is also evident in the countryside around the city of Chiang Mai. Shrines erected at the foot of the mountain of Doi Suthep (on the outskirts of the city) accommodate the Lawa spirits Phu Sae and Ya Saeh who were believed to be roaming in the forest until the Tai erected spirit houses to accommodate them. Interestingly, these Lawa spirits are regarded as the guardian spirits of Chiang Mai, claimed in the Buddhist chronicles to be a Tai city, providing further proof of the complexities involved in the interaction between Tai and Lawa culture.

The Tai portrayal of the Lawa as savages and themselves as Buddhists is easily challenged as there is a strong argument that at least in the Chiang Mai region, the Lawa had converted voluntarily to Theravada Buddhism centuries before the Tai.[5] The earliest physical evidence of Buddhism to the south of Lan Na can be dated to the 7th century AD.[6] In fact the picture is even more complex. The Lan Na princes were active spirit religion practitioners and their authority rested not only on a blameless performance as Buddhist rulers, but equally on spirit religion rites that only they had the power to perform. They conducted these rites at ancient spirit religion shrines as a means to ensure crop fertility and the general well being of the people and the state. Interestingly the shrines themselves are of Lawa origin.[7]

20

Wooden image of a Lan Na *deva*.

Left: Lan Na offering bowls and food containers, temple mural painting, Wat Buak Khok Luang, Chiang Mai.

The tendency in Tai literature to portray the Lawa as uncivilised does not alter the fact that the Tai recognised them as the original inhabitants of the land. The Chiang Mai chronicles records that when Lan Na Tai royalty presided at state ceremonies, the Lawa were prominent participants. Their ritual importance can be measured by their role in the triumphant procession of Prince Kawila (ruled 1781-1813) into the city of Chiang Mai following the defeat of the Burmese. It was the Lawa who led the long and colourful cavalcade of monks, officers and soldiers. The Lawa were also welcomed at other royal events, such as weddings and house warmings. In the late 1920s when Hutchinson (1935) was granted an audience in Chiang Mai with Princess Dararatsami (1873-1933) she informed him that her people respected the Lawa and invited them to their homes, regarding their visits as bringing good luck. This type of recognition applied in other inland principalities, as between the Tai Lao of Luang Prabang and the Khamuk, and the Tai Shan and the Kachin.[8]

Two hypotheses are promulgated in this debate concerning the origins of the Lan Na Tai. One proposes that they came from Sipsong Pan Na as an identifiable group, and that through Buddhism they 'civilised' the existing inhabitants. Another proposes that they moved in gradually, intermarrying with the Lawa and hill tribe groups, but settling in the valleys. It is probably impossible to prove one or the other. In practice, claims of 'Tai-ness' or 'Tai purity' are more closely associated with political circumstances. At various moments in history, as in the political

Two hill tribe men with tattoos and woman in Tai Lue style dress, mural in Wat Phumin, Nan.

environment of the 19th century, great emphasis was placed on 'Tai-ness', while attempts were made to form alliances and exert control over other groups. The Lan Na rulers contained the Lawa in outlying districts, partly achieved by granting them formal written documents and, in at least one recorded case, an inscribed silver plate, legalising their claim to cultivate land in the hills or outer regions of the domain.[9] Lawa villagers were sometimes appointed as Buddhist temple slaves to physically maintain the buildings and grounds and support the monks. The Lawa recognised the authority of the Tai rulers and brought them tribute in the form of agricultural and forest products. In 1886 the British diplomat Sir Ernst Satow witnessed a tribute ceremony in Chiang Mai when the Lawa presented Prince Indra Witchayanon (ruled 1871-1897) with wild orchid plants.[10] At the time of writing, Lawa communities still live in outlying districts of Chiang Mai such as in the Mae Chaem valley south west of Chiang Mai.

The Lan Na princes made pacts with hill-dwelling groups, particularly the Karen who were fierce opponents and did not submit readily to Tai authority. In 1809 Prince Kawila of Chiang Mai sent his deputy to conclude a treaty of friendship with the Red Karen who were raiders in what was considered, at that time, to be Tai territory. The treaty did not last and on at least one occasion they threatened the city of Chiang Mai. Always a force to be reckoned with, the Lan Na princes tried to keep the peace through successive treaties in 1813, 1829, 1870 and 1881.[11]

A river at the end of the monsoon season.

What is important in terms of this book, is how the social and political interaction between the Lawa, Tai and Karen over many centuries affected the way the people dressed. Groups moving from highlands to lowlands made adaptations to climatic conditions. Women were more conservative than men and could be identified by ethnic group, although they made subtle changes to their dress. A joint belief in spirit religion meant some shared iconography for body decoration and protective clothing. Intermarriage and resettlement led to assimilation in the form and patterning of materials. This fascinating issue of conservatism and adaptation will be the subject of later chapters.

The Muang System

One of the defining cultural characteristics of the inland states is the *muang* system. The term *muang* describes a primary unit of political and social organisation. Variations in the term, such as *mong*, *mueang*, are found from Assam to south China. The word encompasses a defined territory and can mean a city, a city with village dependencies, a number of cities each with village dependencies, or a large important village. In a geographical sense, *muang* means a territorial unit centred in a river valley basin.[12] In political terms, a *muang* is based on mutually beneficial relationships with people coming together for reasons of defence, trade and social interaction. The *muang* ruler was usually a prince (*chao*) who came from a powerful local family.

The major city of a *muang* lay in a river valley and its borders were the surrounding mountains. Over the mountains in the next valley would be another *muang* that might be as powerful, or be a satellite of a powerful *muang*. The major city was sited on the banks of a river, with fortified walls, a moat and four gates at the cardinal points. Built on the boundary of the city, but not physically central to the settlement was the city ancestor shrine revered as the soul of the community. The ruling prince made annual sacrifices to the shrine. Important Buddhist monasteries were sited inside the city walls near to the centre and revered Buddha images were kept there. Outside the city walls there were monasteries occupied by so called 'forest monks' seen as inhabiting uncivilised space, but viewed as following a purer religious existence than city monks.

The ruler of the *muang* was ultimately responsible for the building and repair of irrigation systems that provided water for the rice fields. He oversaw the construction and restoration of temple buildings and the welfare of the monks. He conducted the annual ceremony at the city's ancestor shrine. His authority is seen as radiating outwards to the villages and settlements to the farthest reaches of the *muang*.

The people who consider themselves the original Tai inhabitants of Lan Na, call themselves *khon muang*. The significance of the term *khon*

Two Lawa women in loose smocks, striped cotton *phasin* and cotton leggings, Mae Sariang, Mae Hong Son.

A woman wearing an ankle-length Lan Na *phasin*, Mae Chaem valley.

Wat Luang Rat Santan, Phayao. This temple collapsed and was rebuilt in the 1980s.

muang, which in translation means 'people of this *muang*', appears to be primarily social and geographic rather than ethnic. Yet it is also the way the Tai choose to differentiate themselves from hill tribes, and from all people they consider to be foreign. The term was used in the past as a form of cultural identity, implying 'civilised people'. However as a political term it is possible that *khon muang* included, not excluded the Lawa and hill tribe groups living in the outlying districts of the *muang*, if they were controlled by, and paid tribute to, a Tai ruler. Evidence to support this argument comes in the following incantation from the ceremony of the city ancestor shrine (the Inthakin pillar) that lists those who were viewed as foreigners in Chiang Mai, the capital of Lan Na. The incantation is recorded in the 19th century edition of the Chiang Mai chronicle, although the actual ceremony can be traced through earlier manuscripts to the time of the Lan Na Tai ruler King Mengrai (1259-1317).

> *We beg the spirits to accept offerings to protect the Buddha's holy religion, our country and all of us along with the Lord of the* Muang *. . . save us from all calamities and dangers. Ensure our city . . . Chiang Mai of immense power against enemies from whatever directions and make it invulnerable. Do not allow foreigners such as Haw, Khaek, Lan Xang,*

*Ayodhaya, Man, Ngieo and Kula to cross the frontiers. Do not let them
move near, but disperse them by the power of the Inthakin pillar . . .*
(Premchit and Dore 1992: 213).

A domestic scene, Wat Phra Singh, Chiang Mai.

This translation lists 'foreigners' as Chinese Muslims, Indians, Laotians,
Siamese from Ayutthya, Burmese, Shans and *kula* (a general term for
strangers), who, as will be evident later, were immigrants, traders and
administrators in 19th century Lan Na. The Lawa, perhaps recognised as
rightful inhabitants, are not identified in the list.

The term used by neighbours and outsiders to describe the *khon muang*
is Tai Yuan, said to derive from Yon or Yonok, an ancient kingdom which
included parts of present day Myanmar, Thailand and Laos. The term Tai
Yuan is accepted as standard scholarly practice when speaking of those
considered to be the indigenous Tai speakers of Lan Na and is used in this
book. In the 19th century, the majority of Tai Yuan lived in the provinces
of Chiang Rai, Chiang Mai, Lamphun, Lampang, Phayao, Phrae, Nan and
parts of Uttaradit, Mae Hong Son and Tak (*see maps 1 and 2*).

Lan Na women wearing sashes *(pha sabai)* and tubular skirts *(phasin)*. Their hair is dressed in Lan Na style, temple mural painting, Wat Nong Bua, Nan.

19th Century Immigrants

The Lan Na kingdom flourished until the mid 16th century when there was a period of decline, identified with costly religious and secular projects burdening the economy, together with an inability on the part of the ruling council (*khao sanam luang*) to select a strong prince ruler.[13] The Burmese took advantage of these weaknesses and invaded in 1558 AD, remaining in occupation for over 200 years. The wars that led to the final expulsion of the Burmese in 1774 caused a dramatic fall in the population in the towns and countryside of Lan Na. According to the Chiang Mai chronicle, Chiang Mai was left deserted and in ruins. There were not enough people in Lan Na to rebuild the cities, work the land and provide militia to guard the borders against further Burmese incursions.[14] A voluntary resettlement policy brought small numbers back to the country but in order to rapidly increase the population the newly restored rulers initiated forced resettlement campaigns into Sipsong Pan Na, the Shan States and Kayah state (Burma). Table 1.1 and 1.2 list the original domicile of the captive immigrants, their group identity and the year they settled in Lan Na. As can be seen, they are identified as Tai Khoen, Tai Lue, Tai Yai, Karen, Mon and Burmese although the figures reproduced in Table 1.2 *(see page 32)* cannot be proven to be accurate, based as they are on a mixture of factual and fictional accounts.[15] A half century later Prince Phichit, the Siamese Commissioner to Chiang Mai, returned a list of fighting men to Bangkok which recorded 80,000 from Chiang Mai, 80,000 from Lampang and 100,000 from Nan.[16] In contradiction the Chiang Mai Princess Ubonwanna reported to Holt Hallett, a British engineer, that the number from Chiang Mai was closer to 50,000. Such confusion continued and figures remained speculative until the publication in Bangkok of the Statistical Year Book for 1924 that gave the total population of Lan Na as 1,342,000.

Grabowsky (1993) has estimated that as a result of resettlement in the 19th century, between one third and two fifths of the population of Lan Na were immigrants. The majority came from Tai groups who belonged to semi-independent political states and principalities that had differences in speech and custom from the Tai Yuan. Many were allowed to settle with their own leaders and establish their own temple sects. The importance of the men who led the settlers is evident from the monuments later erected in their honour. They established their own neighbourhoods in the cities or set up village communities. All were subject ultimately to the authority of the Lan Na rulers. Some groups were resettled more than once, mainly into border areas after they were deemed safe. For example, some Chiang Mai inhabitants were removed to Chiang Saen and Chiang Rai on the northern borders.[17]

The ethnic groups living in Lan Na in the 19th century have been defined as Tai Yuan, Tai Lue, Tai Khoen, Tai Yai, Tai Lao, Mon, Lawa and Karen.[18]

a) The Tai Lue inhabit areas of Sipsong Pan Na, south China and the

Table 1.1
LATE 18TH & 19TH CENTURY RESETTLEMENT CAMPAIGNS IN LAN NA
(Adapted from Grabowsky 1993).

MUANG	FROM	PPROXIMATE NUMBER	SOURCE*
TO LAMPHUN			
1805	Muang Yong	10,000	TPCM
1809-1810	Muang Yong, Chiang Tung	2,000-4,000[1]	"
TO CHIANG MAI			
1783	Kayah State	1,000	TPCM
1784	Cuat	1,000-2,000	"
	Shan State of Pan, Tong Kai	'numerous'	"
	Chom Chit, Satoi, Soi Rai Wang Lun, Wang Kat		
1798	Muang Sat, Muang Pu	1,000-2,000	TPCM
1802	Muang Sat, Chiang Tung, Muang Pan	6,000[2]	NL
	Muang Pan, Muang Pu, Chiang Saen		PPRI
1804-1805	Chiang Saen	23,000[3]	PPRI
1805	Chiang Tung, Sipsong Pan Na	10,000-20,000[4]	"
1809-1810	Muang Yong, Chiang Tung	2,000-4,000[5]	TPCM
1814-1815	Mon from Burma	3,000	
1837	Muang Sat	1,800-1,900	PCMLL
1869	Mok Mai	No record	
TO NAN			
1790	Muang Yong	585 families	PMN
1791	Chiang Khong	505 families	"
1792-1811	Not given	5,000[6]	"
1812	Muang La, Muang Phong, Luang Phu	Thousands of people	"
1826-1827	Vientiane	600	"
From 1830	Sipsong Pan Na[7]	No record	
TO LAMPANG			
1802	Muang Sat, Pu, Pan and Chiang Tung	6,000	NL
1804-1805	Chiang Saen	23,000	PPRI
PHAYAO	No record		
PHRAE	No record		

Total number of people by forced settlement was 50-70,000.
Hill tribe resettlement: There are general references to numbers of hill tribe people, especially Karen and Lawa, referred to as *kha* or *khikha* (slaves).

*Key to Abbreviations

TPCM	Tamnan Phunmuang Chiang Mai [Chiang Mai Manuscripts]
PMN	Pongsawadan Muang Nan [Nan Chronicle]
PPRI	Phraratchapongsawadan Krung Rattanakosin Rachakan [Rattanakosin Records]
NL	National Library (Bangkok)
PCMLL	Pongsawadan Muang Nakhon Chiang Mai Nakhon Muang Lampang Muang Lamphunchai [Chiang Mai and Lampang chronicles]

[1] Some were sent to Chiang Mai.

[2] This group was divided between Chiang Mai and Lampang.

[3] The total was divided between Lampang, Chiang Mai, Nan and Wiang Can.

[4] This group was divided between Chiang Mai, Lamphun and Lampang.

[5] Some were sent to Lamphun.

[6] 5,000 people were hired to build and dam in Nan.

[7] These refugees fled the anarchy and civil war in Sipsong Panna.

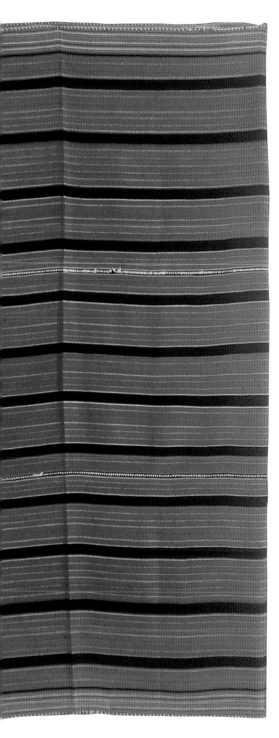

Karen–style cotton *phasin*.
(Bank of Thailand Museum, Chiang Mai)

eastern Shan States and are ethnolinguistically close to the Tai Yuan and Tai Khoen. The majority brought as immigrants were resettled in the principalities of Chiang Kham, Nan, Lamphun and Lampang.

b) The Tai Khoen came from the central and eastern valleys of the Shan States. Within the context of this book it is interesting to note that the Tai Khoen are described as distinguishable from neighbouring Tai populations by slight differences in dialect and by the peculiarities of women's dress. They were resettled in Chiang Mai, Lamphun and Lampang.

c) The Tai Yai (also called Ngio) are from the western Shan States and in ethnolinguistic terms are related to the Siamese and Tai Lao. They were settled in the outlying regions of Mae Sariang, Mae Hong Son, Thaton and Fang.

d) The Tai Lao are ethnolinguistically close to the Siamese and Shan and were resettled in Nam Pat, Uttaradit and Phayao.

e) The resettlement records in Table 1.1 also list the non-Tai Mon described as close cousins of the Khmer, who speak a Mon-Khmer type of Austro-Asiatic language. They were resettled from Pegu (Myanmar), into Lamphun and Lampang.

f) There are also general references to the Lawa and hill tribe people, especially Karen, who are of Tibeto-Burmese origin.

It is important to include the Siamese who although they were not part of resettlement programmes, lived in Lan Na from the 1870s, serving as representatives of the Siamese government. In terms of linguistic affiliation, Siamese is described as an isolative and tonal language related to Tai Lao and Shan.

Ethnic groups are identified above in terms of linguistic affiliation, although language affiliation does not always correlate with culture, political organisation and territorial proximity.[19] When Moerman (1965) attempted to clarify these issues by asking individual Tai Lue what their typical characteristics were, they mentioned cultural traits that they shared with neighbouring groups. The Tai Lue who Moerman interviewed lived in close interaction with other groups and had no exclusive livelihood, language, customs or religion, and he questioned why it was considered appropriate to describe them as an ethnic group. He concluded that someone is Tai Lue by virtue of believing and calling himself Tai Lue and of acting in a way that validates his Lue-ness.

Issues of dress and ethnicity have been the subject of debate and Manning Nash (quoted in Eicher 1995: 1) acknowledged that ethnicity is among the most complicated, volatile and emotionally charged words and ideas in the lexicon of social sciences.[20] It is argued here that throughout the history of Lan Na there was assimilation between hill people and valley dwellers, including among the ruling classes and this affected the way they dressed. In the 19th century there were identifiable forms of court dress that relate to perceptions of ethnic identity and to political, economic, social and cultural conditions in Lan Na. These conditions were not static and, as will be argued, are reflected in the changes that took place in court dress from the beginning to the end of the century.

The people of Lan Na in the 19th century were approximately two thirds to three fifths indigenous population and one third to two fifths immigrants, from what is now south China, Laos, Kayah (Myanmar) and the Shan States (Myanmar). The indigenous people are described as Tai Yuan, Lawa and hill tribe (mainly Karen) and, as they were the inhabitants who preceded 19th century settlers, probably all thought of themselves as *khon muang*. The immigrants are described as Tai Lue, Tai Khoen, Tai Yai, Tai Lao, Mon and Karen. These definitions should be accepted only within the context of the political and cultural environment of the 19th and early 20th century. The Tai far outnumbered other groups and were the dominant political force. All the people, except nobles and monks, were subject to the authority of a Lan Na ruler, either as citizens or slaves.

Citizens and Slaves

The 19th century immigrants to Lan Na were settled with the status of citizens *(phrai)* if they submitted willingly to their captors and slaves *(kha)* if they resisted.[21] Citizens *(phrai)* were divided into two classes, one of scholars, astrologers, scribes, master craftsmen and the relatively well-off, the second class of small farmers, manual labourers, traders and the poor. European writers often referred to this second group as serfs but Thai academics define them as either 'peasants' or freemen.[22] Citizens were expected to fulfil specific duties towards the state. These included providing a portion of their produce as a tax in kind, as well as contributing labour to maintain the courts and militia for defence of the state. Immigrants given status as citizens, as opposed to being slaves, were settled throughout Lan Na. They were forced to labour part of the time for the local ruler and could be mobilised for military purposes. Control of their labour and movements was in the hands of a loosely structured network of delegated village and district leaders who were referred to as *kae ban* and *kwaen*. Whether citizens were severely exploited depended on the whim of successive rulers. It is argued that the further away they lived from the ruler, the less likely they were to be called on for service. Accounts by foreign observers are varied. Some painted a harsh picture, describing citizens as never being left to get on with their own work, being continually forced to serve the purely selfish ends of their masters, who they described as 'lords of life and death' over all. The American missionaries complained that the system forced their converts to work on Sundays, although they admitted that they had not heard of harsh treatment by any 'overlord'.[23] Some rulers never overworked their citizens because they wanted to gain more labourers and keep those they had from running away, or migrating to another district.[24]

The statue of Chao Luang Muang La at Tha Wang Pha district in Nan.

A group of slaves *(kha)*, one is wearing leg irons, temple mural painting Wat Luang Rat Santan, Phayao.

Mural painting on wood showing farmers at work, Wat Phra That Lampang Luang, Lampang.

Slaves were divided into three categories, war slaves, debt slaves and temple slaves. As their name implies, war slaves were captured enemy soldiers and their families, or they were civilians and their families, abducted during raids into foreign territory. They could be bought and sold. However, some poor families gave children into the service of royalty as slaves, hoping that they would be well cared for.[25] Many subjects viewed slaves as having more freedom than citizens. Some sought to change their status to be slaves because then they were exempt from state and military service. Debt slaves were owned as a result of liability and probably had citizen status before they fell into debt. They were in a slightly better position as they could redeem themselves eventually even if the process of repayment was difficult.[26] Temple slaves were villagers given the job of taking care of temple compounds. They tended to be poor villagers and were not allowed to give up this role.

War slaves and debt slaves lived in the compound of their owners, or in a village close enough for them to be called on for service. They provided manual labour in the fields, at the rulers' palaces and gardens, and they could also be hired out to others. Any wages were paid to their owner. Women slaves who worked in palace compounds laboured as domestics, as court dancers and as textile workers, a significant number as weavers. For long periods of service, slaves usually received some monetary compensation or its equivalent in kind. Many slaves lived at court and children born as a result of liaisons between rulers and their female slaves were usually well treated, although their status was ambiguous. If male and female citizens or slaves married, the male became the subject of his wife's owner.[27]

The rulers of Lan Na were entitled to corvée (unpaid labour) from all their subjects, except nobles and monks. This confused the line between citizen and slave. If labour was performed on the basis of obligation, should this be labelled as a form of slavery? It is safe to assume that all subjects, whether citizens or slaves, were bound to a local prince, to some degree. However, they were able to change their allegiance from one ruler to another and, it is argued, this provided a form of escape from serious oppression.[28] It has been suggested that foreigners, especially the British, listened sympathetically to, and reported on, alleged harsh treatment of citizens and slaves because they had secret ambitions to intervene in the area. The 'citizen' system made flexibility of labour possible as men and women worked certain days for their ruler and certain days for themselves, or remitted a specific amount of their produce to the ruler. In the case of trade, the system discouraged an entrepreneurial culture, as citizens could never travel far in case they were called on for labour.[29]

The general impression given in accounts by foreign missionaries, traders and travellers is that they judged the relationship between rulers and subjects, both citizens and slaves, as exploitative, although there was little evidence of physical ill treatment. Many missionaries agreed that the people of Lan Na were better treated than in some other Southeast Asian societies.[30] Where there was cruelty, it was related directly to the character of an individual ruler. McGilvary wrote of the corporal punishment and beheadings which took place during the reign of Prince Kawiloros Suriyavong of Chiang Mai (ruled 1856-1870), and descendants of citizens and slaves have described the harsh treatment and poor working conditions their ancestors suffered.

In summary the rulers of Lan Na were descended, like their subjects, from assimilated groups of Tai, Lawa and hill tribe people who settled in the valleys and practised wetland rice cultivation. When the Tai became the dominant group, described in Lan Na as Tai Yuan, their rulers intermarried with Tai royalty from Sipsong Pan Na, the Shan States and western Laos, defined as Tai Lue, Tai Lao, Tai Khoen and Tai Yai. They also took members of elite Lawa and hill tribe (Karen) women as consorts, although this is underplayed in some versions of the Buddhist chronicles. In the nineteenth century there was a vast resettlement of people from the surrounding inland states who were settled close to, or among indigenous Lan Na people.

There was a common system of social and political organisation based on the *muang*. Control of the people rested with a ruling prince, although the further away from the court, the less authority could be imposed on them. The manner in which the Lan Na princes established and maintained their authority is the subject of the next chapter.

Princess Tippawan of Lampang and Prince Promlue of Chiang Tung on their wedding day in 1922. She wears a white blouse, sash and Lan Na–style *phasin*. Her hair is dressed in Lan Na style. He wears a shirt, *chong kraben* and waist sash.
(River Books Collection)

TABLE 1.2
DISTRIBUTION OF ETHNIC GROUPS AND THEIR OCCUPATIONS
CHIANG MAI CITY c.1850

Adapted from Vatikiotis (1984) and Grabowsky (1993).

ETHNIC GROUP	OCCUPATION	ORIGINAL DOMICILE	SOURCE
Tai Yai	Tanners Pot makers	Western Shan States	Pongsawadan Yonok, 1 Oral history Temple lists2
Tai Lue	Silversmiths	Muang Nai Sipsong Pan Na Chiang Tung	as above
Tai Khoen	Lacquerware makers, Woodcarvers, Gong smiths	Chiang Tung, Chiang Saen	as above
Mon	Boatmen	Pegu	Richardson (1836) Nimmanhaeminda (1965) Temple lists
Burmese	Foresters	Burma	Temple lists Oral hitory
Karen	Forester	Burma	Karen folk history

1 National Library (Ho Samut Hangchat), Bangkok.
2 Wat Chedi Luang, Chiang Mai.

Reference:
Conway S. (2000) *A Hidden Culture : Lan Na Court Textiles and Dress in the 19ed Century.*

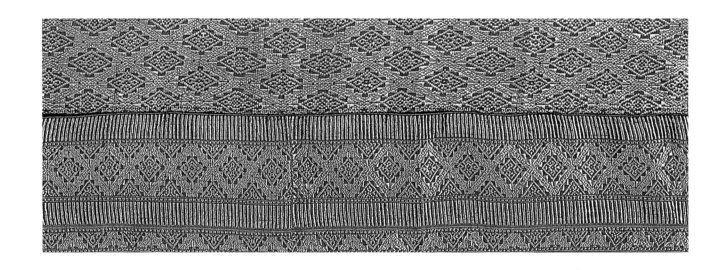

1 Dodd 1923, Seidenfaden 1963, Le Bar et al. 1964, Chamberlain 1972.

2 Hall 1981.

3 The Jinakalamalipakarana Chronicle was written by Ratanapanna in 1516 at the Rattavana vihara temple, Chiang Mai. It gives the Buddha's life history, the history of Buddhism in India and Sri Lanka, and in Laos, Cambodia and Thailand.

4 Wyatt and Aroonrut 1995.

5 Condominas 1990.

6 Pisit and Diskul 1978.

7 The Inthakin pillar of Chiang Mai is one good example of a spirit religion shrine. The Tai chronicles record the Lawa discovering the pillar while preparing a site for a new city (Kaufmann 1971, Premchit and Dore 1992).

8 Interview with Eleanor Gaudoin, member of the royal family of Hsenwi (Brighton, June 1993).

9 Nimmanhaeminda 1965.

10 Brailey 1994.

11 Sethakul 1989.

12 Tambiah 1977: 70, Rhum 1987: 92.

13 Penth 1994: 24-29.

14 Wyatt and Aroonrut 1995: 147.

15 Premchit and Tuikheo 1975, Vatikiotis 1984, Grabowsky 1993.

16 Hallett 1890.

17 McGilvary 1912.

18 Dodd 1923, Le Bar et al 1964, Premchit and Dore 1992.

19 Erikson 1993.

20 Cordwell and Schwarz 1979, Eicher 1995, Welters 1995.

21 Nineteenth century temple records refer to citizens as *phrai* and slaves as *kha* or *khikha*. In Southeast Asia generally, there were acknowledged paths by which a person would enter a state of bondage. These are systemised as inheriting the bondage of parents, or sale into bondage by parents, or capture in war, or judicial punishment such as failure to pay fines and meet debts (Reid 1988).

22 Holt Hallett (1890) and Hugh Taylor (1888-1930) used the term 'serf' while Sethakul (1989: 27) uses the terms 'peasant' or 'freeman'.

23 Peoples 1885, Taylor, H. 1888-1930.

24 Sethakul 1989:45.

25 Interviews with Chao Ja Pa and Khun na Sompan of the Chiang Mai court (Chiang Mai 1996).

26 Sethakul 1989.

27 Brailey 1994.

28 Hallett 1890.

29 Sethakul 1989: 34.

30 McGilvary 1912, Taylor 1888-1930.

Detail of the hem border of a *phasin* from Luang Prabang, woven in silk with silver and gold metal thread.
(Bank of Thailand Museum, Chiang Mai)

Chapter Two

Princes and Politics

This chapter focuses on the rulers of Lan Na in the nineteenth century, their ancestry and their politics and the complex blend of myth and reality that surrounded them. During the third quarter of the century, external forces began to impact on their lives and the way that they governed. By the end of the century their unique way of life had all but disappeared.

Lan Na Royalty: Myths, Legends and Factual Accounts

Following two hundred years of Burmese occupation, it was important for the new Lan Na rulers to establish their legitimacy and to prove their inherited right to control the *muang*. This was achieved by stressing links through ancestors to a Tai monarchy based in antiquity. The Lan Na princes funded compilations of the Tai chronicles that included them in the long line in succession from the time of the first mythical prince who descended from the Tavatimsa Heaven to begin the dynasty.

> *At that time, King Anuruddha Dhammikaraja summoned all the kings and rulers of the Jambu Continent to come together to his court. All the rulers and kings of the principalities assembled / except those of Lan Na Thai, as they had no king. Anuruddha Dhammikaraja therefore prayed to the Lord Indra that Indra would pay attention to Lan Na Thai, because it was a place where the teachings of the Buddha were established, and find a great king to be / overlord of that area. Indra*

Prince Suriyapong Paritdej of Nan, photographed in 1888 while he was still *uparaj* or Viceroy. He was a loyal ally to King Rama V in his fight with the Ho. He is wearing a turban cloth, a sash and *chong kraben* with flowers decorating his right ear. He sit on a mattress leaning on an embroidered cushion, surrounded by his regalia of office.
(River Books Collection)

A portrait of the first ruler of Chiang Mai, Prince Kawila (ruled 1781-1813).

Middle: The sixth ruler of Chiang Mai, Prince Kawiloros Suriyavong (ruled 1856-1870).

Right: Princess Tipkesorn, wife of Prince Indra Witchayanon, the seventh ruler of Chiang Mai.
(Chiang Mai National Museum)

accepted this commission, carefully considered the matter, and saw a son of the gods named Lawacakkradevaputta who was filled with merit and was reigning in the / f 1.09/ Tavatimsa Heaven and meritoriously had served [out his time in the heavens] and was of an appropriate age to leave the heaven [and return to earth].[1] The Lord Indra went directly to the court of that son of the gods and said "Behold thou who knows no suffering! Thou wilt descend to take birth in the world of men at Chiang Rao, and wilt assume the royal condition as a great king as lord over all the rulers / in the Lan Na country, and there maintain the Great Teachings of the Buddha.

Lawacangkara, a son of the gods, consented to the words of Indra, saying, "Sadhu! Good! Fine! He then left the heavens and descended down a bejewelled ladder from heaven with a thousand of his retainers; or, put another way, to the pinnacle of Doi Tung / to take unparented birth as a royal scion of sixteen years, finely dressed on a fine wooden throne/ comported near the Mae Sai in Jayavaranagara- that is Chiang Rao.[2] As for his thousand retainers, they all, men and women alike, came to be born similarly, as princes and princesses sixteen years of age, /possessed of wondrous beauty and complexion, resplendent everywhere.[3]

The Chiang Mai chronicle traces successive rulers from the first mythical prince to actual historic rulers. The genealogy charts based on the chronicle shows that the 19th century Lan Na dynasty was descended from Thip Chang, a forester. He who assumed the name Prince Sulawa Leuchai Songkram when in 1732 he became ruler of the ancient city of Lampang, to the south east of Chiang Mai.[4] Prince Sulawa submitted to Burmese authority and on his death his son Prince Chai Kaew was allowed to succeed him. During the reign of Prince Chai Kaew

the Burmese were expelled from Lan Na and his three sons became the rulers of Chiang Mai, Lamphun and Lampang. From 1781, Prince Kawila ruled Chiang Mai, Prince Setthi Kamfan ruled Lamphun and Prince Kham Som ruled Lampang. Attavorapanyo, a nephew of the Governor of Nan, became Prince of Nan in 1786. Prince Kawila of Chiang Mai was succeeded by Prince Phuttawong of Chiang Mai (ruled 1825-1846). He was followed by Prince Mahotara Phratet (ruled 1846-1854), then Prince Kawiloros (ruled 1856-1870) and Prince Indra Witchayanon (ruled 1871-1897), who was elected from a different branch of the royal family. The son of Prince Indra Witchayanon, Prince Indra Varoros (1901-1911) was succeeded by his brother Prince Kaew Nawarat (1911-1939) who saw the end of the dynasty. Power was then transferred to Bangkok.

The seventh ruler of Chiang Mai, Prince Indra Witchayanon (ruled 1871-1897). (National Archives, Bangkok)

Left: Princess Tipnetra, wife of Prince Indra Varoros Suriyavong, the eighth ruler of Chiang Mai. (National Archives, Bangkok)

The last version of the Nan chronicle covers the period from the first mythical ruler through the historic period to 1918. It includes the governors under Burmese rule who were successively, Chao Phraya Luang Tin Mahawong (1717-1753), Ariyawong Wan Tok (1754-1768), Nai Ai (1768-1769), his brother Nan Mano (1769-1775) and finally Chao Mongkhonvaroyot (1784-1786). The first Prince of Nan, elected with the approval of the other Lan Na princes, was Prince Attavorapanyo (ruled 1786-1810). He was succeeded by his nephew Prince Sumanadevaraj (ruled 1810-1825), followed by Prince Mahayot (ruled 1825-1835) and briefly Prince Achittawongsa (ruled 1836-1837). The son of Prince Mahayot, Prince Mahawong (ruled 1838-1852) was followed by his son Prince Anantayot (ruled 1853-1891) who in turn was succeeded by his son Prince Suriyapong Paritdej (ruled 1894-1918) and finally by Prince Maha Promsurathada (1918-1931).

Prince Indra Varoros Suriyavong of
Chiang Mai (ruled 1901-1911).
(River Books Collection)

Middle: Prince Kaew Nawarat, the last ruler
of Chiang Mai (ruled 1911-1939).

Right: Princess Bua Kieuw, wife of Prince
Kaew Nawarat. (River Books Collection)

There is no translated chronicle listing the rulers of Lamphun, but we
know from historical accounts in Thai that the Lamphun royal family
were descended through the Lampang line, beginning with the accession
of Prince Setti Kamfan (ruled 1781-1826), brother of Prince Kawila of
Chiang Mai. He was succeeded in 1826 by his brother Prince Bunma,
followed by Bunma's son, Prince Noi Indra. Unfortunately no dates for
the succession are available after 1826. Noi Indra was followed by Prince
Luang Kamton and his son Prince Luang Thamma Lungka. The sixth
prince was Chailungka Pisarn Soparkkhun, the seventh prince was Dara
Direkratana and the eighth prince was Hemapintu Paijitt. The ninth
prince was Indrayongyote Choti and the last prince of Lamphun was
Chakrakam Kajornsakdi. Power then passed to Bangkok.

The history of the Lampang royal family is not available from
translated chronicles. We know that Prince Kham Som was a direct
descendant of the Lampang line and his reign ended in 1794. We also
know the names of two successors, one being Prince Duang Thip (ruled
1794-1825) although his ancestry is unknown. The second is Prince
Noranun Chai although we do not know his ancestry or the date of his
reign.

Through the Buddhist chronicles the Lan Na princes established
links with royal ancestors and the modest background of their actual
forebear, the forester Thip Chang later Prince Sulawa Luechai Songkram
of Lampang, was glossed over and given what in modern parlance would
be described as 'spin'. However, it was possible to rule a state without
proving royal precedence. The Tai chronicles record times when men of
humble origin were appointed as rulers of smaller tributary states, either
as a reward for piety and religious acts or because they showed
outstanding loyalty to a senior prince. Their numbers included a convict

Prince *(uparat)* Bunthawong, brother of
Prince Indra Witchayanon (ruled 1871-1897).

Middle: Princess Bua Lai of Phrae with her
daughters in typical Lan Na attire, while the
little boy wears *chong kraben* and a formal
white jacket.

Left: Prince Suriyapong Paritdej of Nan in
later life, wearing the costume of the
Bangkok court.

who was released to rule Chiang Saen, to the north of Chiang Mai, on the assumption that he would be loyal to the prince who had set him free.

The need to legitimise oneself through links with deities and royal ancestors has been analysed in the works of Chinese, Thai, European and American scholars.[5] Some stress that proving legitimacy gave a prince the sole right to perform the annual spirit religion ritual associated with the city shrine, thus assuring the well being of the *muang* and its citizens. Only 'legitimate' rulers could conduct ceremonies that guaranteed crop fertility and granted protection to all the citizens of the state. These ceremonies were of great significance to the personal authority of the Lan Na rulers. Even when Prince Kaew Nawarat, last Prince of Chiang Mai, was deprived of all administrative authority by Rama V of Siam, he continued to preside at spirit religion ceremonies until his death in 1939. The princes cherished this ancient rite and had an equally important role as Buddhist rulers. According to Buddhist cosmology a prince is viewed as a being on the way to Enlightenment *(boddhisatva)* and should reside in a royal palace built as a symbolic celestial mountain, described as a 'sacred centre'. The palace should have in its inner sanctum a tiered, canopied throne and the ruler wears a tiered crown symbolising cosmological and protective forces.[6] Those entering the sacred space of the palace should obey special rules of obeisance. Many ancient cities have palaces and throne rooms built on this model and a specific form of dress was prescribed for all those in the hierarchy of the court.

This was the ideal, but life in late 18th and early 19th century Lan Na was far removed from it. A brief account by McCarthy (1900) gives a sense of the insecurity and instability surrounding the life of a Lan Na prince.

Palace of Prince Kaew Nawarat of Chiang Mai, photographed in 1905 during the visit to Chiang Mai by HRH Crown Prince Maha Vajiravudh (later King Rama VI). The sign over the balcony reads 'Long Live the King'. Sadly the palace has been pulled down to make way for the Nawarat market.
Photo by permission of Khun Suchinda Heavener.

He [the Prince of Nan] is descended from the man who led the Burman army on its way from La to Nan into an ambush where it was slaughtered in the stream now called Sam Pan. He was about fourteen years of age when he fled with his father, a refugee before the Burmese army to Suwankalok in about 1815 AD.

The early dwellings of the Lan Na princes were improvised bamboo palaces and field camps, and they later dwelt for some years in temporary accommodation while ancient royal cities, destroyed during the war with Burma, were restored and fortified. We know from the Chiang Mai chronicle that Prince Kawila camped at Pa Sang, south of Chiang Mai for 'fourteen years, four months and twenty days' before he was able to move to a palace in the city of Chiang Mai.[7] The Nan chronicle states that Prince Attavaropanyo ruled for sixteen years before he moved to a permanent residence in the city of Nan.[8] Meanwhile the princes led military expeditions to outlying districts where they quelled rebellions and established treaties of friendship with those who had the potential to threaten regional stability. Some led raids to the Shan States, Laos and

Back and front of silk shirt with Buddha images, Buddhist monuments *(stupa)*, and symbolic diagrams *(yantra)* of circles, squares and triangles filled with numbers, letters and symbols, read or recited as magical incantation *(gatha)*.
(Barbie Campbell-Cole)

Sipsong Pan Na where they captured whole communities of people and brought them to re-settle in Lan Na. Expeditions to fortify border towns continued until the middle of the 19th century.[9] We know that the principality of Nan did not enter a period of prolonged peace and prosperity until the 1850s.[10]

During this long time of uncertainty the practical garb of warfare was more appropriate than tiered, canopied thrones, elaborate regalia and expensive court dress. However, the Chiang Mai chronicle gives the impression that such grandeur did exist. The victory march of Prince Kawila into the city of Chiang Mai is an example. It seems likely that the protective forces of spirit religion, manifested in body decoration and talismanic clothing that were believed to render the wearer invincible, were as important as the regalia of a Buddhist ruler.

Soldiers going in to battle, temple mural painting, Wat Buak Khok Luang, Chiang Mai.

Marital Alliances

Throughout the 19th century, the Lan Na princes used marital alliances as a way of networking with their allies in Sipsong Pan Na, the Shan States, Laos and Siam. In the 19th century these alliances were a way of deterring the Burmese from future attack. Marital alliances were the bedrock of political union and are described in the Chiang Mai chronicle as 'the customs of yore, of friendship and comity.... following royal customs.'[11] Prince Kawila of Chiang Mai (ruled 1781-1813) accepted consorts from *muang* Luang, *muang* Rai and Chiang Rung in Sipsong Pan Na, and *muang* Wa and *muang* Chiang Khang in the Shan States. According to the Nan chronicle, Prince Anantayot of Nan (ruled 1853-1891) took wives and consorts from Nan, Chiang Mai, Phrae, Chiang Khong, Siam and *muang* Kussawadi. The Nan Chronicle also refers to princesses from Nan sent as consorts to the courts of Vientiane and Luang Prabang.[12] Meanwhile Princess Sri Anocha, sister of Prince Kawila was sent to Bangkok as a consort for the brother of Rama I of Siam (ruled

Table 2.3
MARITAL ALLIANCES MADE IN 1805 AND 1806 BY PRINCE KAWILA
(RULED 1781-1813)

Consorts from the following *Muang* in Sipsong Pan Na and the Shan States:
MUANG LUANG
MUANG LAI
MUANG RUNG
MUANG WA
MUANG CHIANG KHONG

Prince Kawila's sister Sri Anocha was married to the brother of Rama I of Siam.
Source: *The Chiang Mai chronicle* (Wyatt and Aroonrut 1995).

MARITAL ALLIANCES OF PRINCE ANANTAYOT OF NAN
(RULED 1853-1891)
Consorts from:
NAN
CHIANG MAI
PHRAE
MUANG CHIANG KHONG
SIAM
SIPSONG PAN NA

Princesses from Nan were married into the Royal families of:
VIENTIANE,
LUANG PRABANG and
SIAM

Source: *The Nan chronicle* (Wyatt 1994).

Prince Maha Promsurathada, the
last ruler of Nan (ruled 1918-1931).
He was the younger brother of
Prince Suriyapong Paritdej.
(River Books collection)

Prince Chakrakam Kajornsakdi,
the last prince of Lamphun (ruled
1911-1943).
(River Books collection)

1782-1809). In terms of ethnicity, marital alliances can be said to have blurred the identity of the Lan Na royal families who were of mixed Tai Yuan, Tai Lue, Tai Khoen, Tai Yai and Tai Lao stock.[13] This will be an important factor in the analysis of court dress in later chapters.

The Establishment of Government

While in the process of stabilising their principalities in military terms, the princes also re-established a system of government based on the traditional hierarchy of patron-client relationships. The senior ruler *(chao luang)* held the title Lord of Life *(chao chiwit)* and had power of life and death over his subjects, operating within a traditional framework of law *(thammasat)* and the social environment of kingship networks. The ruling classes operated in a three tiered system. Beneath the prince ruler *(chao luang)* was his deputy *(chao uparat)* and three other princes, two of

King Rama I of Siam (ruled 1782-1809).

King Rama III of Siam (ruled 1824-1851).

whom (*chao ratchawong* and *chao ratchabut*) had titles which indicated their loyalty to the prince ruler rather than any specific duties to the state. Brailey (1968) speculates that the role of the third prince *(chao burirat)* was administrative, although there is no conclusive proof. The second tier of authority was composed of thirty-two men who formed the ruling council *(khao sanam luang)* made up of a group of senior Buddhist monks and members of the elite. Physical control over the subject population was achieved by imposing laws that divided society into three levels. There were officials and administrators *(khunnang)*, citizens *(phrai)* and slaves *(kha)*.

Lan Na had a relatively egalitarian system for dispersing status among branches of the royal family and nobility, as opposed to a hierarchical patrilineal system.[14] The appointment of a Lan Na prince did not follow the straightforward rule of male primogeniture. The ruling council *(khao sanam luang)* considered senior prince candidates and, as can be seen from the genealogy charts *(page 262-265)* they sometimes chose a candidate from a branch of the royal family who was not a direct descendant of the previous ruling prince. The process of selection was often complicated by marital alliances as a prince might have several wives and consorts who between them produced many children. The lack of clear succession often led to situations where offspring competed for power after the death of a ruler. The chosen prince ruler was anointed by senior princes and the ruling council in a ceremony which included sanctification with lustral water and a ritual involving circumambulating the city, a symbolic gesture representing the possession of the *muang*. This was followed by a procession to the royal palace.

The Siamese had played a major role in the expulsion of the Burmese in 1774 and from that time the Lan Na princes paid tribute to Siam. Following their anointment in Lan Na they travelled south to the Bangkok court and these visits were repeated at approximately three yearly intervals, both to swear allegiance and report on affairs of state in the north. The journey involved many hazards including exposure to disease, attack by wild animals in the forest and dangerous river crossings that sometimes resulted in fatalities.

According to Yule (1855), the Indo-Chinese token of tribute to a superior state was two small trees bearing flowers, one wrought in gold and the other in silver, which he estimated cost up to 1,000 Spanish dollars. The American missionary Hugh Taylor (1888-1930) described a tree shown to him by the Prince of Lampang. It was made of gold that had been panned from the river flowing through the city and the trunk, the branches, the twigs and leaves were beaten from a base nearly a foot square.

Relations with Siam, Europe and America

Rama I of Siam (ruled 1782-1809) accepted tribute from Lan Na but was unable to maintain a strong influence on the internal politics of the country, nor was he able to control their relations with traditional allies in the Shan States, Laos and Sipsong Pan Na. Lan Na was too remote and Siam had no permanent officials in place to monitor events there. Rama I counted on loyalty from the north by relying on traditional kinship ties, reinforced by the marriage of his brother to Princess Sri Anocha, sister of Prince Kawila of Chiang Mai. The long and arduous journey between Siam and Lan Na meant that contact between the two countries remained limited although this did not mean that the north was totally without obligation to Bangkok. Demands were made for able-bodied men in times of war, for timber from the rich forests and, significantly, as far as this book is concerned, for woven cloth used during important ceremonies such as the cremation of the king.[15] Lan Na royalty and senior officials were expected to perform the 'Water of Allegiance' ceremony twice a year at a temple in their home cities, as a sign of their loyalty to the king of Siam. If their obedience was in doubt they were summoned to Bangkok. At times there was resistance to the summons and the Chiang Mai chronicle records that in 1799 AD Prince Kawila was whipped one hundred strokes for refusing to report to Rama I when ordered to do so. However, the Lan Na princes were aware of the importance of maintaining good relations in general because they relied on the Siamese as a strong ally against Burma, whose military power they continued to fear.

By the reign of Rama III of Siam (ruled 1824-1851) the appointment of the ruling Lan Na prince and other senior officials was subject to approval from Bangkok. This gave Bangkok a voice in solving succession disputes and settling quarrels between the various branches of the ruling families. The increasing intervention from Siam affected traditional kinship networks and patronage systems operating among the Lan Na rulers and their officials in the *muang*.[16] The status of the principalities of Chiang Mai, Nan, Lamphun and Lampang, and their satellites were, to some extent, dependent on the king in Bangkok, although, as the British diplomat Sir John Bowring (1857) observed, their relationship was a complex one. Rama IV (1851-1868) recognised that as Lan Na was at a great distance from Bangkok, the princes could, if they joined together, form strong resistance to any unwelcome interference, thus causing great problems to Siam. Bowring noted that Bangkok managed the crowned vassals gently, and the king always gave them presents when they paid tribute.

Evidence of the independence of the Lan Na princes and their reluctance to accept Siamese interference in their affairs can be glimpsed from their treatment of two Siamese princes who made an official visit to Chiang Mai in 1859, a rare event at that time. According to the British Consul, Sir Robert Schomburgh (1863), neither Prince Kawiloros

Women with ceremonial bowls and dishes, mural painting, Wat Phra Singh, Chiang Mai.

Lan Na *phasin*, of silk and silver and gold metal thread, with horizontal geometric patterns in the central panel and diamond shaped patterns in the hem border.
(Paothong Thongchua collection)

Suriyavong of Chiang Mai nor the second prince *(uparat)* attended the ceremony held in honour of the princes. In 1865 Kawiloros again asserted his independence by planning to exchange embassies with the King of Burma, a move viewed by Siam as treasonable. Kawiloros was tried in Bangkok but was acquitted.[17]

In reality King Rama IV could only approve the appointment of princes who were elected by senior Lan Na royalty and the ruling council. However, during the reign of Prince Indra Witchayanon of Chiang Mai (ruled 1871-1897) Rama V was able to push through a decree that all princes be directly appointed from Bangkok. The Lan Na viewpoint is that Prince Indra Witchayanon was a weak ruler in accepting authority from Bangkok. However, it can be argued that Siamese intervention became inevitable at a time when international relations with Europe and the USA were beginning to have implications in Lan Na, and the Siamese feared the colonial ambitions of the British and French.

At the beginning of the 19th century, the Lan Na princes, in contrast to Siamese rulers had little contact with Europeans. Patterns of thought and behaviour relating to Sinhalese Theravada Buddhism and spirit

Lan Na *phasin*, with a central silk panel and hem border with a pattern called 'snakeskin' or 'tortoise shell'. Chom Thong, Chiang Mai Province.
(Bank of Thailand Museum, Chiang Mai)

religion, and the *muang* system of government dominated society. Lan Na at that time was viewed from outside as a land with few established boundaries and there was the problem of imposing a nation state, with centralised authority and fixed boundaries on a society that was inhabited by a 'quasi floating population'.[18] In the mid to late 19th century European and American explorers, diplomats, missionaries and traders ventured north through the primary forest and mountains to reach the Lan Na kingdom, bringing with them notions of Western politics and diplomacy.[19] They found a people whose language, politics and culture were markedly different from Siam which had diplomatic, political and trade links on an international scale. In contrast Lan Na was a landlocked country whose princes traded and negotiated mainly with surrounding inland states. The Lan Na princes were judged as inexperienced in the skills of international diplomacy, their horizons limited to the surrounding inland principalities.

Throughout the 19th century the colonial power of Britain, Holland and France was extending through countries now called Myanmar, Malaysia, Laos, Vietnam, Cambodia and Indonesia. Successive rulers of

Prince Sakkarinrit, ruler of Luang
Prabang, with his wife.
(River Books Collection)

Siam were increasingly drawn into the politics of the colonists and were anxious to prevent them from occupying their territory. They did this through making concessions, such as agreeing to the presence of diplomatic missions and awarding special status to foreign nationals. The awarding of special status to foreigners was an issue that was to increasingly concern Rama V as it left Europeans and Americans outside the jurisdiction of Thai law. Their numbers included foresters, missionaries and diplomats serving in distant Lan Na. The reason Rama V was so anxious to influence the selection of the Lan Na prince rulers was that he wanted princes in authority who would deal with these difficult and sensitive issues in a diplomatic way.

The main accusation coming from the British was that the Lan Na princes failed to meet legal obligations to foreign nationals, such as Burmese foresters who came under British jurisdiction. The princes were also accused of causing unnecessary conflict with American missionaries who from 1867 were evangelising in the north. The British continued to pressurise Bangkok to intervene in Lan Na to protect their interests, especially in extracting timber from the teak forests. They also accused the Lan Na princes of corruption and mismanagement of timber concessions. Rama V saw that the problem could not be solved locally and responded by appointing a Siamese High Commissioner to Chiang Mai. In a letter of instruction sent to him in 1883, the king wrote that he should consider Chiang Mai as a vassal state *(prathetsarat)*, not part of Siam and he did not want to destroy the ruling families or upset their status. He wanted the High Commissioner to exercise power discretely. He wrote 'we want them to be like a machine which we will wheel forward or backward as we wish'. He cautioned that it was necessary to do this with 'brains and intelligence more than power and force'. He also warned against being oppressive.[20] Thus a policy of gentle political pressure, reasoning and tactful intervention became the rule in dealing with Lan Na.

When the British opened a Consulate in Chiang Mai in 1883, anxiety in Bangkok increased as the Siamese continued to fear British interference in Lan Na. They had also to deal with French ambitions in the area, particularly in 1893 when the French annexed Laos and demanded the land on the east bank of the Mekong River that was the property of the Prince of Nan. In the ensuing peace treaty, the Prince of Nan lost all the land that the French claimed and the size and power of his principality was greatly reduced. In the light of colonial aggression in the area, it is not surprising that gradually over the next two decades, authority from Bangkok was increased. Administrative officers were appointed to deal not only with the political situation, but to supervise local government, tax collection, the law courts and timber concessions.

European reports suggest that relations between Siam and Lan Na were, at times, strained. It was reported that Siamese officials in Lan Na were corrupt although the King of Siam sent commissioners to investigate, and in many cases convict, those found guilty of such offences.[21] Sir Ernst Satow described in his diaries how the Siamese were plundering the people and embezzling the revenue.[22] He reported that during a visit to the Prince of Phrae, a court singer intoned a lament about the hard treatment the people received from the Siamese. Bock (1986: 147) noted that in Lampang Siamese officials were viewed as foreigners *(farang)* in the same way as he was. As with certain other reports, the British probably exaggerated these grievances as a way of furthering their own interests in Lan Na.

As had happened in the time of Rama I, a marriage alliance between Lan Na and Siam eased tensions. In 1877 Rama V took as his fifth consort Princess Dararatsami, daughter of Prince Indra Witchayanon of Chiang Mai (ruled 1871-1897). The marriage improved relations with Bangkok and the Prince of Chiang Mai relied on his new connections at court to solve many local political and economic problems. The Lan Na princes received titles and honours from Rama V and they were awarded preferential treatment when they attended the court in Bangkok. However in reality they had been marginalised. Officials sent from Bangkok were recognised as holding the real power and all levels of Lan Na society gradually accepted Siamese authority. The traditional *muang* polity by which Lan Na had been governed was transformed into a centralised bureaucratic system. With the disappearance of the *muang* went the annual ceremonies to the ancestor spirits conducted at city pillars. This drastically reduced the power the Lan Na princes held over their subject. In the city of Chiang Mai the Inthakin pillar was transferred to the temple of Wat Chedi Luang inside the city wall. The protective power of the princes and the symbolism of the *muang* became part of history. In 1892 Lan Na was officially integrated into the kingdom of Siam and by 1908 Bangkok controlled the Lan Na government, paying the princes fixed incomes.

Gold lacquer bowls being carried in a procession, Wat Buak Khok Luang, Chiang Mai.

At some time after authority passed to Bangkok, the ancient ceremony of the anointing of Lan Na prince rulers is said to have been abandoned although in the opinion of Thai scholars, small, discreet ceremonies were still held.[23] If there was change, it came slowly and the shift in political authority did not alter the respect held locally for the Lan Na royal family. The American missionary Daniel McGilvary described a New Year ceremony in Chiang Mai, called *dam hua*, when the ruling prince underwent a ritual bathing and members of the royal family and the elite came to pour lustral water on him, using silver bowls.[24] This ceremony bears remarkable resemblance to the ancient ceremony of anointment. The first, more exclusive part of the ceremony took part in the palace. McGilvary wrote that the great reception hall was crowded with the prince's family and with 'officials of all degrees'. He described the air as 'heavy with the fragrance of flowers, which loaded every table and stand'. All those assembled were in readiness with their silver vessels filled with water, awaiting the arrival of the prince. McGilvary wrote that the whole company received the prince with the 'lowest prostration, after the old time fashion'. Then there was a long invocation of all the 'powers above or beneath, real or imaginary, not to molest, but instead to protect, guide, and bless His Highness' person, kingdom and people, with corresponding curses invoked on all his enemies and theirs'. The inclusion of the invocation demonstrates that even after authority had passed to Bangkok, the princes continued to be regarded as symbolic protectors of the *muang*.

Authority to Bangkok

The shift of authority to Bangkok meant that the Lan Na rulers were obliged to participate in Siamese court ceremonies. Siamese rulers were Theravada Buddhists, but were strongly influenced by Hinduism. The concept of a king who could be a divinity had been introduced by the Khmer in the 9th century. Hinduism was a religion which supported the pomp and circumstance inseparable from absolute monarchy. The tenets of Theravada Buddhism see the destiny of a king to rule as not dependent on divine incarnation but on religious merit. For all men, the accumulation of merit is rewarded by rebirth in happy conditions while those living in poverty and misery are believed to be paying for the de-merit acquired as a result of evil deeds in former lives. Theravada Buddhism is essentially a religion of the people, tolerating kings merely as protectors. Siamese kings protected Buddhism and looked to it for spiritual consolation. At the same time they surrounded themselves with the paraphernalia of Hinduism, retaining Brahmins at court to perform rituals at state ceremonies.

The form of Sinhalese Theravada Buddhism practiced in Lan Na was described as 'purer' than Siamese Theravada Buddhism and Lan Na

A *phasin* from Nan woven with silver and gold metal thread in the central panel and hem border.
(Bank of Thailand Museum, Chiang Mai)

people are said to have expressed disdain for the Brahminism of the Bangkok court.[25] Le May (1926) had stated that he found no evidence of Brahminical ceremonies in the Lan Na courts.[26] In contrast, at the Siamese court, the paraphernalia of Hinduism was manifested in ritual garments and regalia, some imported from India.[27] Since the time of the Siamese court at Ayutthaya, the dress of the king, his heirs, consorts and court officials, had been graded as to the richness of fabric, colour, pattern and style.[28] Quaritch Wales (1931) has described the hierarchical system and the sumptuary laws that applied to dress and regalia worn at the Bangkok court during the reign of Rama VII (1925-1935).

In the 19th century, when the Lan Na princes went to Bangkok to pay tribute to the King of Siam, they were presented with gifts that included items of dress, textiles and regalia, some intended as symbols of office. These garments gave the Lan Na rulers a formal position in the hierarchy of the Bangkok court, thus symbolically restricting their independence. The type of garments, textiles and regalia presented to the Lan Na rulers, their origin and manufacture will be the subject of later chapters.

British Attitudes to Lan Na

The general attitude of the British, with their vast empire, was to regard Lan Na and Siam in the same way as they regarded Burma, as an outpost of India. India's Burmese dependencies suffered distance from the centre of power although their remoteness lay not in mileage but in the physical obstacles of mountains, primary forests and rivers. Communication did not naturally run towards India to the west, but in a north-south direction along rivers and river valleys. In cultural, as well as physical terms, Burma, and by implication its neighbour Lan Na, were intrinsically part of Southeast Asia, not India. Furthermore, the British made the mistake of imagining that because they were present in other Asian countries, they would be in a position to understand the Tai. The other Asian countries that the British knew were colonised and the people of Lan Na and Siam were not.

In summary, there was a relatively egalitarian dispersal of status among members of the ruling Lan Na families, and new prince rulers were appointed through a selection process involving a council, made up of royalty, senior officials and Buddhist monks. The authority of the Lan Na princes was embedded in a form of Sinhalese Theravada Buddhism and indigenous spirit religion administered through the *muang* system. Although Siamese kings were also Theravada Buddhists, certain Hindu customs were incorporated in their system of government. This affected the way court rituals were conducted and the level of hierarchy imposed on court dress and regalia.

Teachers from Mission School, Lampang, c. 1900. (The papers of Dr. Samuel Craig Peoples in the collection of Payap University, Chiang Mai)

Opposite:
Lan Na *phasin* with a cotton waistband, patterned central panel and silk
and silver and gold metal thread in the
geometrically patterned decorative
hem *(jok)* border.
(Bank of Thailand Museum, Chiang Mai)

The relationship between Lan Na and Siam has been the subject of debate. Some observers saw the Lan Na princes as more or less self-governing, especially those who visited the principalities. Certainly until the death of Prince Kawiloros of Chiang Mai in 1870, there was fierce resistance to Siamese hegemony. The accession of Prince Indra Witchayanon (ruled 1871-1897), who was considered to be a weak ruler, led to a shift in power to Bangkok, although this was not accepted without some grievances being expressed. Private ceremonies that acknowledged the authority of the Lan Na princes were held for some time after control passed to Siam. The traditional role of the Lan Na princes within the *muang* system was marginalised and this in turn affected court ritual and the style of dress and regalia worn on ceremonial occasions.

[1] The numbers /f.109/ refer to the folio pages of the original manuscript. The Tavatimsa Heaven is the thirty-third and highest Buddhist heaven.

[2] Doi Tung, Mae Sai district, Chiang Rai province is the site of Wat Phrathat Doi Tung.

[3] Wyatt and Aroonrut 1995: 5-6.

[4] The genealogy charts on pages 262-265 are based on the Buddhist chronicles of Chiang Mai and Nan, on Thai genealogies and on oral history obtained through interviews conducted with surviving descendants of the Lan Na royal family.

[5] Aroonrut 1977, Quaritch Wales 1977, Ganjanapan 1984, Vatikiotis 1984, Mabbett 1985, Premchit and Dore 1992, Zhu Liangwen 1992.

[6] Heine-Geldern 1942.

[7] Wyatt and Aroonrut 1995: 152.

[8] Wyatt 1994: 99.

[9] Wilson and Hanks 1985.

[10] Wyatt 1994: 120.

[11] Wyatt and Aroonrut 1995: 175.

[12] Wyatt 1994: 115-126.

[13] Europeans ignored the concept of polygamy as a political tool, interpreting the custom according to Victorian moral values.

[14] Abhakorn 1984.

[15] Pritsana 1973.

[16] Sethakul 1989.

[17] Le May 1926.

[18] Wilson and Hanks 1985: 1.

[19] Bock 1884, Hallett 1890, McCarthy 1900, McGilvary 1912, Le May 1926.

[20] Records of the Fifth reign (1883) National Archives, Bangkok.

[21] Hallett 1898 repr. 1988: 406-410

[22] Brailey 1994: 25, 104-105.

[23] Interview with Dr. Udom Roongruangsri, Chiang Mai University, 1997.

[24] McGilvary 1912: 85.

[25] Quaritch Wales 1931.

[26] Steinberg 1987: 67.

[27] Dr. Udom Roongruangsri, Chiang Mai University confirmed this view during an interview at Chiang Mai, Feb. 1997.

[28] Gittinger 1982, Guy 1992.

[29] Gervaise 1688.

54

Chapter Three

Culture and Design

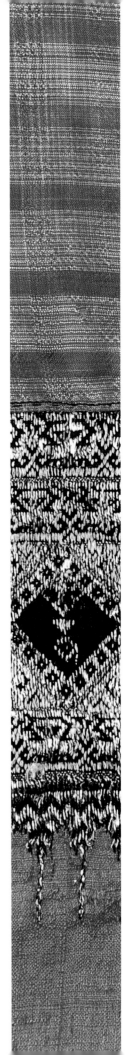

Lan Na textiles are a symbol of the well-balanced rhythms of social and religious custom. They are an expression of women's creative talents, and the knowledge to cultivate, spin, weave and dye yarn was believed to have originally passed to them from the guardian spirits. The complex beauty of Lan Na textiles is echoed in the other decorative arts. Stylised weaving and embroidery patterns derived from religious iconography and from nature are echoed in temple mural paintings and in the gold stencil designs used to decorate temple interiors. There is similarity in the patterns of shimmering inlaid glass and mother of pearl found on interior and exterior temple walls, and on temple furniture and the stunning arrangement of colours used in silk weaving patterns. The sources of colour, dyes for yarn and pigments for painting often came from the same plant and mineral sources. The relationship between mural painting and textiles extends to the depiction of dress and weaving patterns, so closely observed that it is possible to match actual weaving patterns with those portrayed on temple walls.

Textiles, Religion and the Rice Cycle

In Lan Na society the annual cycle of rice production formed the basis of the economy and was linked to those of cotton and silk production, to Buddhist temple rites and to spirit religion practices.[1] Men and women shared work in the rice fields, except for ploughing which is by custom a male job. Women practiced sericulture, cultivated cotton and gathered

Opposite and right: Lan Na *phasin* with a cotton waistband, purple silk central panel and hem border (*jok*) with silk, silver and gold metal thread. (Paothong Thongchua collection)

the raw materials necessary for dyeing yarn. They processed these raw materials and used looms set up under the house to weave cloth.[2] The ruling families were entitled to free labour (corvée) to tend their rice fields and could also take a percentage of the silk and cotton produced by women as tax in kind.

The annual rice cycle begins at the end of the dry season when fields are prepared for the new crop. Suitable land is cleared for cotton growing. Mulberry trees, which provide food for silkworms, are pruned. This activity coincides with Buddhist New Year rites and celebrations *(songkran)* when Buddha images are bathed and displayed in public and human sins are ritually washed away. Respect is paid to Buddhist monks and village elders, and ancestors are commemorated. The awaited monsoon rains are invoked through spirit religion practices that include fertility rituals involving a rain-making ceremony *(bunbangfai)* that is addressed to village guardian spirits.

The start of the monsoon season brings a period of intense agricultural labour. The waterlogged fields are planted with rice seedlings that have been raised in special nursery beds. Cotton is sown and silk worms (caterpillars) are raised from eggs laid by silk moths. As the rice seedlings develop Buddhist Lent *(phansa)* begins, novices are ordained and monks go into retreat. The period of the monsoon brings accelerated plant growth and is a relatively quiet stage of the rice cycle. It is devoted to worship, and is a time for piety and asceticism.[3] It is also a period when silk worms evolve to the cocoon stage and the silk filaments are reeled from them. The cocoons are heated in water to loosen the gum (seracin) allowing the filament to unwind. The filament is spun onto bamboo reels and prepared for dyeing. At around the same time, cotton bolls are ginned to remove the seeds, then washed and prepared for spinning.

Teak temple pillar painted black and decorated with gold stucco and inlaid mirror glass, Wat Phumin, Nan.

Left: Interior of Wat Pong Yang Kok, Lampang.

Opposite:
Top left and right: Painted and stencilled gold leaf decoration of animals and foliage, Wat Phra That Lampang Luang, Lampang.

Middle left and right: Lan Na temple decoration. Painted and stencilled gold leaf on painted wood. Wat Lai Hin, and Wat Pong Yang Kok, Lampang.

Left: Manuscript chest decorated with painted and stencilled gold leaf on painted wood. Wat Lai Hin, Lampang.

Lan Na court dancers performing in a
royal procession to Wat Kaet Karam,
Chiang Mai, c. 1900.
(Payap University Archive, Chiang Mai)

The next stage in the rice cycle occurs when the rice is running to ear, vital for the development of the crop. A spirit religion ceremony *(bun khaw saak)* is held to invoke the spirits of ancestors to guard the crop. Puffed rice is offered in the rice fields so that the guardian spirit of the fields and ancestor spirits will be aware that the fields are cultivated and they will guard the crop. The people believe that puffed rice is a suitable offering to the dead because puffed rice is like death, it cannot produce new growth.

The rainy season and the period of Buddhist Lent end in October when a series of merit-making ceremonies and festivities take place, including the presentation of robes and gifts to the monks *(bun kathin)*. From November to January the rice harvest is gathered in. The agricultural cycle concludes with a grand merit-making ceremony *(bun phrawes)* which celebrates the harvest. The ceremony is described as 'the dedication of nature and man to a higher ethical purpose and thereby securing peace, prosperity and health'.[4] Once the harvest is safely stored in the village rice barns, women turn to a more prolonged period of processing silk and cotton into yarn and preparing warp and weft for weaving. The loom itself is constructed with tongue and groove joints and wooden pins that make it easy to dismantle and store at times in the year when space is needed for agricultural products. It can be quickly re-assembled during the weaving season. Those entering villages after the harvest may be greeted by the clacking sound of loom heddles and cloth beaters in action.

The Culture of Weaving

According to an ancient Tai legend, passed from generation to generation through story telling, the guardian spirits taught women to weave through a male intermediary Khun Borom. The ancestry of the legendary Khun Borom is subject to speculation. In local legends he hails from Sipsong Pan Na, or from Laos or from Lan Na, depending on who is telling the story. Khun Borom taught that weaving was a household duty to be carried out with skill and diligence, to bring respect in this life and the reward of spiritual merit in the next. The legend of Khun Borom has survived in the form of oral homilies and prose.

> *A good wife is like a ploughshare. If she is skilled at weaving then her husband can wear fine clothes. A wife who talks harshly and is unskilled at her loom makes a family poor and shabby in dress.*
>
> *If you want to be rich you must be creative and diligent. Be careful in making merit and give donations to the monastery. Be skilled at the loom and you will be respected and never get into debt. Measure newly woven cloth with skill. Show it to an expert and if she approves keep the cloth until you can get a fair price.*[5]

The link between diligence, wealth and merit applied to village women and to female royalty. Even a wealthy princess was not exempt from 'the necessity for making the silken garments which are the symbol of her rank, any more than the poorer women can do without weaving their cotton clothes'.[6] Most women were taught to spin and weave, regardless of class and being an accomplished weaver was a way of gaining status in society. Female members of the royal family supervised their attendants and slaves who worked together at court.[7] Some princesses were extremely talented weavers and their skills are still acknowledged.[8]

Textile production in traditional Tai society was an integral part of a socialization process for all women, beginning from about the age of five and continuing until the end of life.[9] In their early years girls helped their mothers by performing simple skills associated with the preparation of yarn. At puberty they acquired basic weaving skills and made simple cloths for use at home. From the age of eighteen until marriage they wove cloth for family consumption, for their trousseau and some items for barter or cash. After marriage and the birth of children, they wove for the home and family and sold or bartered any excess cloth. They made robes, pillows and sheets for the monks and textiles such as banners used in religious ceremonies. Once the children had grown they focussed more

A Lan Na weaver working at a frame loom with four heddles, temple mural painting, Wat Phumin, Nan.

A weaver hand picking patterns by inserting a sword into the warp before introducing the weft thread.

on textiles for the temple and acted as teachers and supervisors to younger weavers. Younger women presented them with textiles as a sign of respect. In old age they continued to act as teachers and prepared cloth for 'the final day' which involves weaving a plain white coffin cover for use at the time of their cremation rites. In the scenario described above, every stage of a woman's life is defined through making, giving and receiving textiles, and her status in society is reflected in the social interaction involved in these processes.

Lan Na Women: Followers and Leaders

The Buddhist chronicles generally refer to female royalty as 'followers'.[10] When women are referred to in person they are identified as the dependents of men, living as homemakers, nurturers and pious Buddhists.[11] Tai Buddhist literature has particular ways of explaining away the behaviour of women who do not fit this stereotype. For example, the Chiang Mai chronicle accounts for the feats of a courageous female warrior, Lady Si Muang, by ascribing her 'male' behaviour to the fact that she was pregnant with a male child. Buddhist chronicles use this type of reasoning because the wider world of political and military action was deemed to be a man's world.

This attitude to women is revealed in the 19th century immigrant resettlement records. Women are present by implication only in the use of the term 'families'. In the records that accounted for the distribution of ethnic groups and their occupations, only men and male occupations, tanners, potters, silversmiths, lacquer makers, woodcarvers, boatmen and foresters are listed. Women are excluded from the records although the occupation of spinning, weaving and dyeing cloth was of major importance in supplying textiles for the temple, the court and the household. Women are portrayed in a more positive light in Lan Na temple mural paintings, where their activities, including trading, textile production, farming and religious observation are recorded alongside the activities of men. The temple murals of Wat Phumin, Nan Province include a scene of a princess directing male and female troops into battle from a howdah on the back of an elephant and a mural painting at Wat Phra Singh shows women trading in the marketplace. Women were directly powerful in their role as spirit mediums and some female members of Lan Na royal families wielded extensive political power as a result. Decisions affecting affairs of state, including taxation, were sometimes taken on the strength of pronouncements made by a princess as to what was the cause of spirit displeasure.[12]

Those writing outside the conventions of Buddhist literature recall times when women of high rank took an active role in warfare, politics and diplomacy. In 1545 AD Queen Chira Prapa negotiated with the King of Ayutthaya to prevent warfare, later securing money from him towards the cost of building a temple.[13] In the late 19th century, in his

A princess directing her troops into battle from an elephant howdah, temple mural painting, Wat Nong Bua, Nan.

survey of the Upper Salween River the Siamese government official Nai Bancha Phumasathan wrote respectfully of Nang Mia, an impressive woman leader and administrator in the politically sensitive and unstable border area of Mae Hong Son.[14] Foreign male observers endorsed these views by describing the more unusual female occupations they witnessed while travelling in Lanna.[15] Sir Ernst Satow wrote about a journey from Bangkok to Chiang Mai that he made in the 1880s. He travelled north by river and across country noting that female pilots were operating on the river and female officials were working in the towns. European men imbued with the traditional 19th century values of their class felt uncomfortable when confronted by females in professional roles. This is evident in the disapproving tone they used to report on such matters.

In the 19th century a small group of female American Presbyterian missionaries recorded their impressions of the status of Lan Na women,

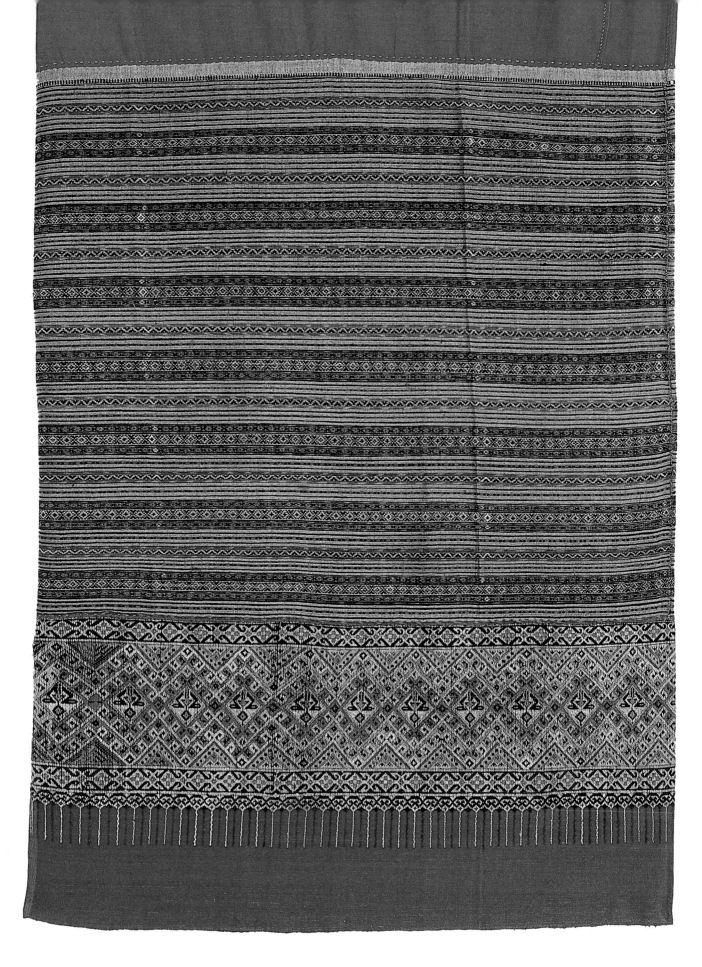

noting that they were relatively liberated when compared with women in China, where American Presbyterian missionaries also worked.[16] These judgements were expressed in a series of articles published under the heading 'Woman's Work for Woman and Our Mission Field', in the Philadelphia Presbyterian Mission magazine (1883-1894). The magazine provided a platform for female missionaries where they described their experiences of life in the field to churchgoers in America who supported their work through donations. The magazine articles cover a wide range of topics and include accounts of the role and status of women in the countries where the missionaries proselytized. Although not overtly feminist, they stress the strength and personal freedom permitted to women in the cities and villages of Lan Na. From their standpoint as Presbyterians, they viewed Lan Na women as 'heathen', but took a less biased view when reporting on daily life and the social interaction that took place between them. The American missionary, Emilie McGilvary went as far as to describe female royalty as a great power in the land. In her descriptions of life at the Chiang Mai court, she states that Princess Tipkesorn, the wife of Prince Indra Witchayanon (ruled 1871-1897), had the reigns of government virtually in her hands and her husband was the nominal ruler. Mrs. Peoples commented on the life style and independent wealth of Princess Ubonwanna, sister of Tipkesorn, who was a landowner, slave owner and inter-state trader in her own right. The missionaries also describe the relatively open lifestyle enjoyed by Lan Na

Lan Na woman with a Luang Prabang-style sash and *phasin* decorated with gold metal thread, temple mural painting, Wat Wiang Ta, Phrae.

Opposite:
Lan Na *phasin* with repeat floral patterns in the central panel and geometric patterns in the hem border.
(Bank of Thailand Museum, Chiang Mai)

Princess Ubonwanna, daughter of Prince Kawiloros Suriyavong (ruled 1856-1870). (Chiang Mai National Museum)

Right: Prince Indrayongyote Choti, the ninth ruler of Lamphun with his wife and son, Prince Chakrakam, who later became the last ruler.

princesses, who were able to visit them in their homes, leaving the palace in the company of female attendants. It was not only women who commented on this independence. Hallett visited Princess Ubonwanna on the advice of the American missionary Reverend Wilson, who had told him that she was by far the best source of information concerning trade in Lanna and the surrounding states.[17] Hallett recorded the statistics she gave him and used them in his reports to the British government. Such freedom of contact with foreigners would not have occurred in the restricted atmosphere of the Bangkok court where the king's wives and concubines lived a segregated life and were forbidden from leaving the confines of the palace.[18]

Before the arrival of female American missionaries, girls of all classes were not taught to read and write, an option only open to boys who could attend temple schools run by Buddhist monks. American Presbyterian missionaries were the first to set up schools for girls in Chiang Mai and other cities in Lan Na.[19] The education of upper class women was restricted to domestic skills such as weaving, embroidery, flower arranging, lace making and cooking. These skills were considered to be invaluable for women living at court.[20] Lan Na Tai women were judged by their weaving skills. Emilie McGilvary (1883) wrote that although women did not know how to read, they were always trained to be useful in their homes, and a girl who could not weave her own dress was considered as ignorant as an American girl who could not read. Given the skills required to set up and operate a loom, which include complex systems for counting threads and intricate patterning techniques, weaving sets a benchmark for intelligence, creativity and artistry.

If there was relative freedom for Lan Na princesses it did not extend to marriage alliances in which women were pawns in political coalitions. The tables on page 43 provide lists of consorts given in arranged marriages to Prince Kawila of Chiang Mai and to Prince Anantayot of Nan. The custom of a royal bride moving to the household of the bridegroom was contrary to traditions practiced in rural communities where men moved from the natal household to the bride's household.[21] The Tai Yuan believed that if a bride moved into her husband's house, there would be conflict between her ancestral matrilineal spirits and the matrilineal spirits of her adopted household.[22] In contrast, a groom was incorporated into his wife's cult group on marriage. Women in rural Lan Na did not have their marriages arranged and the choice of a partner was by consent of both parties.[23] The absence of choice among women of the ruling classes indicates a class-based variation in custom, although there were exceptions. The ubiquitous Princess Ubonwanna resisted arranged marriage by selecting her own partners although they were either murdered or deported by agents of the Chiang Mai royal family.[24]

It was the custom in Lan Na and in the surrounding inland states that princesses continued to wear the dress of their homeland when they married into a foreign royal family and went to live abroad. If a prince gained a number of consorts particularly from more powerful states and from different ethnic groups, then bringing them together publicly in indigenous dress signalled the extent of his influence. This symbolism was important in political terms and in the 19th century was intended for a wider audience, a development that will be examined later.

The relative freedom experienced by Lan Na women has to be placed in the context of their legal status. As was established earlier, women were subject to the authority of the prince rulers, in the same way as men. Women classed as citizens (*phrai*) might be called to work in a ruler's house or in his fields, or be forced to pay tribute in the form of farm produce, including cotton and silk yarn, locally-produced dyestuffs and hand-woven textiles. Those women not called on for labour were often left to bear the brunt of work in the family rice fields when the ruler summoned men. Satow gave this as the reason why he often saw more women working in the village ricefields than men.

Women classed as slaves (*kha*) had little freedom as their working conditions were totally controlled by their owners. Holt Hallett wrote that 'the judicial price of a male slave was 54 rupees, and of a female slave 72 rupees'. This was because 'the woman does most of the work' and 'the woman is decidedly, as a worker, worth more than the man'.[25] If a woman married a slave, the owner of the slave had the right to one male child or a daughter if no son was born to the couple. If a female slave married, it was the custom that her owner purchased her new husband so that the two could live together. This benefited owners of female

A simple Lan Na *phasin* with striped pattern in the central panel and a plain cotton hem border.
(Bank of Thailand Museum, Chiang Mai)

Typical Lanna-style carved wooden pediment and gable of Wat Pan Tao, Chiang Mai.

Opposite:
Top: A Lan Na temple and landscape, temple mural painting on wood, Wat Phra That Lampang Luang, Lampang.

Left: Temple furniture, carved and gilded wood. (Chiang Mai National Museum)

Right: A *boddhisattva* holding a fan, painted in gold leaf on a crimson ground, temple mural painting, Wat Lai Hin, Lampang.

textile workers and any children born to them were allowed to stay in the workshops with their mothers at least until they were weaned.[26] The commercial value of slave women who were good weavers was well known. In Chiang Mai good weavers could be purchased for 50 rupees which was considered to be an excellent investment as they could often earn double that amount in just one year.

The active participation of female royalty in politics, commerce and spirit religion led to a more egalitarian form of society than existed in many Southeast Asian courts. However, the freedom of female royalty was restricted by marital alliances arranged in many cases with distant states where they were sent to live. For most ordinary women, as for men, freedom to trade and move without hindrance in society was hampered by tributary obligations to the rulers.

Lan Na Architecture, Arts and Crafts

According to the Tai chronicles, towards the end of his time on earth the Buddha visited many lands where he left relics. He bequeathed hairs from his head and planted footprints in the earth in the Lan Na cities of Chiang Saen, Lamphun, Nan, Lampang and Chiang Mai.[27] Relic chambers *(stupas)* and temples *(wat)* were built on the sites. The tenets of Buddhism dictate that it is a ruler's duty to maintain religious sites. The Chiang Mai and Nan chronicles list the virtuous acts of the Lan Na kings who throughout history, conserved monuments, constructed new temples, and commissioned the casting and gilding of Buddha images.[28] They sponsored monks to make new copies of sacred manuscripts, viewed as a way of furthering the future of the ruling family. They commissioned artists to paint temple mural paintings, and sponsored wood carvers and carpenters to decorate temple facades and interiors and to make furniture, such as pulpits and manuscript chests. Female royalty produced woven and embroidered covers for palm leaf manuscripts, banners to hang in the temples and textiles for the personal use of the monks.

Lan Na developed an endogenous culture in the 14th century, and its arts, architecture, literature and crafts were exported to the surrounding inland states. It was a tradition from the time of King Mengrai (1259-1317) that the Lan Na rulers employed indigenous craft workers and captives from the surrounding inland states. They were resettled in the cities and in later times of war their descendants were often uprooted and taken to serve another ruler. Throughout the history of the inland states artisans were treated as part of the spoils of war. Skilled architects, sculptors, painters, scribes, metal workers, wood carvers, silversmiths, goldsmiths, potters, weavers and lacquerware makers contributed to the arts and crafts of victorious states. When fortunes changed and a state was weakened those same workers, or their artisan descendants, were

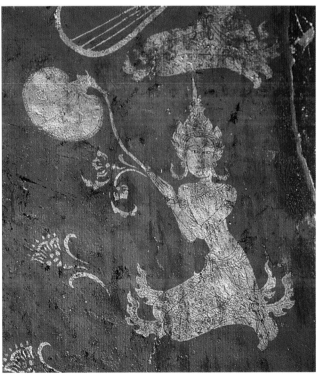

CULTURE AND DESIGN   67

Looking out from the Viharn Luang to the main entrance of Wat Phra That Lampang Luang, Lampang.

Temple exterior, wooden walls stencilled with gold, two dimensional carved and inlaid *deva*, animals and floral patterns, Wat Phra That Lampang Luang, Lampang.

captured and moved to a newly victorious state. In this way temples, monuments, sculpture, paintings and crafts shared common features of construction and decoration.

The Burmese occupation of Lan Na from the 16th to the 18th century could have meant the end of the indigenous Lan Na style. However it has been argued that the prolonged occupation had little impact on art, architecture and literature because the Burmese rulers employed Lan Na craft workers.[29] Temples and Buddha images, it is claimed, are of pure Lan Na style. The art and crafts that are identified as Burmese were actually the work of Tai Yai (Shan) artists. The Tai Yai lived in principalities that were independent of Burma, and had strong political and cultural ties with the Lan Na Tai. Many Tai Yai worked in Lan Na as foresters and some gave part of their profits to build temples and make offerings as a way of making merit and compensating for depleting the forests.[30] An example of a Tai Yai offering, in the form of a miniature Buddhist altar is now on display in Chiang Mai National Museum and bears the dedication:

> In the year 2152 BE [1609 AD] *the second month, this altar gilted with gold was donated by Phraya Choong Gu* [Tai Yai name] *and Phraya Daga Ma* [wife] *and household. May the merit gained be to all Men and Theravada* [Buddhism].

When the Burmese were expelled from Lan Na the new line of princes began a vast programme of restoration and rebuilding. They repaired city fortifications and major religious monuments that had been sacked and plundered during the war. Relic chambers (*stupas*) and temples built of brick and stucco were repaired and although many escaped serious structural damage, royal palaces and buildings constructed of timber and bamboo were razed to the ground. The princes commissioned monk scribes to make new copies from old palm leaf manuscripts, instructing them to add the history of the Burmese campaign, and records of the restoration programmes. The monks and the men and women who contributed to the Lan Na renaissance were indigenous Tai Yuan and resettled immigrants from the Shan States, Sipsong Pan Na and western Laos, not a new formula but a recurrence of labour movements in previous centuries.

The unique quality of Lanna Buddhist architecture is expressed in the building materials, the form of construction, and the decoration. The wood tiled roofs slope outwards in graded steps and form tiers of eaves, often three or seven that have numerical significance as representing domains of creation in the Buddhist cosmology. Most temples are built as beam-frame teak structures with double lines of interior teak pillars that define the interior space of a lofty inner temple and narrower, lower flanking ambulatories. Teakwood is an important element in the decoration of facades, and was carved and inlaid with patterns of coloured stone and mother-of-pearl. Interior teak wall panels were painted and stencilled in gold leaf and the large teak pillars that supported the roof, were painted and stencilled or decorated with stucco and inlaid with coloured glass. Many walls were decorated with mural paintings.

The murals were painted on wood panels, or on stucco, using a fresco technique that involved preparing the walls and allowing the surface to dry before applying the paint. This differs from the wet fresco technique developed in Renaissance Italy. In contrast to Renaissance frescoes, Lan Na frescoes are fragile and paint flakes easily from the walls. This has led to periodic restoration that has sometimes altered the character and style of the murals. Nevertheless the school of Lan Na temple mural painting is an important and unique one with a solid and lasting tradition. Lan Na artists put emphasis on contemporary life in towns and villages and included important historical events in the narrative. Importantly for present-day dress and textile historians, they portrayed textiles and clothing as worn at court and in the villages, often detailing the weaving patterns and trimmings.

Painting materials were obtained locally although wealthy communities funded the use of gold leaf and the import of rarer pigments from China. Indigenous pigments were extracted from indigo plants, from the soil, from special soot, and from trees, plants and their roots. Tree gum or animal glue was used as a binder. The expressive depiction of landscape can be partly credited to the brushes that were made from shredded tree bark, plant roots and stems. Fine, sinewy lines were produced with brushes made of animal hair. The nature of the materials and the free way the artists applied the paint has helped to define Lan Na

Shan men wearing *luntaya* robes, manuscript painting, Wat Nong Bua.

A Lan Na woman seated on a mat, Wat Nong Bua.

Deatail of the carving on a temple manuscript chest, painted and gilded and inlaid with mother-of-pearl and coloured glass.

mural painting as a special school. Another contributing factor is the way that the stories are told in a continuous narrative form with outdoor scenes separated by architectural devices and by landscape and interior scenes by walls and by textile screens. There is little sense of perspective and the paint is applied in a flat, two-dimensional way.

Lan Na Language and Script

The Tai Yuan used a Tai script written in Yuan dialect for secular matters and Mon script, called *tham* for religious texts. *Tham* is the script used in nearly all palm leaf manuscripts stored in Lan Na temples.[31] The use of Yuan dialect can be traced in physical terms to the 15th century when the script was engraved on stone tablets and stone pillars. When Lan Na became a major power in the 15th century aspects of the culture, including script, spread to Lan Xang (western Laos), Chiang Tung (eastern Shan States), and Chiang Rung (Sipsong Pan Na), leading to the description 'Culture of the Region of the Dhamma [*tham*] letters'.[32] Interestingly, script in Yuan dialect is found on mystical symbolic

diagrams *(yantra)* throughout this region. Many scholars have also referred to the mutually understandable dialects of the people, noting only minor regional variations.[33]

This chapter has emphasized the relationship between textile production and the rice cycle and the seasonal rites of Buddhism and spirit religion. As in many other Southeast Asian societies, textiles were almost exclusively the work of women and were a means by which they gained status in village, temple and court society. Weavers employed at court came from a range of ethnic groups, reflecting the origins of male craft workers who over the centuries were captured and resettled from one inland state to another. They produced arts and crafts with many shared designs although there were regional and local variations. The textile workers also created weaving and embroidery designs that were common throughout the inland states, although as will be evident, they skillfully maintained an individual identity.

A carved wooden *deva* amidst foliage on a temple pediment.

A scripture cover embroidered with scenes from the Life of the Buddha. Reading from the right: the Great Departure, the Enlightenment and the Descent from the Tavatimsa Heaven. Details of the donor, Chao Fong Cham of Wieng Yong, aged 72 are included.
(Hariphunchai National Museum, Lamphun)

A scripture cover embroidered with a central deity in silver and gold thread surrounded by a foliage border.
(Hariphunchai National Museum, Lamphun)

74

1 Personal observation, Chiang Mai Province, 1981-1991. The value of women's work in the agricultural cycle has been recently recognized. Dulyapach 1985; Feldstein and Poats 1989; Shinawatra, Diowwilai, Bangliang 1990.

2 According to oral history there were times when men helped with processing. This included wartime when there was a premium on cloth production (interviews In Chiang Mai and Nan 1985).

3 Tambiah, 1970: 155-156.

4 Tambiah, 1970: 160.

5 These homilies were recorded by Jeruwan Thamawat (1980) and translated from central Thai into English by Acharn Seurat (Conway 1992).

6 Bock, 1884, repr. 1986: 322-323.

7 Hallett, 1898 repr. 1988.

8 Interview with *Chao* Nid and *Chao* Vilai na Chiang Tung, Chiang Mai 1997.

9 Smutkupt, 1993.

10 Interview with Dr. Roongruangsiri, Chiang Mai University, February 1997.

11 Rhum, 1994: 156-157.

12 Hallett, 1898, repr. 1988: 105.

13 Le May, 1926: 26.

14 Nai Bancha Phumasathan, 1890: 36.

15 Bock, 1884, Satow 1885-1886, Brailey 1994: 30, 43.

16 McGilvary E.1883, Cort 1889, Peoples 1890.

17 Hallett, 1898, repr. 1988: 103-104

18 Quaritch-Wales, 1931.

19 Bock, 1884, Swanson, 1996.

20 Viravaidya, 1994.

21 Tambiah, 1970, Davis 1974, Potter 1977, Rhum 1994.

22 Davis, 1974: 53-62

23 Moerman, 1975, Potter 1977

24 Bock, 1884 repr. 1986: 395-396.

25 Hallett, 1898 repr. 1988: 131.

26 Interview at the Lamphun workshop of Chao Patpong (1996).

27 Identified in the Chiang Mai and Nan chronicles.

28 Rajadhon (1961) states that Buddhists regard temple building as a highly meritorious act and a praise worthy sacrifice of time, labour and wealth.

29 Penth, 1994.

30 Panichphant, 1993.

31 *Tham* script is taught at university and in some monasteries as a way of preserving Lanna culture.

32 Penth 1994.

33 Grabowsky, 1993: 20, Moerman, 1965.

An interesting Lan Na *phasin* with a cotton waistband, wide horizontal bands of cotton and silver metal thread and plain hem border, Nan Province.
(Darabhirom Museum, Chiang Mai)

Chapter Four

Status, Protection, Identity:
Lan Na Court Dress: 1781-1871

This chapter examines Lan Na court dress in the time frame 1781-1871, beginning with the accession of Prince Kawila of Chiang Mai (ruled 1781-1813) and ending in 1871 with the accession of Prince Indra Witchayanon, seventh Prince of Chiang Mai. These ninety years saw the transformation of Lan Na from a war-torn bankrupt country to a stable agricultural society. This was a time of regrouping and some major inland principalities and their satellites that had paid tribute to China and Burma changed allegiance to Siam. Initially Prince Kawila and his brothers were faced with many problems. Skirmishes in the isolated border areas were extremely difficult to prevent as the forests and hills provided a haven for small armies and gangs of bandits. However, by the 1860s there was a degree of stability and trade flourished between the inland states as pack animal caravans travelled to and from Yunnan and the Shan States avoiding areas where there was still conflict.

Dress and textiles were an important way of communicating the identity of groups of people living in the inland states. In the time frame of 1781-1871 there were common features of dress and methods of patterning cloth that were ascribed to certain groups. As new settlers joined existing populations, interesting adaptations took place. However, some components and characteristics of dress defined as 'essential elements', were not altered so that a particular style of dress could still be viewed as 'traditional'.[1] This happened in the villages and at court, as a result of inter-marriage, resettlement and adaptation to changing political and economic circumstances.

Lan Na *phasin* with a cotton waistband, silk and silver and gold metal thread in the central panel, with a silk, gold and silver hem border.
(Bank of Thailand Museum, Chiang Mai)

Prince *(uparat)* Bunthawong of Chiang Mai with his attendant, c. 1875. (National Archives, Bangkok)

Opposite:
Top left: Lan Na princes going into battle on elephants, temple mural painting, Wat Buak Khok Luang, Chiang Mai.

Top right: Lan Na soldiers with guns, spears and swords, temple mural painting, Wat Phumin, Nan.

Middle left: A young man with loin cloth twisted high on the hips to reveal his thigh tattoos, temple mural painting, Wat Buak Khok Luang, Chiang Mai.

Middle right: Soldiers carrying weapons, temple mural painting, Wat Phumin, Nan.

Below: A sword blade with a decorated silver handle, Chiang Mai National Museum.

Lan Na Male Military Dress

In order to deal with attacks on the borders, the princes assembled troops in the major principalities of Chiang Mai, Nan, Phrae, Lamphun and Lampang and in villages throughout the *muang*. Village headmen were expected to provide a quota of military conscripts who received no formal training but learnt military skills in the field. No standard military uniforms were issued to them. Troops were led by a prince ruler (*chao*) or by his prince deputy (*uparat*), or by another member of the elite to whom they swore allegiance. The armies crossed the valleys and difficult hill terrain on elephants, on horseback or on foot, with oxen carrying supplies. Mounted cavalry officers and foot soldiers were armed with swords and spears with dangerous curved and hooked blades. Swords and spears carried by senior officers had tooled silver handles decorated with floral patterns and officers mounted on elephants had swords with elongated shafts and special long-handled spears. The Tai Lue had an excellent reputation as sword makers and in Chiang Mai they manufactured arms in the silversmith district on the Wualai Road.[2] Other cities also had special districts where weapons were made.

Although the princes used locally-made weapons, to be known to possess a cache of firearms was significant in the power struggles of the time, even if they were unreliable and often malfunctioned. Their use, alongside spears and swords, is illustrated in mural paintings and was recorded in the Tai Buddhist chronicles. In his official report to Prince Phuttawong of Chiang Mai (ruled 1825-1846), the intelligence agent and government official Thao Sittimongkhon reckoned that the Prince of Chiang Tung [Keng Tung] had a weapons store of 200 guns (*puen lek*) and 2,000 flintlock rifles. Thao Sittimongkhon also described a skirmish on the Shan borders in which enemy soldiers were armed with another type of gun (*priab*) and some carried flintlock rifles.[3]

Temple mural paintings show Lan Na officers and soldiers, and Burmese and Shan enemy soldiers, engaged in battle. Surprisingly the Lan Na princes and their troops are portrayed without helmets or any kind of body armour. Tai Yuan and Tai Yai foot soldiers have bare chests and wear loincloths although a few, probably officers and foreign troops, wear shirts. They have short hair cut in a circle on the crown with the sides shaved although Tai Yai soldiers have long hair often coiled in a topknot and secured with a white headband.

A photograph of Prince (*uparat*) Bunthawong, brother of Prince Indra Witchayanon (ruled 1871-1897) and his attendant shows us how unprepared for battle they were, by European standards of the time. Prince Bunthawong was an accomplished soldier and commanded the army in campaigns on the northern Lan Na borders. He has no helmet, his hair is cut in Lan Na style with a short circle on the crown that stands up like bristles on a stiff brush, he has a bare chest and wears a plaid *chong kraben* and open sandals. He holds a sword across his lap and the military attendant at his feet is similarly dressed. This type of clothing

78

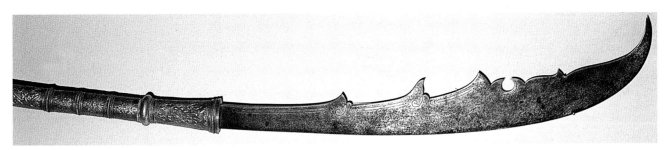

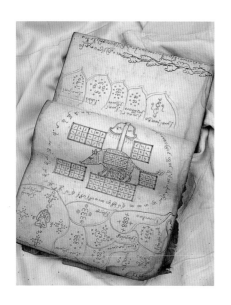

Book belonging to a spirit doctor with ink *yantra* diagrams, and texts, ink on hand-made paper.
(Barbie Campbell-Cole)

Right: Soldiers marching into battle, Wat Phra Singh, Chiang Mai.

Silk trousers with anthropomorphic animals and symbolic diagrams *(yantra)* of circles, squares and triangles filled with numbers, letters and symbols, read or recited as magical incantations *(gatha)*.
(Barbie Campbell-Cole)

was acceptable in battle because the Lan Na princes and their men believed that strong protection was provided by spirit cloths, body decoration and spirit religion rituals. In fact there was a common belief among the people that charismatic princes like Kawila and Bunthawong were imbued with supernatural powers that made them invisible to the enemy and immune from injury.[4]

To ward off evil spirits soldiers carried cotton cloths or wore cotton vests or jackets covered in mystical symbolic diagrams *(yantra)*.[5] The diagrams were drawn in squares, circles and triangles with mythical figures and animals placed strategically among and around them. Some included images of the Buddha and his disciples and angels *(devas)*, others had grotesque animals, giants and local spirits. The circles and squares were filled with numbers, letters and symbols that were read or recited as magical incantations *(gatha)*.[6] Numbers appearing in the *yantra* represented stars, suns and planets, or their mythical gods and goddesses, and were often selected according to the horoscope of the person for whom the magic was created.

The earliest known *yantra* is Pa Kua, the Eight Trigrams, created by the Chinese Emperor Fu Hsi around 2852 BC. He drew lines in configurations to represent natural energy and the elements and they were inscribed in stone and bronze. The Eight Trigrams were the basis of alchemy and were viewed as a way of channelling positive power in nature and as a means of protecting against negative power. This basic formula evolved and changed to suit the beliefs of different societies. In Ancient Greece it had developed as a form of mathematical mysticism that expressed a unique order. Script and numbers set within grids and circles aimed to represent a perfect concept of man, society, and culture situated in harmony with the natural world. In inland Southeast Asia, ancestor spirits, ghosts, demons and spirits of the valleys and forests were incorporated in the diagrams. When Buddhism became the prominent religion, images of the Buddha and his disciples were incorporated in the *yantra*.

Spirit doctors composed the *yantra* and skills were passed down from one generation to the next.[7] Induction included drinking water in which the ashes of magic scrolls had been dissolved. Some practitioners studied meditation and mysticism with recognised masters and received reference books that contained *yantra* diagrams and texts written in Lan Na, Shan or Burmese language. Interestingly Lan Na script is found on *yantra* cloths in Sipsong Pan Na, the Shan States and Luang Prabang. If the spirit doctor was very experienced he might draw the *yantra* directly onto cloth with a stylus, although wood blocks were often used to print frequently repeated images. The spirit doctor kept his book and tools on a special altar in his house.

Tattooing the skin was also seen as a way of warding off evil spirits, and was common among valley and hill tribe groups in the inland states. Correctly formulated, tattoos acted like armour and were capable of bestowing special knowledge and guile to defeat the enemy. The earliest record of a people using *yantra* tattoos were the P'u of southern China, referred to in a history of China dating to the 4th century AD.[8] In Lan Na, contrary to many other societies where tattooing was common, there were no special marks or signs to denote rank, leading to the comment 'beggar and king were equal in the hands of the professional tattoo artist'.[9] The Lan Na princes employed their own tattoo masters who were considered to be particularly accomplished practitioners of the art.[10] Opium was administered to ease the pain of the process.

Lan Na temple mural paintings portray extremely fierce soldiers with black tattoos on their thighs and around their waists. They wear narrow loincloths *(yak rung)*, drawn tight and twisted between their legs so that the tattoos are clearly displayed. The designs include mythical beasts, animals and birds, contained within a decorative border at the waist and the knee. Some soldiers were tattooed with *yantra* diagrams in red pigment, on the chest and back. Tattoos were considered to have advantages proportional to the pain endured in the process of acquiring them and were therefore a sign of courage. Not all men endured the suffering and discomfort involved and some chose to have the designs in isolated areas, others gave up before the tattoos were completed. Foreign observers noted that men were prepared to undergo the pain and discomfort to please women and that in this context, tattoos were perceived as a way of 'being made beautiful forever'.[11] There is plenty of evidence from oral history that tattoos were seen as an expression of male sexuality and that many women would not marry a man who did not have his thighs tattooed.

There were other ways of protecting the body that involved inserting small objects in incisions made in the skin of the chest and upper back.[12] Rubies and other precious stones or fine gold wires or small gold and silver discs were the most common. The discs had engraved symbols of a fish, a monkey, a crab and a peacock, separated by etched lines. These

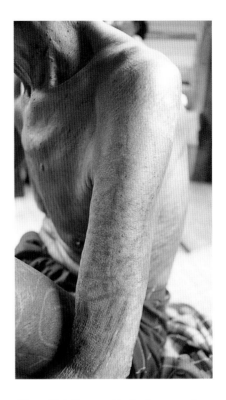

Man with tattoos on his chest, arms and back, 1981.

Above and opposite: Silk jackets back and front with anthropomorphic animals and symbolic diagrams *(yantra)* of circles, squares and triangles filled with numbers, letters and symbols, read or recited as magical incantations *(gatha)*.
(Barbie Campbell-Cole)

were animals whose form the Buddha had assumed in previous lives before taking the appearance of a man, and they were considered to be intelligent and wise. Wearing their representations carried a measure of protection from all types of injury and endowed the soldier with their attributes. *Yantra* were inserted into metal amulets that were strung on cord worn around the waist, around the upper arm, around the neck and around each ear. They were put through a kind of test and if they passed were believed to protect against bullets and cuts from swords. A Buddhist monk bestowed a blessing, without which they were not considered effective. *Yantra* were also punctuated on thin ribbons of silver foil, or written on paper that was rolled up and carried in a small pouch or in a metal container attached to a necklace or bracelet.[13] Although *yantra* provided a major form of protection for soldiers, blessings given by

Buddhist monks were seen as a form of reinforcement. Of course many *yantra* were drawn with Buddha images and *deva* because a combination of Buddhist and spirit religion iconography was considered to be a particularly potent force.

Although great faith was placed in *yantra* there were also strongly held beliefs concerning the protective role of women. If a soldier carried a piece of his mother's *phasin* with him it would help to ward off evil spirits. He might wear a piece of the garment as an armband or a scarf, or a smaller piece could be inserted in a container attached to a chain around his neck.[14] The skirt was particularly potent if it had been worn while his mother was in the process of giving birth to him, as it was seen as a manifestation of a benevolent guardian spirit *(khwan)* that ensured her safe delivery.[15] As her child survived the dangerous journey of birth,

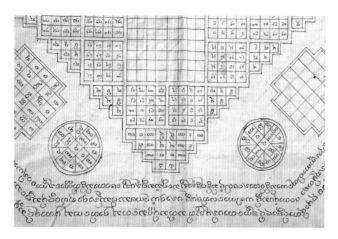

Cotton *yantra* cloth with ink diagrams and script.

Right: An amulet made of silver foil punctuated with inscriptions and protected inside a strip of leather. (Reproduced courtesy of the Board of Trustees of the National Museums and Galleries on Merseyside, accession no. 56. 26. 279).

so it was believed that the power of her skirt would continue to protect him as a young man.

A woman's skirt would protect her son, but could be a negative force for other men. This ancient belief is expressed in the Jinakalamali Chronicle that tells the story of Queen Chamdevi of Lamphun who reigned in the 7th century AD. She sent a skirt polluted with menstrual blood to an enemy chief. Disguised as a turban, he unknowingly wore the skirt in battle and suffered a major defeat. The belief in this form of pollution is widespread and women's lower garments are still hung out to dry on a pole suspended below waist level so there is no chance of a man brushing his head against them.[16]

Women conducted spirit ceremonies *(suu khwan thahaan)* before men left home to go into battle.[17] A soldier sat in a circle with his family and members of the community and a female medium led the chant to call his spirit and bind it to his body. She tied his wrists with cord made from local cotton and hand spun by mature women in the village.[18] When the soldier came back home a similar binding ceremony was held to recall his spirit in case it has been left behind on the battlefield.

A silk waist decorated with figures of animals, diagrams and incantations. Such waist believed to protect against numural dangers.
(Oriental Collection, The British Library)

84

Lan Na Male Court Dress

The Chiang Mai chronicle describes the triumphant entry of Prince Kawila into the city of Chiang Mai, following the defeat of the Burmese. The prince was publicly acknowledged for his bravery and the brilliance of his military campaigns. The victory celebrations included poetry readings, musical performances, dancing and feasting. The following passage describes the dress of those attending the celebrations.

> *As for all the officials civil and military, the slaves and freemen, there were elephantry officers and cavalry officers dressed in fine uniforms, like divinities from the Tavadimsa [Tavatimsa] Heaven, the abode of the gods.*[19]

The reference to the Tavatimsa Heaven places Prince Kawila in the tradition of former Lan Na Buddhist kings who for the sake of legitimacy were viewed as descendants of the first Prince Lawacangkara who came down from the Tavatimsa Heaven. As a legitimate Buddhist ruler, Kawila was also viewed as a being on the way to enlightenment *(bodhisattva)*. Interpretations of the dress worn by *bodhisattva* are portrayed in Buddhist art throughout Southeast Asia, and include representations in sculpture, temple mural paintings and manuscripts. The exterior bas relief of the 15th century temple of Wat Ched Yot, Chiang Mai, and the 15th century murals of Wat Lai Hin, Lampang provide examples of early Lan Na style. They portray divinities wearing gold headdresses, bracelets, anklets, and gold robes with wing-shaped scalloped panels on the shoulders, waist and skirt. We should therefore expect to see the Lan Na princes similarly attired, as they were in some other Southeast Asian states.

There is no evidence that the Lan Na princes actually wore *bodhisattva*-style costumes in the period 1781-1871. In an official portrait Prince Kawila of Chiang Mai (ruled 1781-1813) was portrayed wearing a simple front-buttoned, round-necked shirt, a *chong kraben* and metal belt with an ornate buckle. In a court photograph taken over forty years later, Prince Kawiloros Suriyavong of Chiang Mai (ruled 1856-1870) wore an equally modest outfit. At the beginning of his reign, Prince Indra Witchayanon of Chiang Mai (ruled 1871-1879) also wears a round-necked shirt, *chong kraben* and waist sash. The Chiang Mai rulers and senior princes were bareheaded and barefoot, their hair is cut in a circle on the crown and shaved at the sides and they were clean shaven.[20]

Why did the Lan Na princes dress so simply in what were clearly meant as official court portraits? At the time when Kawila ascended the throne, the princes lacked funds for elaborate displays and they did not have a court infrastructure. However Prince Kawiloros could have changed that if he had wished because by the time of his reign in the 1860s there was a degree of political stability and wealth from agriculture and trade. Perhaps *bodhisattva*-style dress was not appropriate for the Lan Na princes except for Prince Luang Tin Mahawong of Nan who was

Image of a *deva*, exterior bas relief, Wat Ched Yot, Chiang Mai.

Detail of a golden elephant howdah, temple mural painting, Wat Phumin, Nan.

related to the Lan Na elite.[21] The other princes were descendants of the forester Thip Chang who assumed the title prince when he became ruler of Lampang. Prince Kawila had gained the throne because he was an outstanding military leader and he probably encouraged this image because it inspired the confidence of the people. It is also possible that a simple form of court dress was more in keeping with Sinhalese Theravada Buddhism that was less hierarchical than other forms of Buddhism.

If Prince Kawila did not wear ornate *bodhisattva*-style court dress it is probable that the princes of Lamphun, Lampang, Nan and Phrae would not have done so either. Chiang Mai was the seat of Lan Na authority from the time of its founding by King Mengrai in 1259 and in the 19th century, following the expulsion of the Burmese, resumed its position as first city with its prince as 'supreme ruler'.[22] This hierarchy was acknowledged within Lan Na, but there were to be later external pressures, particularly from Siam, which judged and rewarded the Lan Na princes according to a different set of criteria.

Although there is no evidence of *bodhisattva*-style costumes worn at court in the period 1781-1871, we know that the rulers were revered as *bodhisattva* after death. The American missionary Daniel McGilvary made a visit in 1870 to pay his last respects to the deceased Prince Kawiloros of Chiang Mai, whose face, he reported had been covered in gold leaf. A funeral chariot *(prasat)* built to resemble Mount Meru in the Tavatimsa Heaven, was reserved for the funeral.[23] The dress of the princes was simple and not hierarchical but in contrast court regalia was expensive and decorative. Lan Na regalia included gold and silver water vessels, parasols, gilded thrones, gilded and painted elephant howdahs, ceremonial bowls, gold and silver betel box sets and silk pillows and cushions, embellished with gold and silver metal thread. When the princes built new palaces they had their regalia displayed permanently in a ceremonial hall. Some items were carried in procession when the ruler took part in public ceremonies. Minor princes and senior officials were entitled to regalia graded according to rank and the system radiated outwards from the court to minor officials in the remote reaches of the *muang*. It is not clear whether the Lan Na princes were able to strictly control these codes. Enforcement probably depended on distance, the further a dependency was from the centre of power the less control could be exerted.

There were designated areas in the Lan Na cities where goldsmiths, silversmiths, wood carvers, lacquerware makers, jewellers and other craft workers lived and worked. A distinctive Lan Na style was evident in their woodcarving, stucco, inlay work and gilding, metalwork, painting and stencilling. The smaller objects they made, water vessels, jugs, betel nut trays, food containers and pillows were displayed in official court portraits and photographs of the Lan Na rulers and senior princes.

Ceremonial offering bowls, temple mural painting, Wat Phra Singh, Chiang Mai.

Silver and gold water vessels were of particular significance because they held the sacred water that was poured over the prince during the consecration ceremony confirming his appointment. Special vessels were also used in ritual bathing ceremonies and in allegiance rites. The Chiang Mai chronicle describes a ceremony in 1802 when Prince Kawila was 'lustrated with the holy water of consecration' in the presence of the ruling council *(khao sanam luang)*, his family, senior Buddhist monks, court officials and his troops.[24] The pouring of water appears to have been the key ritual because there is no reference to a crowning ceremony. A gilt umbrella was the symbol of the ruler's authority and was displayed in his throne room and carried in state processions. The umbrella was the most ancient symbol of regal authority in Southeast Asia, derived from the Buddhist Jataka 539 that describes a battle in which a royal umbrella is the prize and symbol of the kingdom, not a crown.[25] Temple mural paintings and photographs show that Lan Na umbrellas were not tiered, in contrast to the Hindu-Buddhist courts of Siam and Burma and their satellites where the number of tiers was strictly controlled to denote rank.

The throne and footstool of the court of Chiang Mai.
(Chiang Mai National Museum)

Chewing betel was a social custom practiced among Lan Na royalty and commoners alike. Carl Bock wrote that the people were 'perpetually chewing' from infancy to old age, and enjoyed betel at every friendly interaction.[26] This was the practice throughout Southeast Asia, and betel juice has been described as the lubricant of society 'to be dribbled, spat and enjoyed' on all social occasions.[27] As water vessels were a symbol of consecration, so betel box sets represented the sociability of the Lan Na princes. They commissioned designs from local metalworkers who worked in silver and gold, using repoussé (hammering the patterns into relief) and embossing techniques. A betel box set included a number of containers for storing the ingredients of areca palm nut *(areca catechu)*, betel leaf *(piper betle)*, tobacco and white lime. To prepare a quid, a piece of areca palm nut is wrapped in a betel leaf along with a small amount of lime and tobacco and this is placed in the side of the mouth. This concoction stains the inside of the mouth and the saliva bright red. At court, gold and silver spittoons were provided for expectorating the juice and decorative cloths were used to wipe the stains from the mouth.

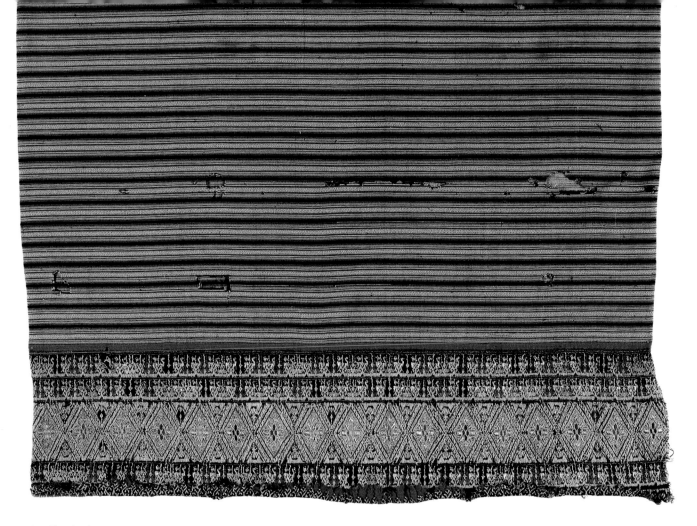

Lan Na *phasin* with a striped cotton central panel and geometric *teen jok* hem bordered by rows of birds.
(Paothong Thongchua collection)

Opposite:
Above: Triangular cushions *(maun)* decorated with couched silver metal thread embroidery and mother-of-pearl sequins. Their function is clearly demonstrated in the photograph of the Prince Suriyapong Paritdej of Nan, page 30.
(Duangchit Taweesri collection)

Left: A wiping cloth (*pha chet*), black lacquered cotton panel with red velvet end panels decorated with couched embroidery of silver metal wire inset with mirror glass. Used to wipe betel juice from the mouth.
(Private collection)

Right: A cushion (*maun*), green velvet cover, grey silk end panels decorated with multicoloured floss silk embroidery and mother-of-pear sequins. Chiang Tung, Shan States. (Duangchit Taweesri collection)

The Lan Na rulers slept on kapok filled mattresses spread on a wooden dais. Weavers of the royal household produced decorative bed sheets, blankets and pillows, decorated with silk and silver and gold metal thread. Before the fashion for European furniture, the Lan Na princes received their guests from a raised platform, seated on special cloth mats with triangular or rectangular cushions as back rests. The cushions were covered in cotton, silk and velvet with flat end panels decorated with floss silk embroidery, metal sequins and couched gold and silver metal wire. Cloth floor mats and cushions were also provided for guests.

Court Dress in the 'Extended Cultural Area'

In the Shan States, Luang Prabang and Sipsong Pan Na, court costume varied according to tributary relations although distance from a major power centre often meant virtual independence from dress codes. Some states in Sipsong Pan Na and Laos paid tribute to China, some Shan States were tributary to Burma and some paid tribute to Siam. In 1798 the ruler of Muang Pu (eastern Shan States) migrated with his people to Chiang Mai and offered allegiance to Siam. In 1805 minor principalities in Sipsong Pan Na and western Laos also changed allegiance to Siam. Some states, like Chiang Rung, the capital of Sipsong Pan Na remained loyal to existing tributary arrangements. Although these were early days

STATUS, PROTECTION, IDENTITY: 1781-1871   89

The French Commission is received by the King of Xieng Hong. Etching based on a drawing by Delaporte, in Garnier (1885).

Right: The King of Muang You, Sipsong Pan Na with two of his consorts. Etching based on a drawing by Delaporte, in Garnier (1885).

The Francis Garnier Mission is received by the King of Muang You. Etching based on a drawing by Delaporte, in Garnier (1885).

for European explorers in the region, there are etchings by the artist Delaporte who was part of a French Mission in the 1860s, led by Francis Garnier. They explored the Upper Mekong River region and Delaporte made drawings of the princes wearing side-fastening shirts, *chong kraben* and patterned turbans. Some female consorts are portrayed in hill tribe dress and jewellery. Garnier described dress at some of the courts as Chinese with princes attired in dragon robes and Chinese-style hats. There is little evidence of *bodhisattva*-style dress although scalloped gold collars like those worn at the Burmese and Siamese courts are seen in some of Delaporte's etchings.

Burmese and Siamese Court Dress

In comparison with the style of court dress worn by the Lan Na princes, and by princes in many of the inland states, the ceremonial dress of the courts of Burma and Siam was lavish and hierarchical. The collection of 19th century Burmese court costumes in the Victoria and Albert Museum, circa 1853, is a perfect example. The collection includes the fabulous court dress of the Secretary of State *(atwinwun)* in Mandalay. It consists of an ankle-length plum-coloured velvet robe trimmed with lavish gold embroidery. It has a scalloped collar, also embroidered with gold, and an elaborate gold belt. The court dress of the Siamese kings was constructed in similar fashion, with gold scalloped decoration on jackets and loincloths worn under flat panels of scalloped gold embroidery. This type of dress is seen in the portrait of King Rama V of Siam taken on his coronation day in 1868. The embroidery techniques and the designs are

These women from Souei-Sa wear typical northern Laos (Sam Neua) *phasin.* (White Lotus)

King Rama V of Siam (ruled 1868-1910) on his coronation day.

A Shan prince, temple mural painting, Wat Pa Daet, Mae Chaem.

similar in Siamese and Burmese court costumes. Silver and gold metal wire, sequins and beetle wings are couched in scallops containing floral patterns. However, it is possible to differentiate Burmese and Siamese court dress by the style of the *chong kraben* and skirts worn under these elaborate clothes. The Burmese generally wore silk tapestry weave *(luntaya)* with a characteristic 'wavy line' appearance. In Siam men and women both wore silk made in India to Siamese specifications.[28] The difference in the Siamese and Burmese designs is so marked that when they are portrayed in mural paintings it is easy to identify them.

Gifts to the Courts of Lan Na

Textile gift exchange among the courts is recorded in the Chiang Mai chronicle, as when silk clothing from Chiang Mai was sent to the Shan States as part of a peace settlement in the 18th century.[29] The Nan chronicle lists Burmese and Chinese silks among the presents sent to the Nan princes from courts in Sipsong Pan Na in the early 19th century.[30] In exchange the chronicles say that the Shan rulers sent textiles which included a set of curtains. When at the end of the 18th century, Lan Na became tributary to Siam the princes travelled to Bangkok once every three years to present the King of Siam with gold and silver trees and gifts of cloth. In exchange the princes received gifts whose value depended on how well they had performed in their relations with Siam.

When he established his court in Bangkok, Rama I of Siam (ruled 1782-1809) instigated a reform programme that included dress codes modelled on the court of Ayutthaya, the capital of Siam until 1767. Tunics with decorations at the collar, shoulders and cuffs were strictly graded according to rank. Senior officials could wear brocaded silks while lower ranks were restricted to plainer fabrics. Court jewellery was also graded and senior officials were allowed to wear gold and diamonds. Jewellers who supplied the court were ordered to obey the rules and sell to clients according to their seniority.[31] Rama I applied these codes when he sent gifts of dress and textiles to tributary states.

The Nan chronicle records that in 1786 Prince Attavorapanyo went to Bangkok to pay tribute to Rama I although there are no records of gifts presented to him. He may have received little or nothing as Nan was in a state of post-war political uncertainty and Rama I was in doubt as to the prince's loyalty to Siam. However by the time of his second visit to Bangkok in 1804, Prince Attavorapanyo had distinguished himself in battle against the Burmese and delivered to Bangkok the Burmese Deputy Governor of Chiang Saen as a prisoner of war. He received gold jewellery and regalia as a reward. In 1856, Prince Anantayot of Nan, whose loyalty was vital to create stability in the north-east borders of Siam, was rewarded with the highest honour of a six-tiered parasol; one tier less than the king of Siam. In contrast, the Siamese king reserved

A sleeping princess, Wat Buak Khok Luang, Chiang Mai.

single tiers for princes of minor states.[32] The Prince of Lamphun, whose principality was less strategically important than Nan, was presented with a felt parasol and the rulers of satellite principalities received satin parasols. At other times, gifts appear to have been more even handed, Prince Attavorapanyo of Nan received a robe with gold flowers and a gold flowered shirt, Prince Anantayot received a tunic with gold binding and the Prince of Lamphun received a 'glittery [gold decorated] garment'.

Some textiles presented to the Lan Na princes can be identified by their Siamese names. Silk brocade was *pha yok,* fabric with Siamese patterns was *pha pok rui thong* and fabric designed exclusively for court use with a Siamese flame motif was *pha kan yaeng.* Gifts to the Lan Na princes included printed and painted cloths made in India to Siamese specifications.[33] There is fabric described as 'silk cloth with a gold royal pattern' that could be of Siamese or Indian origin. The lists also include 'Chinese-style cloth' that was either made in China or copied in Siam from a Chinese design.

Two Lan Na women in a doorway. Wat Phumin, Nan.

It is important to acknowledge the skill of Siamese weavers who produced cloth of the highest quality and many of the fabrics in the court lists were probably made in Bangkok. Some of the most costly garments worn by people of high rank were manufactured in their palaces and not imported. A British diplomat observed that the Siamese 'pride themselves on being able to produce textures more valuable than any they import from foreign countries'.[34] It is necessary to stress this point because it is often assumed that all high quality court textiles were imported from India. Although it is certain that printed cottons and some fine quality brocades were imported from India, excellent silk fabrics were also produced by weavers working in the southern provinces of Siam and in Bangkok.

In summary, dress and textiles were part of tribute and gift exchange between the courts of Lan Na, the Shan States, Luang Prabang, Sipsong Pan Na, China, Burma and Siam. Burmese and Chinese silks were exchanged as part of the tributary system operating in the inland states. Siamese textiles and dress, possibly including cloth made in India, were sent as gifts to the Lan Na princes. These gifts were an acknowledgement of loyalty to the political interests of Siam and were intended as a symbol of the relationship between individual princes and the king of Siam. The traditional hierarchy that existed among the Lan Na princes was not recognised by successive kings of Siam who dealt with the princes on an individual basis and judged them according to their loyalty. Significantly there is no evidence to show that the Lan Na princes wore the items of dress and regalia sent from Siam. Court portraits show them in Lan Na dress. Oral history suggests that gifts from Siam were displayed in ceremonial halls. [35] As there was no official Siamese presence in Lan Na before 1874 there was no way to enforce dress codes there even if that had been the intention. Contact between courts was limited to tributary visits and it was not until the third quarter of the 19th century that this changed.

Lan Na Female Court Dress

Lan Na female court dress in the period 1781-1871 includes that worn by the wives and consorts of rulers in the principalities of Chiang Mai, Lamphun, Lampang, Nan and Phrae and their satellites and dependencies. It also includes court dress worn by wives and consorts who came to the Lan Na courts as the result of marital alliances with the surrounding inland states of Sipsong Pan Na, Luang Prabang and the Shan States. The Chiang Mai and Nan Chronicles record 19th century alliances that brought women of Tai Yuan, Tai Lue, Tai Lao and Tai Khoen origin to live at the Lan Na courts.

The custom of marital alliances between states explains the variety of ethnic dress worn at court. Women who married into the Lan Na royal

A Lan Na woman arranging her hair.
Wat Phumin, Nan.

Left: A princess with fine gold jewellery,
Wat Phumin, Nan.

family from another state or ethnic group continued to wear the dress of their homeland. Archibald Colquhoun had noticed this among female immigrants from the Shan States and wrote that 'the ladies of Chiang Mai are more conservative than their male folk and still adhere to costumes worn by their race previous to leaving the Burmese Shan States for these parts'.[36] William Dodd saw this in other inland states and reported that when Princess Wen Tip who was Tai Khoen (probably from Chiang Tung) married the Prince of Chiang Rung (Sipsong Pan Na) her new home was 'in the Lu [Lue] country' although she retained her Khoen style of dress.[37]

In terms of weaving patterns and structure, the dress of female royalty can be identified with village women belonging to the same ethnic group. Class and wealth was displayed through the cost of yarn and trimmings. Female royalty and the wealthy wore clothes made from silk yarn and silver and gold metal thread, woven in refined patterns by skilled weavers working at court. In contrast, village women usually made their clothes from cotton yarn although they often used colourful, intricate weaving patterns for best dress. As the line between rich and poor, and high and low status was not subject to formal regulation there was room for a great deal of flexibility. The wives and daughters of minor rulers and officials, of powerful village leaders in satellite domains, and of wealthy farmers, owned costumes made with expensive imported

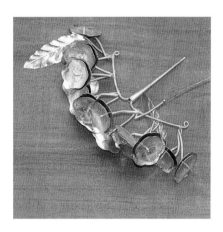

Modern copies of Lan Na style hair decorations, purchased in Chiang Mai.

materials obtained from itinerant traders. In years when there was a good harvest even poorer women could afford to buy a little silk yarn if they could not produce it themselves and some even bought gold and silver metal thread to decorate a hem border for their best skirt.[38]

It was believed that female royalty, like male royalty could be reborn as *deva* if they observed the Buddha's teachings.[39] However, like the princes, they did not wear court costumes associated with *deva* or *bodhisattva* but were allocated regalia that indicated their rank. This was displayed when they were present at court ceremonies and was carried in procession by attendants. They were fond of jewellery that was manufactured in the main cities. Local jewellers were famous for their gold and silver chased work, and beautifully designed gold and silver ornaments, bracelets and necklaces.[40] There are portraits and photographs of Lan Na princesses wearing gold and silver necklaces, silver bracelets and large cylindrical earrings.

Dress, Religion and Group Identity: Karen, Lawa and Tai Yuan

The Tai Yuan consider themselves to be the original Tai inhabitants of Lan Na and, as was argued earlier, they were probably the descendants of assimilated Tai, Karen and Lawa.[41] The argument for assimilation is examined here in terms of the similarity in their dress. Young, in his study of the Lawa, wrote that 'the dress of the more assimilated Lawa is identical to that of the Lao-Thai [Tai Yuan]. He later added that 'much of this dress is borrowed from the Karen'.[42] In contrast Prangwatthanakun and Cheesman noted that the Tai Yuan 'absorbed influence from the Lawa in Mae Chaem district and weave a Lawa *phasin* [skirt]'.[43]

Some revision in the style of female dress can be explained as adaptation to environmental and climatic conditions as groups moved from uplands and forests into lowlands. In the more remote hilly districts of Lan Na, Lawa and Karen women wore horizontally striped skirts to the knee, and leggings from knee to ankle. This type of dress was adapted to suit difficult hilly terrain and protect the legs from thorny plants, insects and leeches. In the valleys, in settled village communities, leggings were not worn and the Lawa and Karen who settled at lower altitudes wore ankle-length skirts. All three groups wore skirts with horizontal stripes arranged in repeat patterns that involved simple weaving techniques. Red, blue, black and white stripes are common among all three groups probably because the dyes were available locally or could be cultivated in home gardens.

The similarity between Karen, Lawa and Tai Yuan dress is particularly evident in women's skirts. E. M. Hinton, who interviewed Karen women concerning the meaning of skirt patterns, was told that black stripes were referred to simply as 'the skirt's black' *(ning a saa)* and that narrower combinations of stripes were called the 'skirts eyes' *(ning a mea)*.[44] Less obtrusive single stripes were called 'dividers of

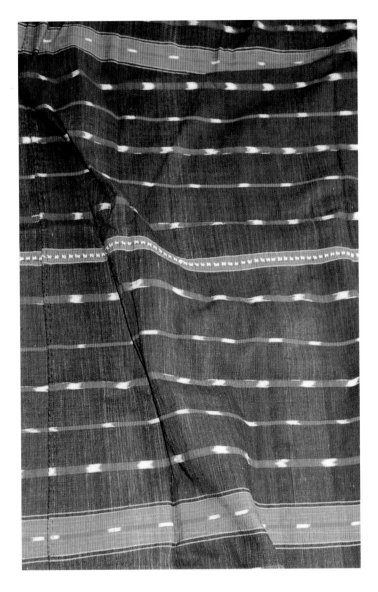

Portrait of a Tai Lue woman, Wat Phumin, Nan.

Left: A Lawa *phasin* from Mae Chaem.

the red' *(chii a chaw)* and as their name implies, divided solid blocks of red. Hinton was also told that the choice of colours for the stripes was left to individual women, but yellow and green were the most common. The terms that the Karen women gave him relate to the layout of the design although Hinton either was not told or failed to report the meaning of the term 'eye'. However, Cheesman (1988) refers to 'eye' in describing Tai Lao textiles noting that in Lao the term means 'star eye', interpreted as 'third eye' or 'seeing eye'.

In comparison with Karen skirts the Lawa cotton skirts were made of indigo cotton rather than red cotton and have horizontal blue and red stripes usually subdivided by blue, white and red. Tai Yuan skirts also have horizontal stripes. Lawa, Karen and Tai Yuan skirts share design elements that have been noted by many scholars. What is significant is the shared patterning system of horizontal stripes and the use of the term

Women wearing village-style Lan Na
phasin, temple mural painting,
Wat Pa Daet, Mae Chaem.

Right: A Lan Na couple,
Wat Nong Bua, Nan.

'eye' to describe the way the stripes are laid out. The Lawa and Karen skirts are balanced so that there is no obvious waist or hem but the Tai Yuan skirt has a distinct waistband and hem border. This relates to Buddhist conventions that define the head as the most sacred part of the body and the feet as the most polluting.[45] It was important for Buddhists to be able to differentiate the waist from the hem so that the potentially polluting hem is always worn closest to the feet. If the Karen and Lawa practiced spirit religion, this convention would not have applied to them. However, there are samples of Karen and Lawa skirts that are structured with a distinctive waist and hem. George Young used the term 'animistic-Buddhist' for those Lawa who had contact with Buddhism and 'strictly animist' for others who were isolated. Lawa and Karen skirts with waist and hem borders were worn by those living in close contact with Buddhists or were practising Buddhists themselves.[46]

In summary, women of Tai Yuan, Karen and Lawa groups woreskirts with horizontal stripes and used similar weaving patterns, suggesting a common root of design. The finished fabric was sewn lengthways to form an ankle length tube, or the skirt was worn to knee length with leggings. Samples of these skirts can be recognised in 18th century temple mural paintings, although the designs probably long pre-date the 18th century. Tai Yuan, Lawa and Karen skirts have common characteristics that raise issues about the origins and assimilation of ethnic groups within the hills and valleys of Lan Na and the surrounding inland states.

Tai Yuan Court Dress

In his diary of April 20th 1855, the British Ambassador Sir John Bowring described a visit to the Bangkok palace of Prince Krom Luang Wongsa where as a special privilege he was allowed to meet the prince's favourite Lan Na wife. Unlike Siamese women, she had a fine head of hair that he described as 'very prettily arranged with a garland of fragrant flowers'. Lan Na women were proud of their long hair which they dressed with large fancy pins, or with silver and gold chains set with precious stones or with fresh flowers. The beauty of their hair decorations is often captured in temple mural paintings.

Tai Yuan female royalty at the Lan Na courts wore a style of dress that was common to their group. The skirts were hand woven without mill-produced fabrics in any part, and indigenous and imported yarn was used for weaving. At the courts of Chiang Mai, Lamphun, Lampang, Phrae and their satellites, Tai Yuan women wore a sash *(pha sabai)* and a horizontally striped tubular skirt *(phasin)*. The sashes were draped either across one shoulder or both, or worn loosely around the neck or tied in a knot over the breasts. The different ways of wrapping the *pha sabai* can be seen in photographs of royalty and village women. Although sashes were regularly produced at the Lan Na courts, in the 19th century traders brought finely woven samples decorated with gold and silver metal thread from Luang Prabang.[47]

Women walking to the market in Chiang Mai. (Payap University Archive, Chiang Mai)

A Lan Na princess, Wat Nong Bua, Nan.

Lan Na temple mural paintings tend to portray women wearing *pha sabai* only, although in portraits and photographs princesses often wear blouses. The introduction of white blouses is generally credited to American Presbyterian missionaries who established themselves in Lan Na in 1867. The missionaries tried to ensure that women covered their breasts with a more substantial garment than a sash that was often worn with one or both breasts exposed.[48] In reality sashes could easily be worn to cover the breasts. The missionaries may have persuaded some women, including their converts, to wear blouses, but they were by no means successful with other women. Covering the breasts became accepted practice for Lan Na princesses when they were in the company of strangers, and particularly for photographs but otherwise female royalty wore *pha sabai*.

Tai Yuan princesses wore horizontally striped skirts made up in three sections, a waistband, a central panel and a hem border. The waistbands were made of cotton, with black, white and red the most popular colours. Cotton was preferred for the waistband because it was less inclined to slip when tucked in a pleat.[49] The central panels were woven from imported Chinese silk yarn or indigenous silk yarn. The patterning techniques included plying (twisting) yarns together to create a two-tone effect, multi-coloured plain weave horizontal stripes and continuous supplementary weft stripes, often incorporating gold and silver metal thread. The hem border *(teen jok)* was woven in one piece with two distinct pattern areas. The top, with a band of complex discontinuous supplementary weft patterns *(jok)*, used multicoloured silks and gold and silver metal thread. The wealthier the family, the more gold and silver thread was used. A plain border of red cotton or indigenous red silk formed the band nearest the feet.[50] Skirts similar to the expensive samples described here were not confined to the major courts and were also worn at satellite courts in the further reaches of the *muang*.

A Lan Na princess fastening her skirt, Wat Nong Bua, Nan.

Prince Ubonwanna of Chiang Mai, daughter of Prince Kawiloros Suriyavong. The princess was a well-known Lan Na business woman. (Pitt Rivers Museum, Oxford)

Four silk sashes (*pha sabai*) from Luang Prabang.
(Bank of Thailand Museum, Chiang Mai)

Tai Lue Court Dress

According to the Tai chronicles between 1790 and 1830 thousands of Tai Lue from principalities in Sipsong Pan Na were forcibly resettled in Lan Na. Sipsong Pan Na traditionally paid tribute to China although in the 19th century both Siam and Burma exercised nominal authority in certain states. James McCarthy described the territory as in dispute for at least forty years.[51] Tai Lue princesses were living at the Lan Na courts as a consequence of marriage alliances. Prince Kawila of Chiang Mai was presented with three Tai Lue consorts, and Tai Lue princesses also married into the Nan court.

Tai Lue women were renowned weavers and following resettlement were employed at the courts of Lamphun, Nan and Chiang Mai. In the 19th century, there were major settlements in the villages surrounding Lamphun and Nan.[52] The women were able to make the dress worn in their homelands because the raw materials could be purchased from itinerant tradesmen. The capital of Sipsong Pan Na, Chiang Hung was situated on the caravan route operated by Yunnanese *(Ho)* traders, who travelled from Dali *(China)* through Chiang Hung and on to Chiang Mai and Phrae, calling at other Lan Na cities on the way.[53] Moerman wrote

Detail of the *phasin* shown opposite.

Hem borders (*teen jok*) of Lan Na skirts.
Silk with silver and gold metal thread.
(Darabhirom Museum, Chiang Mai)

Right: Detail of *teen jok*.

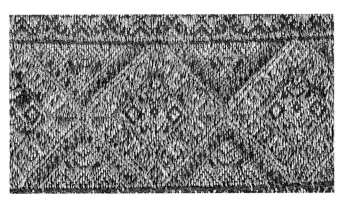

Hem borders (*teen jok*) of Lan Na skirts.
Silk with silver and gold metal thread.
(Chaba Suwatmekin collection)

Left: Border detail shows birds within
the diamond lozenges.

Opposite: A Lan Na *phasin* and detail above.
(Bank of Thailand Museum, Chiang Mai)

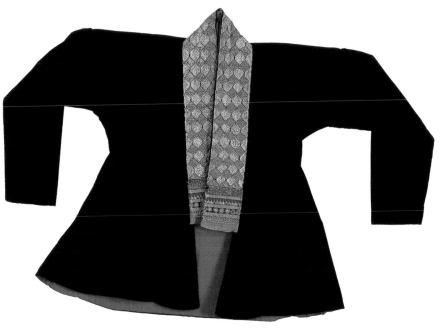

that Tai Lue women were particularly fond of light blue ribbon brought by the Yunnanese, which they used to decorate their jackets.[54] From the dress described below it seems that they also purchased Chinese brocades and trimmings and silk turban cloths from the same traders.

Tai Lue princesses wore silk turbans, in pastel colours that were plain or patterned. They wore long-sleeved side-fastening blouses *(seua pat)* in summer and lined jackets *(seua kop long daeng)* in winter. Their blouses, made of Chinese silk or cotton for everyday, had crossover front panels that fastened at the side and long fitted sleeves. The neckline and front borders were trimmed with ribbons, appliqué and embroidery. The cold season Tai Lue jacket had long fitted sleeves and was often padded. More elaborate jackets were made of black velvet lined with red flannel, with front and neck trimmings of couched gold wire laid in diamond patterns. The front openings, bodice edges and vents were sometimes trimmed with Chinese brocade and the borders decorated with couched gold wire embroidery, beetle wings, Chinese brocade, and red and turquoise cotton.

A Tai Lue skirt is tubular with, a cotton waist band and a central panel and hem border. The central panel contains horizontal bands of continuous supplementary weft *(muk)*, woven with silver and gold metal thread. If the patterns are evenly spaced, they are called *sin pong* and if irregularly spaced *sin man*.[55] Some skirts have horizontal bands of tapestry weave set amid multicoloured stripes.

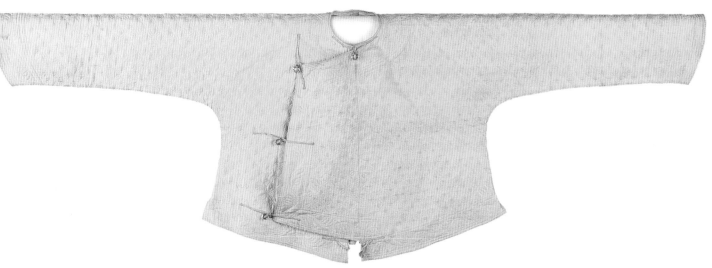

Two blouses, the top one of silk, worn in warm weather. The one below is padded for the cool season. (Paothong Thongchua collection)

Opposite:
Women's velvet jackets decorated with gold and silver metal thread embroidery and bands of brocade.
(Bank of Thailand Museum, Chiang Mai)

Above: Details of the hem borders of *phasin*. Silk and silver
and gold metal thread.
(Chaba Suwatmekin collection)

Right: A Lan Na *phasin* from Nan.
(Bank of Thailand Museum, Chiang Mai)

112

Detail of the central panel of a *phasin* from Nan.
The geometric patterns are tapestry weave.
(Chutinart Songwattana collection)

Right: Detail of the central panel of a *phasin* from Nan. The
geometric tapestry weave pattern is often referred to as 'running
water' (*lai nam lai*).
(Bank of Thailand Museum, Chiang Mai)

Princess Sukhantha of Chiang Tung who
married Prince Intanon of Chiang Mai
(see page 164).
(River Books Collection)

Tai Khoen Court Dress

The Tai Khoen inhabit Chiang Tung, the largest of the eastern Shan
States. From the 13th to the 16th century, Chiang Tung was regarded as
a 'younger brother kingdom' or as a dependency of Chiang Mai. In the
17th and 18th centuries Chiang Tung was tributary to Burma. In 1807
the second Prince (uparat) of Chiang Mai led a military mission to
Chiang Tung where the ruling prince accepted his authority and allowed
members of the royal family and hundreds of families to move to Chiang
Mai and transfer their allegiance to Prince Kawila. Tai Khoen royalty
were allowed to build residences outside the Chiang Mai gate on the
south side of the city. Following resettlement, a marriage was arranged
between Princess Chantima, daughter of Prince Setthi Kamfan of
Chiang Mai (ruled 1822-1825) and Prince Mahaprom, younger brother
of Prince Sirichai of Chiang Tung.[56] Tai Khoen traders from Chiang Tung
travelled between Chiang Tung and Lan Na carrying fabrics and notions
for use by Tai Khoen women who continued to wear their traditional
dress.

A Tai Khoen princess wore a silk turban in cream or pastel colours,
a long sleeved silk blouse in summer (sua pat), a quilted or lined jacket
in winter (sua kop long daeng), and a tubular skirt (sin mai kam). A Tai
Khoen blouse has a basque-shaped bodice, a side fastening wrap-over
front and long fitted sleeves. Padded jackets in similar shape were worn
in the cool season. Tai Khoen skirts have waistbands, central panels and
hem borders. The waistbands are made of cotton and the central panels
have horizontal bands of gold metal thread woven in plain weave,
interspersed at regular intervals with bands of gold supplementary weft
in floral patterns. The hem borders have bands of brightly coloured silk
brocade and embroidery sewn together along the selvage. The hem
borders of Tai Khoen skirts are extremely colourful. The top band is
usually silk, decorated with Chinese floss-silk embroidery in repeat
floral and leaf patterns and couched with silver and gold metal wire and
mother of pearl sequins. Below this there is usually a band of Chinese
satin appliqué with silver sequins set in triangles at the top and bottom
edge, and below that a narrow strip of Chinese silk brocade with floral
patterns. The hem borders are bands of silk with mother of pearl sequins
arranged in triangles.[57] These skirts were worn with a cotton petticoat
with a patterned border.

There is some similarity in the blouses and jackets worn by the Tai
Khoen and the Burmese at the Mandalay courts. We know that the Tai
Khoen court of Chiang Tung maintained a style of pomp and ceremony
that could be identified with the Burmese courts, to which they had
earlier been tributary in the 17th and 18th centuries.[58] When they
resettled in Lan Na, Tai Khoen women relied on itinerant traders from
Chiang Tung for Chinese silk brocade, Chinese satin and strips of
Chinese embroidery for their blouses and to decorate their skirts. The
central panels of their skirts were hand-woven and they resemble the

supplementary weft patterns produced by the Tai Lue. Interestingly, both the Tai Lue and the Tai Khoen wear turbans. As these groups lived in close proximity before being resettled in Lan Na, it is possible that their dress was hybridised before the 19th century.

Above right: Tai Khoen style padded jacket and *phasin*.

Above: Details of the embroidered hem borders.

Above: The front and back of a Tai Khoen jacket decorated with sequins. (Paothong Thongchua collection)

Right: Tai Khoen *phasin* decorated with sequins. (Darabhirom Museum, Chiang Mai)

Detail of a Tai Lao *phasin*.

Tai Lao Court Dress

The kingdom of Luang Prabang (Lan Xang) has a long history of political and cultural relations with Lan Na and Sipsong Pan Na, and is considered to be part of the extended cultural area (defined earlier). The Nan chronicle records that in the late 18th century, men from Luang Prabang joined the combined forces of Chiang Mai, Lampang and Phrae to defeat the Burmese.[56] Marital alliances were arranged between the Lan Na principalities and Luang Prabang and are described in the Nan chronicle as a means to cement ties of friendship with Luang Prabang. In 1828 Luang Prabang became tributary to Siam and remained so until 1893 when it was annexed by France.

A Tai Lao princess wore a silk sash *(pha sabai)*, and a *phasin*. In the cool season, heavier jackets were worn. The *pha sabai* were rectangular in shape, with bands of supplementary weft of silver and gold metal thread, like the *pha sabai* traded from Luang Prabang to Chiang Mai. A Tai Lao skirt is structured in three sections, distinctive from other groups because of the vertical patterning system. The waist band may be plain or have vertical stripes of multicoloured silk and cotton interspersed with stripes of supplementary weft in cotton, silk and gold and silver metal thread. There are two ways of patterning the central panel; one is with vertical stripes interspersed with supplementary weft containing silver and gold metal thread or vertical bands of ikat. The second design has no vertical definition and the supplementary weft patterns in silk or gold and silver metal thread are repeated in a diagonal form. The hem border contains horizontal bands of supplementary weft patterns in gold and silver metal thread. The continuous supplementary weft patterns cover the whole area of the hem, making them distinctive from Tai Yuan *teen jok* hems.

A Tai Lao style jacket.
(Paothong Thongchua collection)

Opposite: A Tai Lao *phasin*.
(Chutinart Songwattana collection)

122

Above and left: Two Tai Lao *phasin*.
(Bank of Thailand Museum, Chiang Mai)

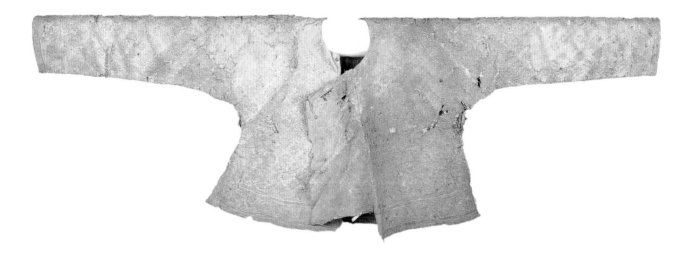

Tai Yai style jacket (*ein gyi*).
(Paothong Thongchua collection)

Details of *luntaya* weaving patterns from
woman's skirts (*hta mein*).

Opposite:
A silk *phasin* in *luntaya* weave.
(Chutinart Songwattana collection)

Tai Yai Court Dress

The Tai Yai (Ngio) live in the Shan States to the west of the Salween river and until 1882 were tributary to Burma. Tai Yai script closely resembles Burmese script, placing the Tai Yai outside the extended cultural area. Most of the Tai Yai living in Lan Na were foresters and many were wealthy from the logging trade. Samples of Tai Yai dress are found in Lan Na collections and it is possible that elite Tai Yai families made marriage alliances with Lan Na royalty. Princess Ubonwanna of Chiang Mai married a wealthy Tai Yai forester without permission from the royal family and the union was not accepted at court.[59] The samples shown here are costumes worn by dancers at the Chiang Mai court.

The dress of a Tai Yai princess was composed of a breast cloth *(yin-zi)* a long-sleeved fitted jacket or blouse *(ein gyi)* and a floor-length skirt *(hta-mein)*. The skirt is a flat rectangle with a cotton waistband and a central panel and hem border woven as one piece. The central section has a wide band of tapestry weave *(luntaya)* and the hem is a band of plain silk interwoven with bands of silver and gold metal thread. In contrast to the other skirts described so far, the is fabric not sewn in a tube but wrapped around the body with an opening left at the front so that the ankles are revealed as the woman walks. A short train forms behind.

Conclusion

The Lan Na princes practiced a form of Sinhalese Theravada Buddhism that did not involve the same degree of hierarchy as established at Burmese and Siamese courts and the Lan Na princes were not subject to complex sumptuary laws. Early portraits and photographs illustrate their simple form of dress. In the surrounding inland states the style of court dress varied between restrained versions of Burmese or Chinese court dress, probably related to tributary relationships and inland trade. The Lan Na princes received tributary exchange gifts of textiles, dress and regalia from Siam that were displayed but probably not worn, a situation that was to change later in the century when Siamese officials were appointed from Bangkok.

Spirit religion was a strong force in Lan Na and its iconography was used on cloth, on paper, on metal and in tattoos, intended as protection for men. Spirit mediums in Lan Na, in the Shan States, in Sipsong Pan Na and Luang Prabang shared a visual language of mystical symbolic diagrams *(yantra)* and a language of magical incantations *(gatha)*.

In contrast to male dress, female dress expressed ethnic identity and for that reason was viewed as 'conservative'. The Lan Na princes used female dress as a vehicle for displaying their political allegiances. Women from foreign states who married into the royal family continued to wear the costume of their group. This custom was particularly important in the period 1781-1871 when the stability of Lan Na depended on successful treaties and marital alliances with surrounding inland states. In practical terms, it was possible for women to continue wearing a particular style of dress because Yunnanese and Shan traders were able to supply the same fabrics, yarns and notions that they had used in their original homelands. The pressure on women to wear 'conservative' dress probably put a curb on change, although a few princesses did occasionally wear European-style blouses.

The strongest expression of ethnic identity is represented in the female skirt *(phasin)*. The most expensive fabrics and the most complex patterning went into its production. The *phasin* was valued as an expression of female creativity, stability and continuity. It could serve as protection for a warrior son but in other circumstances could pollute and weaken men. Because women's skirts carried such complex meanings and values, many have survived as family heirlooms.

A Lan Na *phasin* for everyday wear.
(Darabhirom Museum, Chiang Mai)

1 Shils, 1981: 14.

2 Seidenfaden 1958: 26.

3 Wilson and Hanks 1985: 14-25.

4 McGilvary 1912: 84.

5 Wimolrat Jenjarassakul, Vichai and Lee J. Chinalai (2000) pp. 11-16.

6 *Gatha* is the Pali word for magical chanting.

7 Interview with Dr. Henry D. Ginsburg, The British Library, 1998.

8 Wimolrat Jenjarassakul, Vichai and Lee J. Chinalai 2000: 11-16.

9 Bock 1884, repr. 1986: 170-174.

10 This custom was observed by the British diplomat Sir Ernst Satow when he visited the principality of Phrae (Brailey 1994: 102).

11 Bock 1986.

12 Hallett 1898 repr. 1988: 138, Le May 1926 repr.1986: 120-121.

13 The Liverpool Museum has an amulet in this form, coiled inside a protective strip of leather (access. no. 56.26.279).

14 Suriya Smutkupt (n.p. 1983) observed a similar practice in Northeast Thailand where a young man leaving home for an extended period carries with him a skirt belonging to his mother.

15 Tannenbaum n.d. 13-23.

16 Personal observation, Chiang Mai Province, 1983.

17 Feikje van der Haak 1987: 117-118.

18 Interview with Khun Rattana Craig, Chiang Rai (Chiang Rai, 1985).

19 Wyatt and Aroonrut 1995: 179.

20 Sir John Bowring (1856) also recorded the custom of cutting hair at the time of a full moon.

21 The Tai chronicles do not tell whether members of the old ruling house of Chiang Mai survived Burmese occupation or the Burmese wars.

22 Sethakul 1989: 18.

23 McGilvary 1912.

24 Wyatt and Aroonrut, 1995: 206.

25 Quaritch Wales 1992: 70.

26 Bock, 1986: 254.

27 Hoskins 1998: 26.

28 Gittinger 1982, Guy 1990, 1999.

29 Wyatt and Aroonrut 1995: 152-164.

30 Wyatt 1994: 108-109.

31 Chumbala 1983: 17.

32 Quaritch Wales (1992: 93) sees Cambodia as the source of the tiered umbrella.

33 Gittinger 1982, Guy 1990, 1992.

34 Bowring, Sir J., 1857: 238.

35 Interviews with Chao Patpong and Chao Nid, descendants of the royal family of Lamphun (Chiang Mai, 1996).

36 Colquhoun, 1885: 127.

37 Dodd, 1923: 201.

38 Interviews conducted with weavers (Chiang Mai and Nan Province, 1985).

39 A being of indeterminate rank living on earth, in trees, caves and mountains, or inhabiting the mountains near, or on the summit of, Mount Meru, in a succession of celestial levels (Boisselier 1976).

40 Bock, 1884 repr.1986: 152.

41 Most other hill tribe groups migrated into Lan Na in the late 19th and throughout the 20th century (Penth 1994: 39).

42 Young, 1962: 57-58

43 Prangwattanakun and Cheesman, 1987: 67.

44 Hinton, 1972. Ruth Barnes (1989: 41, 68) in reference to Lamalera (Indonesia) describes the term *mata* (soul) as an alternative to the translation 'eye'.

45 Interviews with Ba Saengda Bansiddhi, Chom Thong, 1983, Akadej Nakbunlung, Chiang Mai, 1983, Princess Vilai na Chiang Tung, Chiang Mai, 1996.

46 Young, 1962: 55.

47 Sethakul 1989: 68.

48 Johnson Curtis, 1903.

49 Interview with Ba Saengda Bansiddhi, (Chom Thong, Chiang Mai Province,1983).

50 Interviews with Acharn Paothong Thongchua, Chao Nid and Chao Vilai na Chiang Tung (Chiang Mai, July 1996).

51 McCarthy, 1900: 163.

52 Prince Patpong of Lamphun and his sister Chao Nid provided information concerning the Lamphun court (Lamphun 1996).

53 Chiang Hung was also locally known as Chiang Rung. It was called Keng Hung by the British and Xieng Hong by the French.

54 Moerman, 1975: 157.

55 Prangwattanakun and Cheesman, 1987.

56 Sethakul 1989: 14.

57 Informants state that the sequins were made in Chiang Tung (interviews with Khun Duangchit Taweesri, Khun Akadej Nakbunlung, 1983).

58 Wyatt 1994: 88-115.

59 Bock, 1884: 395-396.

A Lan Na *phasin* for everyday wear. There are rows of twisted black and white yarn (*hang krarok*) in the central panel.
(Bank of Thailand Museum, Chiang Mai)

Chapter Five

Power Dressing *(1871-1919)*

This chapter examines Lan Na male and female court dress in the period 1871-1919 beginning with the accession of Prince Indra Witchayanon of Chiang Mai (ruled 1871-1897) and ending during the reign of Prince Kaew Nawarat of Chiang Mai (ruled 1911-1939). This is a time frame when the Lan Na princes changed from being autocratic rulers to figureheads in a nation state with centralised authority controlled from Bangkok.

From 1874 when the first Commissioner was appointed from Bangkok to Chiang Mai, the Siamese began to change the administration of Lan Na. The aim of the Commissioner and his officials was to create a Siamese version of the nation state. He developed his own system of contacts in the country, often by-passing traditional Lan Na kinship networks operating within the *muang* system of government. This process was hampered to a degree by poor communication between the Lan Na cities and by the long and arduous journey to and from Bangkok. The round trip took 70 days in the rainy season when river transport was relatively reliable and four to five months in the dry season when the rivers were not negotiable. Some Siamese commissioners sent to Lan Na considered the posting to be so far from the centre of power that they saw it as a kind of banishment. This state of affairs began to change in 1905 when telegraph lines and a Siamese postal service were introduced between Chiang Mai and Bangkok. However, the greatest change came in 1919 when a railway line was completed between Chiang Mai and Bangkok and the journey time was reduced to less than 14 hours.[1]

A formal photograph of Princess Dararatsami of Chiang Mai at the Bangkok Court. She was the fifth consort of Rama V of Siam. (River Books collection)

Lao women from Muang Payap.
(White Lotus)

The Siamese Commissioners and their officials must have worked diligently even before communications improved because British officials reported that by the 1890s being powerful in Lan Na depended more on having influential contacts in Bangkok than at the Lan Na courts.[2] Meanwhile the shadow of colonialism hung over Lan Na and in 1893 the French annexed all the territory belonging to the Prince of Nan that lay to the east of the Mekong River. This greatly reduced the power of Nan and created a feeling of insecurity throughout Lan Na.

The border areas of Lan Na included vast tracts of primary forest and lowland that because it was uninhabited was particularly vulnerable to colonial exploitation. The British claimed that their interests did not extend beyond logging and the expansion of trade, but in order to secure the territory against further colonial expansion a new policy of forced resettlement was sanctioned by the Prince of Chiang Mai and King Rama V of Siam. Groups of indigenous Tai Yuan and immigrants who had been resettled in Lan Na from the early 19th century were uprooted again in the third quarter of the 19th century and sent to start new settlements. Chiang Saen was resettled by at least a thousand people from Lamphun, Phayao was resettled by moving people from Lampang, and Fang by individuals sent from Chiang Mai. This added to the diverse nature of the population in the outer reaches of the *muang* and the forms of dress and weaving patterns that were worn there.

By the 1880s the senior Lan Na princes were wealthy. They owned large numbers of slaves and vast tracts of agricultural land and primary forest, including hunting reserves.[3] One of the main sources of income was teak and taxes on timber provided high revenues. The logs were moved by elephant and floated down river to Moulmein in Burma or to Bangkok where a large percentage was exported to Britain for the shipbuilding industry. The Lan Na royal families also benefited from taxes levied on increasing trans-state and trans-regional trade, and they capitalised on the free goods and services received as tribute from their citizens and slaves. They were moneylenders and charged interest rates as high as 36%.[4] They gained additional income from a monopoly on gambling houses. It is important to note that female members of the royal family, also made fortunes during this period of expansion and princesses at the minor courts were similarly engaged in trading.[5] However, one of the great ironies of this period is that as the Lan Na royal families became very wealthy, their political power actually diminished. Even their personal wealth was eventually curbed when in 1908 Siam removed their right to monopolies and paid them fixed incomes.

Until that time the princes spent their money on restoring and refurbishing Buddhist temples and built grand palaces reflecting their wealth. They used indigenous and immigrant labourers and many were classed as slaves. Their large households included court musicians and troupes of dancers. The Lan Na rulers were polygamous and although senior members of the royal family maintained an expensive lifestyle, wealth did not extend to all the royal children and many struggled to

make a living. A senior prince in Chiang Mai had fathered 106 children, and a prince in Lamphun had 95 children. Some of the younger princes were so poor that they were forced to act as lowly paid guides and interpreters.

As power was transferred from Lan Na to Bangkok, the princes were drawn into a system of hierarchical dress codes operated from the Bangkok court. Interestingly, their resistance can sometimes be glimpsed in the dress they chose to wear for local ceremonies. Meanwhile, female members of the royal family continued to wear the dress of their homelands and their conservatism was to have interesting consequences at the Bangkok court.

Lan Na Male Military Dress

The early 19th century was described in chapter four as an age of charismatic military leadership when the Lan Na rulers led armies of local conscripts, over whom they had power of life and death, against their traditional enemy, the Burmese. The soldiers wore indigenous costume and believed that they would be protected against injury by the power of mystical symbolic diagrams *(yantra)*, magical incantations *(gatha)* spirit ceremonies and Buddhist blessings.

When the Siamese surveyor Nai Bancha Phumasathan visited the Lan Na-Shan States border in the 1890s he reported that the Burmese were no longer perceived as the enemy and the Shan States had replaced them as a threat to regional stability. Some Shan rulers had declared independence from Burma in 1881 and then a series of feuds and rivalries

Prince Chai Worachakra and his wife
Princess Duangchan na Chiang Mai.
(National Archives, Bangkok)

broke out between them. The ensuing chaos led to banditry on the borders and Lan Na soldiers were involved in quelling the disturbances, using the tactics of guerilla warfare at which they were experienced. Fear of British colonial ambitions in Lan Na, and distrust of the intentions of the princes (Prince Kawiloros was known to be negotiating with the Burmese), led Rama V of Siam to intervene. He stationed Siamese soldiers and militia on the borders, thereby introducing professionally trained and uniformed men. According to Nai Bancha Phumasathan they were well received by border inhabitants who resented the presence of undisciplined and untrained Lan Na troops.[6]

The first Siamese Commissioner to Chiang Mai was accompanied by 60 Siamese troops. In the mid-1880s the British Ambassador Sir Ernst Satow described a Siamese expeditionary force stationed at Phitsanalok on the southern border of Lan Na. There were between 250 and 300 soldiers clad in *khaki* uniforms with white leather helmets, equipped with mountain guns and Snider rifles.[7] Their chief of staff was Phra Amorawisai Soradet who had trained at the Military Academy, Woolwich, England. King Rama V of Siam sent officers for training in Europe including his son Crown Prince Vajiravudh, later Rama VI (1910-1925), who went to the British Military Academy, Sandhurst. At the end of the 19th century, a Military Academy, based on a European model, was established in Bangkok.

Lan Na princes were issued with Siamese-style military dress some time during the reign of Prince Indra Witchayanon of Chiang Mai (ruled 1871-1897). This dress was modelled on 19th century European uniforms and included jodhpurs and leather riding boots, straight-legged trousers and a range of fitted tunics and helmets set with Siamese insignia, denoting regiment and rank. Prince Chakrakam Kajornsakdi of Lamphun was photographed in this style of uniform. He wears a fitted round-necked jacket with gold epaulettes and gold insignia on the collar and sleeves. His straight–legged trousers have a line of gold braid down the outside seam and he is wearing a military helmet. Medals and insignia are pinned on his chest (*see page 43*). In a similar formal photograph taken in Bangkok, Prince Chai Worachakra of Siam wears a white tunic with gold epaulettes, tasselled waist sash, jodhpurs and leather boots. His helmet is decorated with the military insignia of Siam. Military uniforms were ordered from Europe and were copied by tailors in Bangkok. It is interesting to note that the leather helmets made for officers bear the label 'Made in Britain' in the lining.

The change in Lan Na military dress that took place towards the end of the century was radical. The photograph of Prince Bunthawong of Chiang Mai taken in the 1870s, and Prince Chakrakam Kajornsakdi in the 1900s, demonstrate this dramatic transformation. Prince Bunthawong wears indigenous dress, simple *chong kraben* and sandals that carry no symbols of hierarchy. In contrast Prince Chakrakam's Euro-Siamese uniform, insignia and medals establish him within the military hierarchy of Siam. Even the traditional haircut has been restyled to make him look like a European officer. This type of transformation took place among the elite throughout Lan Na.

Euro-Siamese military uniforms were worn by Lan Na officers, but it is not clear whether they were issued to regular soldiers and whether the soldiers were also issued with modern weapons. Lan Na soldiers believed in protection provided by *yantra* and spirit rites and belief in spirit religion remained overwhelmingly strong.[8] Lan Na soldiers were familiar with the tactics of guerilla warfare in forested, hilly terrain, traversed by mountain tracks and hill passes used by pack animals. Guerilla tactics were suited to the forests and uplands of interior mainland Southeast Asia where European uniforms and complex military machinery were no match for local men who understood the difficult forest terrain. In fact they were at a great advantage as they could disappear into the forest with no uniform to identify them.[9]

King Rama VI's helmet which was manufactured in Britain.
(Wat Supatanaram, Ubol province, permission of Miss Sharon o'Toole)

Lan Na Male Court Dress

The period 1871-1919 was a time of significant change in the style of male court dress. In the first half of the century the Lan Na kingdom had been re-established within the tenets of Sinhalese Theravada Buddhism and spirit religion. Political instability and the parlous state of the economy meant a modest court style, particularly in comparison with the grandeur of Bangkok and Mandalay. Dress worn at the Lan Na courts was

The water of allegiance ceremony held inside the *Ubosot* of Wat Phra Singh in front of the portrait of King Rama V. The official group on the left is from the Bangkok court with the princes of Chiang Mai on the right, c.1907.
(River Books collection)

Prince Indra Witchayanon, the seventh ruler of Chiang Mai (ruled 1871–1897).

Prince Suriyapong Paritdej of Nan who in 1903 was installed as Chao of Nan by King Rama V. (Payap University Archive, Chiang Mai)

made from cloth woven locally by skilled weavers and from imported Chinese silk. Textiles and clothing were sent as gifts from Siam in an attempt to formalise the status of tributary principalities but the princes resisted interference in their internal affairs. However, after 1874 as Siam increased her authority in Lan Na, the rulers were drawn into a hierarchy of dress codes that had been developed at the Ayutthaya court in the 17th century and later revived at the Bangkok courts in the reign of Rama I (ruled 1782-1809). Added to this was a new Euro-Siamese style.

Euro-Siamese court style developed in the reign of Rama V. He was not interested in slavishly copying European fashion but he hired European experts in a number of disciplines considered essential to Siamese progress. He made state visits to Europe and Russia in 1897 and 1907. One of his letters includes the statement 'we do not wish to be Westerners, but wish to know as Westerners know' and is generally quoted as a way of understanding his intentions.[10] In the arts, a fusion of European and Siamese style developed. For example, the Chakri Maha Prasat throne hall in Bangkok has a European frame, a Siamese pagoda roof and Siamese and European decorative features. This assimilation is reflected in the style of court dress that emerged at this time.

The transition to Euro-Siamese dress at the Lan Na courts is clearly demonstrated in two formal photographs of Prince Indra Witchayanon of Chiang Mai (ruled 1871-1897). At the beginning of his reign he wore a simple silk shirt, *chong kraben* and waist sash and was barefoot. His head was shaved at the sides with a circle of hair on the crown. His rank as ruling prince was communicated through his regalia displayed on tables at his side. Later in his reign he wore a white tunic with braided collar and braided cuffs and a silk sash. His *chong kraben* was draped and tucked to resemble breeches and he wore white stockings and buckled shoes. He carried a dress sword and wore a white helmet and medals awarded to him by Rama V. Awards given to the princes of the tributary states included the Order of the Crown of Siam, the Order of the White Elephant, the Chakri Order and the Chulachomklao Order. There were designated classes for each award.

Although Euro-Siamese court dress was de rigeur at official Siamese functions and on tributary visits to Bangkok, the Lan Na princes attempted to maintain their own regalia at court functions that did not involve a Siamese presence. This is demonstrated in photographs of Prince Suriyapong Paritdej of Nan (ruled 1894-1918). In Bangkok Prince Suriyapong posed in front of a painting of the Royal Palace. He wore a dark tunic cut in the style of a Victorian frock coat and matching straight-legged trousers. The front panels of his coat, the collar and sleeves are decorated with couched gold wire embroidery and edged with gold braid. The prince wears a three-tiered Siamese crown, a gold chain of office, a silk sash, and ribbons and medals awarded to him by King Rama V. This Euro-Siamese uniform was worn with a traditional Siamese coat draped over the shoulders. At home in the Nan palace Prince Suriyapong is photographed seated on his carved and gilded Lan Na throne. He has his

Prince Suriyapong Paritdej
shown wearing his crown
and the Chulachomklao sash
and decoration (First Class).
The photograph was by the
German photographer,
Robert Lenz).
(Payap University Archive,
Chiang Mai)

A view of the Maha Chakri throne hall with its fusion of western and Thai architecture.
(River Books collection)

Right: Prince Suriyapong being welcomed home in Nan by his attendants following a tributary visit to Bangkok.
(Payap University Archive, Chiang Mai)

regalia of office displayed on a table at his side. His uniform is similar to that worn in the Bangkok photograph, but he is not wearing the three-tiered Siamese crown.

A crown was an important symbol of status within the hierarchy of the Bangkok court where the king was entitled to seven tiers and Prince Suriyapong, as ruler of an important tributary state was designated three tiers. But as was argued earlier, a crown was not the ultimate symbol of authority in Lan Na. Anointment with holy water was the ancient rite that confirmed the appointment of a Lan Na ruler, hence the prominent display of ceremonial water vessels in the photograph taken at the Nan court. When Suriyapong was on tributary visits he accepted a position in the hierarchy of the Bangkok court and wore a three-tiered crown, a symbol of inferior status to the King of Siam. In contrast, when he resided at the Nan court he presented himself as an independent ruler by displaying his Lan Na regalia. Suriyapong walked a difficult path in his attempt to separate his personal authority from that imposed from Siam and in the long term he did not succeed. The annexation by the French of large tracts of his land contributed to his loss of authority. In a photograph taken around 1910 his dress includes a colonial-style pith helmet and his courtiers wear Siamese dress. At around this time, Prince Indra Waroros of Chiang Mai (ruled 1901-1911) made a similar transformation. He was photographed in Chiang Mai in Euro-Siamese uniform with a colonial-style pith helmet.

Court uniforms imposed from Bangkok were modelled on those worn by officers of His Britannic Majesty's Far East Consular Service, as in the photograph of Reginald Le May, British Vice Consul to Chiang Mai and Lampang (1913-1915). Le May wore a white tunic with embroidered and braided collar and sleeve cuffs, straight-legged trousers, a pith helmet bearing the British Imperial coat of arms and insignia, and a dress sword and gloves.[11] The Governors of British colonies wore similar uniforms with insignia according to rank, and pith helmets decorated with ostrich plumes. By issuing Prince Indra Waroros of Chiang Mai and Prince Suriyapong of Nan with white pith helmets with ostrich feathers, King Rama V was symbolically changing their status as prince-rulers to Governors under his jurisdiction. At the same time Rama V reserved for himself the right to wear a seven-tiered crown.

The decision to model uniforms on those of the British Colonial and Consular Service was a mirror of Siamese government policy. Rama V used the British administrative systems of India and Burma as a prototype for his own reforms. Under this system the authority of Bangkok, like that of the British in their colonies, radiated outwards, absorbing former vassals and consolidating administrative control. Queen Victoria lavished titles and honours on the princes of the Raj while her administrators limited their real power. Rama V acted in a similar way in his relationship with Lan Na.

Although the uniforms were Euro-Siamese, the princes also received traditional Siamese exchange gifts, as in the first half of the century. Gifts of dress and textiles from Siam can be categorised as Siamese designs, designs made in India to Siamese specifications, Indian designs, Chinese designs and Chinese and Indian designs copied in Siam. The most significant Siamese item of clothing (as opposed to Euro-Siamese), was the gold coat that formed part of court regalia from the time of Rama I (ruled 1782-1809). Rama V issued gold coats as part of official uniforms throughout the tributary states, and to his Ministers of State in Bangkok. Brocaded shirts were also sent as gifts to the rulers of tributary principalities. According to the Chiang Mai chronicle lengths of brocaded silk described as 'fabric with gold and silver patterns' were also distributed. Some samples have been identified as *pha yearabab* [khemkhab cloth], a type of brocade imported from India.[12] This fabric was used to wrap manuscripts and ceremonial regalia, such as swords and water vessels. Larger pieces were used as floor mats.

Under the new administrative reforms, government officers were issued with white tunics. On a journey north from Bangkok to Chiang Mai in the late 1880s Satow noticed that all officials in the towns were wearing close-fitting white jackets and *chong kraben* with the addition of white stockings and shoes for senior officers.[13] At court the Prince of Chiang Mai 'donned a white jacket and a silk sarong, or waist cloth worn Siamese fashion'.[14] However the princes did not always wear a white jacket and there are many accounts of more colourful dress. When he went on a state visit to Chiang Rai, a satellite of Chiang Mai, the Prince of Chiang Mai 'looked resplendent' in a bright red silk *chong kraben*, a blue jacket with gold buttons, and shoes and white stockings.[15] Prince Indra Witchayanon of Chiang Mai (ruled 1871-1897) received tributary offerings from the Lawa wearing a black silk jacket, silk

Reginald Le May, in the uniform of His Britannic Majesty's Far East Consular Service. Le May was British consul to Chiang Mai and Lampang from 1913 to 1915.
(White Lotus)

chong kraben and was barefoot. His son, who was present at the ceremony, wore a green satin jacket and yellow silk *chong kraben*. Many princes wore embroidered slippers made in Chiang Mai rather than European-style shoes. At his wedding the Prince of Lampang wore a blue silk jacket embroidered with gold, purple *chong kraben* and black velvet cap with a gold band.[16] Many princes in the minor principalities continued the custom of wearing flowers and carrying cigars in their pierced earlobes. Some kept their hair in the traditional Lan Na style, shaved at the sides with a circle on the crown.[17]

Senior Siamese princes closely related to Rama V undertook state visits and inspection tours in Lan Na to boost the profile of the Siamese government. Extensive preparations were made for the state visit of Prince Phichit Preechakorn, half brother of Rama V, to Lampang and Chiang Mai in 1876, two years after the appointment of the first Siamese Commissioner. A procession of approp-riately adorned elephants, groups of dancers, musicians and regalia bearers took part in the ceremony.[18] Although there are no photographs of this event, there are photographs of a similar state visit made to Chiang Mai in 1906 by Crown Prince Vajiravudh, later Rama VI

A gold embroidered ceremonial coat sent from Bangkok to a Lan Na prince.
(Hariphunchai National Museum, Lamphun)

Detail of the coat shown opposite.

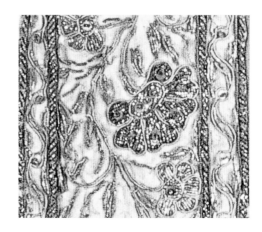

Phaya Prachakitkornchakra (Chup Osathanonda) (1875–1955) who was of governor of several provinces throughout Siam. On this occasion he was wearing his gold embroidered coat and European-style uniform to receive the order of Chulachomklao Second Class.
(National Archives, Bangkok)

Left: A gold coat worn by a member of the royal family or a senior official. Couched gold wire embroidery on a cotton net backing.
(Paothong Thongchua collection)

(ruled 1910-1925). The elephant howdah prepared for King Rama VII (ruled 1925-1935), shows the sumptuous decoration associated with such royal event (*see page 143*). The way Siamese royalty were treated during this period was a great change from 1859 when two Siamese princes made a state visit to Lan Na and were virtually ignored by Prince Kawiloros of Chiang Mai and the second prince *(uparat)*. The Lan Na princes now honoured the Siamese royal family.

As part of the changing political climate, ceremonies acknowledging Siamese authority received ever-increasing attention. The bi-annual 'Water of Allegiance' ceremony to the King of Siam required the participation of all senior Lan Na royalty and government officials as well as Siamese officials serving in Lan Na. Female members of the royal family took the oath at their palace residencies.[19] The photograph of army officers and civilian officials at the ceremony held at Wat Phra Singh, Chiang Mai shows a variety of Euro-Siamese military and government uniforms.[20] The military officers wear tunics, sashes and straight-legged trousers and hold military helmets. Government officials wear jackets

A formal shirt (*sua*) of purple silk and silver metal thread brocade. The repeat floral patterns are set within diamond shapes.
(Chiang Mai National Museum)

Opposite:
The 1906 state visit to Chiang Mai of Crown Prince Vajiravudh (later King Rama VI).
(Payap University Archive, Chiang Mai)

Left: Prince Rajasampan of Chiang Mai with his daughter, Princess Chomchuen.
(Payap University Archive, Chiang Mai)

Right: The howdah prepared for the state visit of King Rama VII to Chiang Mai in 1926. He was the first king of the Chakri dynasty to visit Lan Na. (River Books collection)

and trousers, or jackets and *chong kraben*. From their uniforms it is impossible to distinguish between the Lan Na and Siamese officials.

The new uniforms represented civil, provincial authority and cast the princes in the role of state Governors rather than independent Buddhist rulers. Some princes attempted to reconcile their traditional authority as 'Lords of Life' with the loss of real power, managing to maintain a degree of independence while Siam remained a relatively remote authority. Ancient Lan Na rituals, including the annual ceremony of the Inthakin Pillar and the New Year *dam hua* ceremony in which the Lan Na people swore allegiance to their prince, were continued for a time. Other ceremonies that were linked to the traditional *muang* system, like the formal acceptance of Lawa and hill tribe tribute, gradually faded out. As communication with Bangkok improved, particularly after the completion of the railway line in 1919, and as increasing numbers of Siamese officials were stationed in the towns, the Lan Na rulers could no longer avoid their authority.

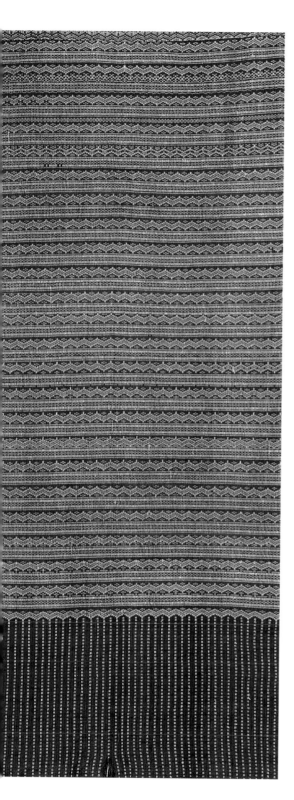

Detail of a Lan Na silk *phasin*.
(Darabhirom Museum, Chiang Mai)

Lan Na Court Life

For many years after the war with Burma the Lan Na princes had lived in modest dwellings. The Prince of Chiang Rai resided in a bamboo and thatch palace for some years before moving into a building of teak construction. The Prince of Lampang also lived in a bamboo and thatch dwelling with teak floors and although the Prince moved the old palace was not demolished until 1957. In 1886, the British diplomat Sir Ernst Satow paid an official call on the Prince of Lamphun who lived in a new teak palace with an audience hall and Satow described it as superior to the audience hall of the Prince of Lampang.[21] Satow noted that the second prince *(uparat)* Bunthawong of Chiang Mai had a more impressive palace with giant teak pillars, bands of carving on the interior and exterior walls and handsome carved wooden screens.

The grandest palace of the time belonged to Prince Indra Witchayanon of Chiang Mai, and was described from the exterior as a mixture of Chinese and Lan Na style. Hallett wrote that it was a substantial brick building rendered with cement and that it had a tiled roof. The audience hall had a wooden inlay floor and the ceiling was hung with chandeliers and the walls with gilt framed mirrors. One of the main rooms was papered like an English drawing room. The palace contained European-style furniture and elegantly carved latticework partitions that served as screens to the private apartments. Emilie McGilvary who lived in Chiang Mai at the time thought the palace was an imitation of a house the Prince had seen during a tributary visit to Bangkok. The adoption of an English drawing room style was possible because of changes to protocol. In 1868 King Rama V had abolished the custom of prostration and allowed visiting dignitaries and officials to sit on chairs, thus creating a demand for European-style seating, tables and other furniture. The costly European furniture in the Bangkok palace had been imported from London, probably following the king's visit there. In Chiang Mai, Lan Na craft workers copied pieces of European furniture that were shipped upriver from Bangkok. When Sir Ernst Satow and his colleague W. J. Archer dined with the Prince of Chiang Mai, all the principal guests sat on chairs at a long table and were served from imported china and cutlery.

Some Lan Na princes accepted the new European etiquette but others did not. While visiting Phrae, Satow and Archer were given chairs, while the ruler and his son sat on carpets on the floor laid on top of velvet mattresses, leaning against wedge-shaped pillows. The Prince of Lampang held audience while sat on a carpeted dais, reclining on cushions. In Lamphun Hallett was provided with floor mats and pillows and was invited to sit on the floor. Floor pillows for reclining were densely filled with kapok to make them rigid and were covered in imported Chinese silk and silk velvet, embroidered with Chinese floss silk, sequins and gold and silver metal thread.

In keeping with their status as 'Lords of Life' the Lan Na princes held audiences in staterooms furnished with gilded wooden thrones, silk

umbrellas, silver and gold repoussé water vessels and other silver and gold regalia. The senior Prince of Lamphun sat surrounded by his consorts, retainers and emblems of rank that included gold spittoons, betel utensils, trays and water vessels. The Prince of Chiang Mai was known to be proud of his collection of gold boxes and repoussé bowls that he showed to Sir Ernst Satow who judged them to be antique.

A Lan Na prince, his consorts, children and household staff.
(Payap University Archive, Chiang Mai)

Some items of regalia accompanied members of the royal family when they went beyond the palace compound. The wedding procession of the Prince of Lampang was led by musicians and dancers followed by servants and slaves carrying flowers, silver-hilted swords and a big red umbrella on a long silver shaft.[22] The fourth Prince of Chiang Mai visited Holt Hallett for tea and was accompanied by fifteen attendants bearing his gold betel boxes, water goblets and other paraphernalia of rank.[23] Sir Ernst Satow received the Prince of Phrae who was escorted by a band of drummers and fiddlers, and when the Prince of Lamphun came to call, he was carried on a bier by a group of attendants and protected from the sun by an enormous red umbrella. Senior foreign officials were also fêted. When he arrived at the city limits of Phrae, Sir Ernst Satow was led in by a man bearing a large silver vase filled with flowers and wax tapers. Servants and porters carrying muskets, silver-shafted spears, drums, gongs and a huge gilt umbrella followed and two elephants with gilded black howdahs brought up the rear of the procession.[24]

As Siam widened its administrative power, regalia was strictly graded according to a ranking system established by Siamese decree. Hallett refers to this as 'The Chronicle of the Governors'. By the end of the

The palace of the Prince of Lampang, built in 1872 and demolished in 1957.
(Payap University Archive, Chiang Mai)

His Majesty King Sisawangwong of Luang Prabang (ruled 1905-1959), photographed by Sesmaisons of Paris.

19th century, regalia that had previously symbolised Lan Na authority was relinquished. Satow was made aware of this change while on an official visit to Lampang. He described the Golden Hall (audience hall) with its red and black pillars decorated with gold leaf and the throne of Lampang, which, he decided 'must once have been a gorgeous object'. The room and its contents had been allowed to fall into disrepair, the throne was no longer used although, significantly, as a symbol of the new order, a photographic portrait of King Rama V of Siam had been placed on the seat.

Court dress in the 'Extended Cultural Area'.

While the Lan Na courts went through a process of change, the fate of states in the extended cultural area of Luang Prabang, the eastern Shan States and Sipsong Pan Na took a different course. Luang Prabang was tributary to Siam until it was annexed by France and became a French protectorate. Rama V was forced to agree to French claims and tributary relations between Siam and Luang Prabang ceased. In order to gain favour with the princes in their new Laotian territories, the French encouraged a grand court style, actually freezing the Luang Prabang court in time and place.[25] A photograph taken at the court of King Zacharine of Luang Prabang (circa 1895) shows the king seated on a raised seven-tiered throne, wearing a seven-tiered crown and surrounded by tiered umbrellas, fans and kneeling courtiers. His son, King Sisawangwong (ruled 1905-1959) was later photographed early in his reign wearing a brocaded silk shirt, a *chong kraben*, stockings and embroidered slippers. A wing-shaped collar has been overlaid on the neck and shoulders of his silk shirt. It is interesting to speculate on what court dress would have been if Luang Prabang had remained tributary to Siam. Presumably the princes would have worn Euro-Siamese dress as issued to the princes of Lan Na and the King of Luang Prabang would not have been entitled to such high-ranking regalia.

In Sipsong Pan Na and Upper Laos the French and British disputed territory. In terms of court life it made little difference as both France and Britain curried favour with the princes and encouraged the continuation of existing court style. In photographs taken during a French expedition (1894-1896) the King of Muang Sing is seen dressed in a patterned turban and a wide-sleeved silk robe in Chinese style. His son wears a turban, a patterned shirt and loose-legged trousers. This type of dress demonstrates tributary and economic relations with Sipsong Pan Na and China.

Meanwhile the Shan States maintained a degree of autonomy from the British, whose authority they constantly challenged. The British aimed to keep the loyalty of the Shan princes by supporting them and their elaborate courts. In a photograph from the James Green Collection,

The king of Luang Prabang in his throne hall c. 1895. (White Lotus)

Brighton Museum, a Shan ruler *(sawbwa)* wears a patterned hat and turban cloth and a tunic in Chinese style over ankle length *chong kraben*. This style of dress also demonstrates earlier political and economic relations with China. In contrast the Shan State of Chiang Tung [Keng Tung] maintained a court style that can be related to dress at the Burmese court of Mandalay.

In summary, at the end of the 19th century, dress codes in the Lan Na states where the Siamese held sway, were different from the surrounding inland states where the British and the French exercised authority. The King of Siam imposed Euro-Siamese dress on the Lan Na rulers and detached the Lan Na people from their traditional relationship with the princes by substituting Siamese ceremonies in place of ancient Lan Na rites. In contrast Britain and France dealt with the rulers of Luang Prabang, Sipsong Pan Na and the eastern Shan States by encouraging traditional court style that varied from court to court. They restricted the administrative power of the rulers while in no way diminishing the ceremonial and religious traditions that linked them with their people.

With great skill and diplomacy, Siam resisted British and French colonisation. Rama V personally chose to Europeanise his country and the tributary courts, curtailing some indigenous religious and ceremonial traditions that were in conflict with his authority. He introduced civil and military uniforms based on those worn by the very colonial powers he successfully resisted. In terms of dress history, this was a most fascinating and unusual course of action, and in historical terms one of the greatest ironies of the Colonial Period in Southeast Asia.

Opposite:
A Shan ruler (*Sawbwa*) wearing a Chinese silk
robe and silk hat.
(The Green Centre for non-Western Art at the
Royal Pavilion Art Gallery and Museums,
Brighton)

Lan Na Female Court Dress

The Lan Na female court dress described here includes that worn by consorts, their attendants and female children in the principalities of Chiang Mai, Lamphun, Lampang, Nan and Phrae, and their satellite courts. Marital alliances between the royal families of Sipsong Pan Na, western Laos and the Shan States continued, although a shift in the balance of power meant that marriages with the Bangkok royal family became the most politically significant. Fear of British colonial ambition was rife in Chiang Mai. A rumour was circulating that Queen Victoria was interested in a marital alliance between a member of the British royal family and the daughter of a Prince of Chiang Mai, as a way of increasing British influence in the region.[26]

Women who married into the Lan Na royal family, and Lan Na female royalty who married out, continued to wear a form of dress that conveyed ethnic group and could be identified with village women belonging to the same group. Although it was important that women maintained their group identity, court dress was not frozen in time and there were subtle changes. Increasing communication with Bangkok brought Lan Na women in contact with hybrid fashions based on Siamese and European designs. This was not in one direction only and Lan Na textiles, particularly women's skirts, became fashionable at the court of Bangkok. Lan Na textiles were also admired in Burma where they fetched a high price. High quality textiles were also available in many villages and Hallett named Ban Nang Eng, to the south of Chiang Mai as one source.[27]

The increasing wealth of the Lan Na courts was reflected in the amount of money female royalty spent on dress in comparison with village women. Bock compared the cost of two *phasin*:

> *When the body is made of silk, this border is made of the same material, often beautifully interwoven with gold and silver threads. These rich borders sometimes cost as much as 60 rupees apiece, while the whole garment, when made entirely of cotton, strong and durable as it is, does not cost more than from one and a half to two rupees.*[28]

The king of Muang Sing, his family and
court, circa. 1890.
(White Lotus)

A Lan Na woman wearing jewellery made by local silversmiths.
(Payap University Archive, Chiang Mai)

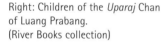

Right: Children of the *Uparaj* Chan of Luang Prabang.
(River Books collection)

Chao Kam On, wife of Prince Mahintrathep Nipaporn, governor of Luang Prabang, c.1905.
(River Books collection)

Bock also noted that weavers preferred to use Chinese silk yarn which they purchased in considerable quantities from Yunnanese traders. Throughout the 19th century Lan Na women continued to wear their hair loose or drawn into a knot on the crown of the head, decorated with fresh flowers, jewellery and metal pins. Wealthy women decorated their hair with gold and silver chains. Satow described a young princess of Phrae who wore her hair 'done up in a knot behind, tied with a gold chain, a tiara pin being thrust through it'.[29] These elaborate hairstyles contrasted favourably with the short and often rather severe looking hairstyles favoured by Siamese ladies.

Increase in wealth at the Lan Na courts also meant more money spent on jewellery. Local craftsmen, many of Tai Lue origin, took orders from the Lan Na courts. The American missionary W.A. Briggs (1894) described a Lan Na princess who he said shone with gold rings, gold bracelets, necklaces, earrings and anklets. The gold and silver necklaces were inset with semi-precious and precious stones, particularly rubies that were mined in Burma. Like hill tribe women, Lan Na women also wore earplugs. Young girls had their ears pierced and small wooden plugs were inserted and replaced over time by ever larger plugs until the holes were large enough for cylinders of gold, silver or semi-precious stones.

Court Regalia for Women

The American missionary Emilie McGilvary described the regalia of Princess Tipkesorn, wife of Prince Indra Witchayanon of Chiang Mai.

> *As the queen walks out a maid walks behind, carrying over her majesty a large lined and fringed silk umbrella with a silvered handle, which may be about six or eight feet long. Behind this maid is another, carrying a gold betel nut box, while dozens of others follow her, all walking in single file. . .[30]*

In 1889 Princess Ubonwanna made a visit to Holt Hallett, accompanied by her eldest son and her niece, the daughter of Princess Tipkesorn. A row of attendants accompanied them bearing silver-handled umbrellas, gold betel boxes, water vessels and cigarette platters.[31] At a dinner at the Chiang Mai palace the royal ladies were seated on a platform surrounded by gold and silver water vessels, betel nut sets and goblets.

Tai Yuan Court Dress

Tai Yuan women wore a sash *(pha sabai)* and a horizontally striped *phasin*. The sashes were woven using silk and silver and gold metal thread, and were made locally and imported from Luang Prabang, a trade that was established earlier in the century. These sashes were heavy, due to the weight of silver and gold thread and were less easy to wear over the light decorative blouses that were fashionable at this time. In the 1880s lighter sashes were imported from Bangkok.

One new style of blouse was called a 'jersey' after the actress Lily Langtry (called the 'Jersey Lily') who was a mistress of Edward, Prince of Wales (1841-1910). This style did not become widely popular in Lan Na, probably because the tight-fitting bodice and sleeves were uncomfortable in the tropical climate. Bock described the garment as a 'jacket' and wrote disparagingly.

> *A few Lao [Lan Na Tai] women are beginning to wear tight-fitting jackets, cut to the shape of the figure, with equally tight sleeves, something after the style of the "ladies jerseys" recently so fashionable in Paris and London, and involving no small amount of labour to get on and off, being made not of elastic knitted work, but of unyielding cotton or silk.[32]*

Between 1894 and 1910 another style of European blouse became fashionable and was popular at the Bangkok court. It was designed with a high collar, had a fitted waist and long sleeves, often cut in a 'leg of

Phrae beauty, c.1900. She wears a simple Lan Na *phasin* and silk sash.
(River Books collection)

Princess Dararatsami's court dress. A long lacy blouse and sash worn with a *phasin*. (Darabhirom Museum, Chiang Mai)

Opposite:
Right: A frilly blouse trimmed with lace, fashionable among court ladies at the end of the 19th century, (Duangchit Taweesri collection)

Far right: Princess Dararatsami at the Bangkok Court.

Below right: Detail of a red silk *phasin* with gold and silver metal thread woven in tapestry weave *luntaya*. (Duangchit Taweesri collection)

mutton' shape. Light filmy fabrics such as silk chiffon and fine linens and cottons were used and the neck, yolk and sleeves were trimmed with copious amounts of lace. This type of blouse was popularised by Princess Alexandra, wife of the Prince of Wales. At the Bangkok court Queen Saowabha, consort of King Rama V, was particularly taken with the style and other ladies of the court followed her example. This new fashion was eventually introduced at the Lan Na courts. The blouses worn in Lan Na were decorative but did not reach the level of fussy flimsiness that characterised the style worn in Bangkok. This was because it was difficult to get chiffon, and lace was not available in the Chiang Mai markets. Princess Ubonwanna resorted to asking Holt Hallett if he could arrange for some to be sent from London.[33] Most Lan Na royalty made do with satin, lightweight silks and fine cottons carried by itinerant Yunnanese and Shan traders. However a few fine fabrics were brought up from Bangkok.

Although they adapted their blouses and sashes to suit current fashion, Tai Yuan women continued to wear traditional *phasin* with some minor changes in the materials. When Hallett took some Tai Yuan skirts from the town of Hot, south of Chiang Mai, back to England to show a textile expert in Manchester, he reported that the waistbands were 'of English manufacture' and the central panel and hem border were produced 'by native looms'.[34] Factory-produced cotton was generally restricted to waistbands while the central panels and hem borders remained almost exclusively the work of indigenous Tai Yuan weavers. There was criticism of women who used imported fabrics other than for waistbands, and skirts made that way were derided as 'lazy women's skirts'.[35]

In 1886 Princess Dararatsami, daughter of Prince Indra Witchaya-non, became the fifth consort of King Rama V of Siam. She lived in her own quarters in the Bangkok palace compound with a group of Lan Na attendants. There had been previous marital alliances between Lan Na princesses and Siamese princes, but this union is notable because it marked a particularly important stage in political relations. Rama V needed to strengthen relations with Lan Na to counter the British presence in Burma and the Shan States and French occupation in Laos.

In keeping with Lan Na custom, Dararatsami wore Lan Na skirts. but combined them with European style blouses and flimsy sashes. The princess often wore silk chiffon blouses trimmed with lace at the neck, yolk and sleeves and sashes of similar fabrics draped over one shoulder. She also wore broderie anglaise trimmed with lace. During her time in Bangkok, the distinctive appearance of Dararatsami and her ladies provided an interesting contrast to the dress of the Siamese princesses who cut their hair very short and wore *chong kraben* in the same style as men. Dararatsami was a creative woman and once she had established herself at court she began to invent her own style of dress. She wore lacy chiffon blouses and narrow silk sashes, Edwardian style chokers and brooches, and Lan Na skirts heavily decorated with gold thread in the

hem borders. However, on informal occasions shared with other female members of the court and in the privacy of her apartments she dressed in the type of *phasin* worn by village women.

Dararatsami's court skirts, and those worn by her attendants, were greatly admired by Siamese princesses who requested copies. Dararatsami's mother Princess Tipkesorn of Chiang Mai organised the weaving and dispatch of skirts to Bangkok.[36] As demand increased, extra weavers were employed at the Chiang Mai court, and work was also sent to Lamphun. Reginald Le May reported on the trade from Chiang Mai:

> ...the trade in piece goods has been given a great fillip by the fact that nearly all Siamese ladies of good social position are adopting the sin [phasin] instead of the phanung [chong kraben] for daily wear- much to their own personal advantage.[37]

Princess Dararatsami was an innovative designer and combined the weaving patterns she had learnt from her mother with other patterns taken from brocades made in Bangkok and the southern states of Siam. She also designed skirts with lengths of Burmese tapestry weave *(luntaya)* in the central panels and traditional Lan Na hem borders *(teen jok)*. Dararatsami was photographed in skirts in this style, as were other fashionable ladies. Her niece Princess Ladakham also wore skirts with supplementary weft pattern in the central panel and new *teen jok* designs in the hem border. Lady *(khunying)* Boonphun Rajamitri wears a skirt with Burmese tapestry weave in the central panel and *teen jok* in the hem border. According to Le May the craze for Lan Na style did not end with skirts as some Siamese women even stopped cutting their hair.

Princess Dararatsami and her attendants at the Bangkok court, c.1900.
(National Archives, Bangkok)

Khunying Boonphun Rajamitri (Singholaka), who used to be in the palace of Princess Dararatsami and can be seen seated at the far left front row in the photograph at left. She is wearing a Lan Na *phasin*.
(National Archives, Bangkok)

Opposite:
A Lan Na *phasin* with a machine-printed cotton waistband. *Phasin* with panels of imported, printed trade cloth were uncommon in Lan Na.
(Bank of Thailand Museum, Chiang Mai)

An informal photograph of Princess Dararatsami combing her hair. In contrast, Siamese ladies wore their hair cropped. (National Archive, Bangkok)

Princess Sroydara (1899-1909) was one of Princess Dararatsami's favourite nieces. She was photographed aged 7 on a visit to her aunt in Bangkok. She died aged 10 after being bitten by a rabid dog in Chiang Mai (National Archives, Bangkok)

Opposite: A silk *phasin* of *luntaya* with a plain cotton waistband. Skirts of this style were worn by court dancers. (Bank of Thailand Museum, Chiang Mai)

When Princess Dararatsami first moved to Bangkok, Lan Na court dress was a vehicle for expressing ethnic identity and a way of signalling a royal marital alliance. During her time at court she added a fashion dimension. However, her world was centred at the Bangkok court, and the hybrid skirt designs that she and her attendants wore were not initially accepted at the regional courts, where women were more conservative in their dress. The courts of Chiang Mai, Lamphun, Lampang, Phayao, Phrae and Nan, and satellite courts such as Mae Chaem continued to produce Lan Na designs for home consumption. Chiang Mai and Lamphun provided the new designs for the Bangkok market.

A Burmese-style *phasin* with fine silver and gold metal
thread embroidery of stylised butterflies and foliage.
(Duangchit Taweesri collection)

Opposite: A silk *phasin* with a central panel of *luntaya*
in a gold and silver wave and flowers pattern.
(Duangchit Taweesri collection)

Tai Lue Court Dress

At the beginning of the 19th century a Tai Lue princess could be identified by a long-sleeved, side-fastening blouse *(seua pat)* worn in summer, a lined jacket *(seua kop long daeng)* in winter, a turban, and a tubular skirt with a patterned central panel and plain hem. By the 1880s the turban had become optional as female royalty portrayed in Lan Na photographs are usually bare headed, although turbans were still worn by village women. Some Tai Lue princesses at the major Lan Na courts began wearing the new European-style blouses, although the fascination with European fashion never threatened indigenous design. Many women continued to wear the traditional *seua pat* and *seua kop long daeng* made of imported black velvet or black Chinese satin and lined with red flannel. The collars and front panels were trimmed with couched gold metal thread embroidery laid in patterns on a cotton or a silk backing decorated with strips of brightly-coloured Chinese silk and silk brocade, floss silk embroidery, beetle wings and beads.

In the 1890s Holt Hallett described the typical Tai Lue skirt as having horizontal red stripes interwoven with lines of gold metal thread with bands of black, blue and red in the border. Dodd wrote a similar description of a Tai Lue skirt adding that a band of green silk was worn at the hem.[38] These skirts, with patterned central panels and plain, or *teen jok* hems, are referred to as hybrid designs.

Princess Ladakham, niece of Princess Dararatsami, c.1910. She wears a silk *phasin* with repeat floral patterns in the central panel. She later married HRH Prince Purachatra Chaiyakorn, Prince of Kamphaeng Phet.
(National Archives, Bangkok)

Left: Detail of a Lan Na *phasin* with *teen jok*.
(Bank of Thailand Museum, Chiang Mai)

Opposite:
A silk *phasin* with a central panel of *luntaya* worked in floral and wave patterns.
(Chutinart Songwattana collection)

Opposite:
A *phasin* worn by Tai Lue and Tai Khoen women who lived in close proximity in the eastern Shan States and frequently intermarried.
(Duangchit Taweesri collection)

A Lan Na *phasin* with a cotton waistband of red and white cotton, a central panel containing silver metal thread in a continuous supplementary weft pattern, and a hem of multicoloured silk in diamond and hook patterns.
(Bank of Thailand Museum, Chiang Mai)

Tai Khoen Court Dress

The centuries-old tradition of marital alliances between the courts of Chiang Tung and Chiang Mai continued, at least until the 1940s. Like other Shan courts the Tai Khoen court of Chiang Tung maintained a style of pomp and ceremony that was encouraged according to British colonial policy in the region. In 1930s Prince Intanon of Chiang Mai, son of Prince Kaew Nawarat, last Prince of Chiang Mai (ruled 1911-1939) married the Tai Khoen Princess Sukhantha of Chiang Tung. On her wedding day the princess wore a long sleeved jacket with wing and scallop shaped attachments at the collar, shoulders and sleeves, a style of court dress associated with Burma. Her hair was fastened in a topknot decorated with gold chains. She wore a tubular skirt with a striped central panel, and patterned hem border, decorated with rows of embroidery, sequins and brocade. The stunning beauty of the Tai Khoen skirt was captured in the following passage:

Prince Intanon, son of Prince Kaew Nawarat of Chiang Mai, and his bride Princess Sukhantha of Chiang Tung on their wedding day in 1933.
(Private Collection, Chiang Mai)

> *The skirt with the many coloured stripes and the dark green border is the ordinary court dress. To this is added a second border of large flowers solidly embroidered in gold thread, each flower four or five inches in diameter and costing a rupee a flower. In the body of the skirt also is there wove much gold thread, and the border of green velvet is bordered on either edge with sequins in silver tinsel put on in points. The same sequins trim the two or three inches of underskirt showing, which usually trails on the ground. With gold embroidered slippers, gold bracelets and many gold ornaments in the hair set with spangles, you want to get a kun [Khoen] princess out in the sunshine to see her sparkle.* [39]

At the beginning of this passage there is a reference to ordinary court dress, devoid of the decorated hem. Later in the same passage the author notes that there is little difference between Tai Lue and Tai Khoen 'ordinary court dress' except that the Tai Khoen used more colour. It was common for both Tai Lue and Tai Khoen skirts to have multicoloured stripes and green hems. These hybrid designs resulted from trade and intermarriage between the Tai Khoen and Tai Lue who lived in close proximity to each other. In 1918 it was calculated that approximately 50,000 Tai Lue were living among the Tai Khoen in Chiang Tung. [40]

Below: Detail of the embroidered hem band on the Tai Khoen *phasin* shown opposite.

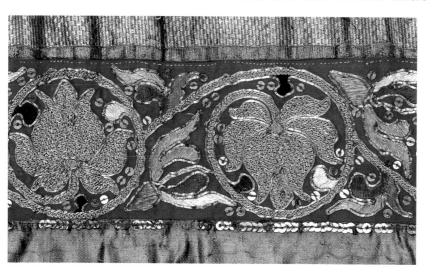

Opposite: A Tai Khoen *phasin*.
(Bank of Thailand Museum, Chiang Mai)

A *phasin* which could be either Tai Lue or Tai Khoen.
(Paothong Thongchua collection)

Opposite:
A *phasin* from Chiang Tung with a cotton waistband,
striped woven central panel and a satin hem, the latter
purchased in the market.
(Paothong Thongchua collection)

Tai Lao Court Dress

Luang Prabang was tributary to Siam until 1893 when it was annexed by France. In consequence a large population of Tai Lao left Luang Prabang, crossed the Mekong River and took refuge in Isaan (now Northeast Thailand) under the authority of King Rama V. After resettlement the nobility among them continued the custom of intermarriage with the Lan Na and Siamese courts.

At the end of the 19th century many Tai Lao women wore sashes although some chose to wear European-style blouses. The Tai Lao skirt continued to be made in a distinct styles with the patterns of the waistband and central panel set in a vertical plane, in contrast to the horizontal direction worn by other groups. The waistband has vertical stripes interspersed with supplementary weft patterns of silk and gold and silver metal thread, and the central panel also has vertical stripes interspersed with silk and silver and gold metal thread. In some samples, the repeat patterns were set in a diagonal field. The hem borders, narrower in design than skirts worn by other groups, have bands of horizontal supplementary weft. Although unusual, a few Tai Lao skirts contained imported fabric in the central panel thus matching the description 'lazy woman's skirt'.

Opposite: Prince Pakinaya (standing at back), later *Uparaj* Boonkong
of Luang Prabang, photographed with his sisters, c.1893.
(River Books collection)

Opposite below: Girls photographed in Luang Prabang, c. 1912.
They wear Lao-style *phasin* and sashes.

A shimmering silk *phasin* with gold and silver
metal thread and multicoloured silk in the central
panel and hem border.
(Bank of Thailand Museum, Chiang Mai)

A Tai Lao *phasin*.
(Darabhirom Museum, Chiang Mai)

A Tai Lao *phasin* with vertical silk stripes in the waistband, vertical stripes of continuous supplementary in the central panel and gold and silver metal thread in the hem border. (Bank of Thailand Museum, Chiang Mai)

Hybrid Dress in Lan Na

It was generally possible to identify Lan Na princesses and female royalty from the surrounding prin- cipalities by their complex costumes, in spite of adaptations and changes in style that had resulted from intermarriage and resettlement among ethnic groups and the vagaries of fashion. Women selected and combined elements of the dress of other groups while maintaining a distinctive style that confirmed their association with a particular group. However, there were instances when dress could not be identified with a particular group. For example, the dress of Princess Poon Pismai, shown opposite at first posed a problem of identification. She wears her long hair in a topknot, decorated with fresh flowers, a style associated with the women of Lan Na and the surrounding inland states. Her side fastening black

The wife and children of Phraya Somtrai, an important Siamese official in Nan. She wears Siamese dress, her daughters are dressed in Lan Na style and her little son wears European-style clothes.

jacket, trimmed with ribbons and embroidery is in Tai Lue or Tai Khoen style, her skirt has a Tai Lao-style waistband and central panel but a typical Tai Yuan hem border. Her dress can be defined as 'traditional' because it contains essential elements that relate to the dress and weaving patterns of the inland states but cannot be identified with a particular Tai group. It almost seemed as if she might be a descendant of mixed Tai Lue, Tai Yuan and Tai Lao families and was demonstrating her affiliation with her various ethnic origins. In fact, as the daughter of the Siamese prince, HRH Prince Damrong, she has assembled all the elements of Lan Na style that she most liked into a delightful ensemble.

Female Siamese Court Dress

Siamese officials and their wives and families were sent to Lan Na after the appointment of the first Siamese High Commissioner in 1874. Hallett called on a Siamese Commissioner and his family in Chiang Mai and noted that the dress of the two sexes was 'exactly alike'. He described the short hairstyles and *chong kraben* worn by men and women, noting that they also wore stockings 'often of gay colours'.[41] The photo of the wife and family of Phraya Somtrai (a Siamese official stationed in Nan) shows her wearing a white blouse with high neck and three-quarter length sleeves, a narrow sash, *chong kraben*, shoes and stockings. Interestingly their daughters are wearing Tai Lue or Tai Khoen skirts and white blouses. Their son is dressed in a scaled down version of Euro-Siamese uniform. Dressing boys in copies of men's uniforms was fashionable at the court of Queen Victoria.

Conclusion

Euro-Siamese civilian uniforms worn by the Lan Na elite redefined them in a hierarchy established in Bangkok. As an independent sovereign Rama V chose to apply a British colonial administrative system to the tributary states and operated it within a traditional Siamese court hierarchy. The Euro-Siamese uniforms he issued represented administrative and military reforms, while the Siamese gold coats were a symbol of Bangkok court hierarchy. Rama V also regulated Lan Na court regalia by introducing an entitlement system that operated according to Siamese sumptuary laws. The presence of Siamese officials in the main Lan Na cities ensured that new dress protocol was observed. Those princes who chose to accept the new order, and showed loyalty to Siam, were rewarded with titles, medals and regalia. In previous times the Lan Na princes had led troops who were bound to them by kinship ties and by obligations as citizens or slaves, now the 'Water of Allegiance 'Ceremony ensured that their loyalty was pledged to Siam.

In terms of dress history, the course taken by King Rama V was particularly interesting and in many ways unique. He introduced the hierarchical uniforms of the colonial powers himself while at the same time resisting their hegemony. In return, the colonial authorities respected him and accepted him as part of a world aristocratic system which they dominated at that time. Later Mahatma Gandhi and Jawaharlal Nehru took the opposite course and used indigenous dress as a symbol of idependence. Of course, India was colonised while Siam had only the threat of colonisation hanging over her, but in their own ways they used dress as a political statement.

Britain and France adopted a different strategy in their relations with courts in the Shan States, Luang Prabang and Sipsong Pan Na. The colonial powers controlled principalities that had previously been

Princess Poon Pismai Diskul, daughter of HRH Prince Damrong, dressed in Lan Na style. Her hair decorated with fresh flowers. Her *phasin* is a hybrid of Tai Lao and Tai Yuan design.
(Payap University Archive, Chiang Mai)

tributary to Siam, Burma or China and court dress varied in style from state to state. Like Rama V, Britain and France restricted the administrative authority of the princes but they did not interfere in ceremonial and religious traditions that bound the princes to their subjects. Male court dress did not change radically and a grand court style was positively encouraged as a way of securing the co-operation of the ruling elite.

While Lan Na male dress reflected change, in contrast court female dress remained conservative and women could be identified with their homeland and with other women of the same ethnic group. Unlike male court dress, the Siamese made no attempt to change female court dress; in fact it was in their interest to keep the system as it was. A Lan Na princess, or a princess from any state who married into the Siamese royal family, represented her home country and was the symbol of an alliance between powerful families. The Siamese were particularly anxious to demonstrate strength through alliances in a period when they were vulnerable to colonisation.

Within this framework of conservatism, there was some adaptation and assimilation. Women selected and combined new elements in their dress while keeping certain constituents that confirmed their association with a particular ethnic group. In Lan Na this involved assimilating weaving patterns, trying new fabrics and adopting some new fashions. As there were no sumptuary laws, princesses at the major courts, at satellite courts and members of the elite in the outer reaches of the *muang* might be dressed in a similar way, if they were wealthy enough and had access to the materials. The main problem for fashionable women who wanted to copy European fashions was distance from the Bangkok markets.

The craze for new fashions was not in one direction. Lan Na skirts became all the rage in Bangkok due to the presence of Princess Dararatsami of Chiang Mai and her attendants. Women with no connections to the Lan Na royal family and with little understanding of the cultural meaning of the skirts asked for copies. What was intended as an expression of ethnic identity and royal marriage alliance, became fashionable. This did not alter the importance of the skirt in Lan Na where its meaning was transmitted through a series of complex visual messages that included ethnic identity and the aesthetic and cultural significance of yarn and weaving patterns.

A silk *phasin* with a brocaded silver pattern in the central panel.
(Duangchit Taweesri collection)

Right: Detail of the hem border of a Tai Lao *phasin* with gold metal supplementary weft worked in geometric patterns.
(Darabhirom Museum, Chiang Mai)

1   Penth 1994: 38.

2   Hallett 1890.

3   The governor of Ban Mae Soo-ay informed Hallett (1890: 147) that the whole of the Mae Soo-ay valley to the north of Chiang Mai was the private game reserve of the Prince of Chiang Mai. Hildebrand (1875) reported that some members of the royal family owned up to a thousand slaves.

4   Bock 1986: 157-159.

5   Bock 1884 repr. 1986: 313, Hallett 1898 repr. 1988: 103-104.

6   Wilson and Hanks 1985.

7   Brailey 1994.

8   Hallett 1890, Dodd 1923, Le May 1926, Brailey, 1994.

9   The effectiveness of this warfare was understood by British officers such as General Wingate in Burma in World War II (Hall 1981); similar guerilla tactics secured French and American defeat in Vietnam.

10 Included in the Letters of the Fifth Reign (Ho Samut Hangchat [National Library] Bangkok) and quoted from the Rama V display sections of the National Museum, Bangkok.

11 The style of Reginald Le May's uniform indicates that he occupied a relatively junior post in the Consular Service at that time.

12 Prangwatthanakun and Naenna 1994.

13 Brailey 1994: 31.

14 Colquhoun 1885: 173.

15 Hallett, 1890 repr 1988: 154.

16 Bock 1986: 178-180.

17 Bock 1986: 223-226, Hallett 1988: 158.

18 Hallett 1988: 283, 373, 381-383.

19 Quaritch Wales 1931.

20 The 'Water of Allegiance' ceremony took place in the Chapel Royal in Bangkok and one temple in the seat of each provincial government (Quaritch Wales 1992: 193). Participants took an oath of loyalty to the King of Siam.

21 Brailey 1994: 45, 199, 159-60.

22 Bock 1986: 152-153.

23 Hallett 1988: 298.

24 Brailey 1994: 97-98,123-125.

25 Steinberg 1987:192.

26 Interview with Khun Benjawan Thongsiri, Chiang Mai, 1996.

27 Hallett 1988: 87.

28 Bock 1986: 324-326.

29 Brailey 1994: 103.

30 McGilvary, E., 1883.

31 Hallett 1988: 117.

32 Bock 1986: 327.

33 Hallett 1988: 327.

34 Hallett 1988: 392-393.

35 Interviews with weavers from Chiang Mai (Chiang Mai, 1987).

36 Kanchanajari 1990.

37 Le May 1926: 102.

38 Dodd 1923: 183.

39 Dodd 1923: 201.

40 Collis 1938.

41 Hallett 1988: 113-114.

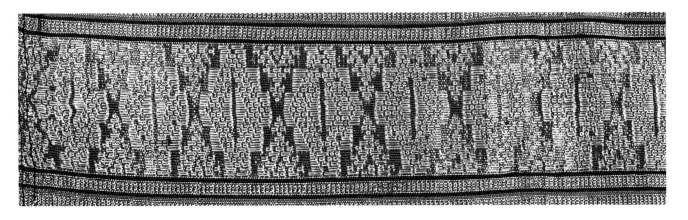

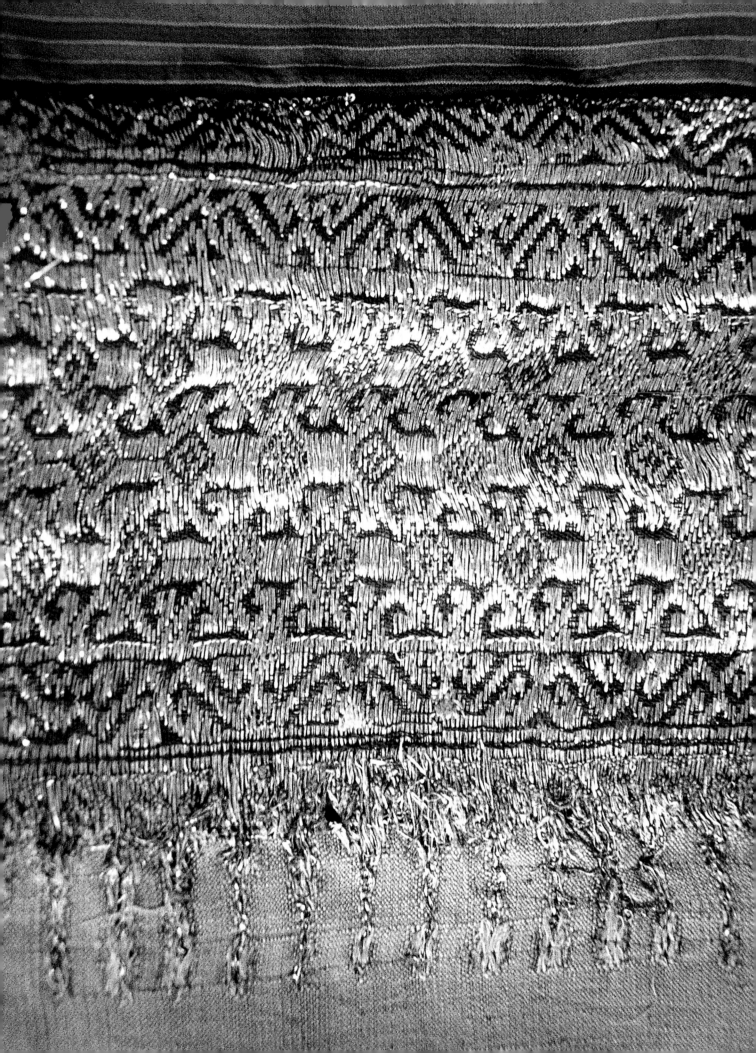

Chapter Six

Textile Design

This chapter examines patterns and techniques used to produce cloth in Lan Na, the eastern Shan States, Sipsong Pan Na and Luang Prabang. There is also reference to Chinese, Siamese and Burmese fabrics that were imported over many centuries, and sent as part of tributary exchange gifts to the inland courts.

Yarn: Aesthetics and Prestige

Textile enthusiasts readily admire colourful fabrics with complex weaving patterns while underestimating the importance of the skilful reeling and spinning of yarn. Yarn is fundamental to the aesthetic and tactile qualities of cloth and is the basic structure on which all other characteristics are developed. At the Lan Na courts, imported Chinese silk yarn was valued for its smooth handling qualities and glossy surface, enabling the production of cloth with a sheen and soft drape that was highly prized. The Chinese silk trade with Lan Na can be traced back at least 1,000 years, although the records do not state whether silk yarn and woven silk fabric were imported at that time. In the 19th century, traders from Yunnan brought Chinese silk yarn to Lan Na cities where it was dyed and woven for court dress. We know its use was extensive. The British diplomat Sir Ernst Satow recorded in his diary that he had seen Chinese raw silk being processed at the court of Lampang.

A hem border of a *phasin*. This discontinuous supplementary weft pattern contains silk and silver and gold metal thread. The design is called 'snakeskin' or 'tortoiseshell'.

A *pha chong kraben* of silk plaid. Each square is bordered by bands of white silk.

Chinese silk yarn was a symbol of prestige and sophistication while indigenous silk yarn was looked on as an unsophisticated product of village sericulture.[1] In practical terms, weavers preferred Chinese silk yarn because the filaments are less prone to tangling and knotting during reeling and spinning. Indigenous silk yarn is uneven, knots easily and takes longer to reel and spin although it is possible to produce smooth yarn by using the inner filament and discarding the coarser outer filament of the cocoons.[2] When supplies were hard to come by, women who were not normally involved in sericulture bred wild silk moths and reeled and spun silk.[3] The aesthetic value of the inner filament of indigenous silk is expressed in courtship prose *(payar)*. A male suitor will compare his beloved to the inner filament while referring to himself as the coarse outer thread.

> *You are like the finest silk cloth and the most delicate silk thread. You are as cool and beautiful as silk. You beat cloth with the finest teeth beater to make the finest silk cloth.*

> *I wish I had thread for you to weave, but I do not know if you are interested in me, or if you think I am an undyed, inferior yarn.*[4]

Inner filament silk was used to produce textiles for the court when supplies of Chinese silk were not available. It was often practical to combine silk and cotton. Cotton provides a strong ground weave support for supplementary weft containing dense patterns of gold and silver metal thread. Waistbands of even the most expensive *phasin* were made of cotton because it does not slip when tucked at the waist, as silk is prone to do.[5] Weavers used indigenous silk and imported Chinese silk yarn in different sections of their garments. For example, some skirts contain Chinese silk yarn in the central panel and in the upper hem *(jok)* while indigenous silk is used in the lower hem that touches the feet, considered to be the most polluted part of the body.[6] The ability to select yarns for specific purposes was possible where imported yarns were affordable. The type of materials used at any one time in history is an indication of the state of the local economy. In hard times the use of indigenous silk and cotton was prevalent.

It has been argued that Buddhist rulers in Southeast Asia wore silk that was processed by non-Buddhist communities because silk production involves killing silk worms when the cocoons are heated in water to melt the gum and release the silk filament.[7] This religious restriction may have applied to royal families in the Shan States but it did not apply to those processing indigenous silk for the Lan Na courts.[8]

Right: A detail of a silk *phasin* showing the supplementary weft (*teen jok*) design.

A dye expert in the Mae Chaem valley. Her hands are stained with indigo dye.

Right: A pot of indigo dye prior to adding cotton. A first dip will produce a light blue. Darker hues are achieved by further dip dyeing.

Dyes and Mordants

The royal families of Lan Na obtained dyestuffs and mordants as part of tribute from their subjects. In the 19th century yarn was dyed with a variety of natural substances harvested locally from forests and fields and raised in home gardens. Dyes were extracted from bark, roots, core wood, seeds and seedpods, leaves, fruit and flowers. Red dye for silk was obtained from the secretions of insects in the form of stick lac. Purple and cerise aniline dyes were first imported into China in the 1870s and at some time after that date were carried on the trade routes to Lan Na. The first trade records listing aniline dyes imported from Bangkok, appeared in 1893.[9] By the early 20th century aniline dyes were available in the main markets.

The mordants used to fix dyes were obtained from local soil, animal excreta and plant extracts. For example, to fix black, blue and yellow dyes on cotton the fibres were immersed in mud extracted from buffalo wallows, from certain riverbeds and from cow dung. Tree bark ash was used to fix dye on cotton. Tamarind juice was a mordant for silk, as was the water collected from rusted metal. Other recipes involved plant extracts, fruits, animal fat and salt.

Plant Dyes

COLOUR	BOTANIC NAME	THAI/ENGLISH NAME	PART USED
red/pink	*Caesalpinia sappan*	*mai fang*/sappan wood	corewood
red/pink	*Areca catechu*	betel nut	nut
red	*Carthamus tinctorius*	*kham foi*/safflower	flowers
red	*Morinda citrifolia*	*yo pa*/Indian mulberry	wood bark roots
red	*Baccaurea sapida*	Burmese grape	wood
red	*Bixa orellana*	*khamsaed*/annatto	seeds
yellow	*Tamarindus indica*	*makham thai*/tamarind	leaves
yellow	*Garcinia mangostana*	*rong*/mangosteen	sap
yellow	*Cudriana javanensis*	*kae lae*/mulberry family	corewood
yellow	*Aegle marmelos*	*ma tum*/bael fruit tree	fruit seedpods
yellow	*Curcuma longa*	*khamin chan*/turmeric	rhizome
yellow	*Nyctanthes abortristis*	night-flowering jasmine	corolla
yellow	*Rauwenhoffia siamensis*	*nom meo*	bark
yellow/brown	*Artocarpus integrifolius*	*khanun*/jackfruit	corewood
khaki	*Oroxylon indicum*	*pheka*/sword-fruit tree	bark
khaki	*Tectona grandis*	*mai suk*/ teak	corewood
green	*Terminalia belerica*	*samoe phiphet*/myrobalan	bark, fruit
green	*Terminalia catappa*	*hu kwang*/wild almond	leaves, bark
green	*Ananas sativa*	*supparot*/pineapple	leaves
green	*Garcinia tinctoria*	*ma hud*	corewood
green	*Sesbania grandiflora*	*ke* or *ke ban*/leguminous tree	leaves
black	*Harrisonia perforata*	*si fan kon ta* or *kon ta*/bitter bark	fruit
black	*Piper methysticum*	*phrik*/pepper	root
black	*Canarium kerrii*	*kakoem*	fruit
black	*Diospyros mollis*	*ma kleua*/ebony	fruit
brown	*Rhisophora mucronata*	*kong kang bi yai*/mangrove	wood
brown	*Peltophorum inerme*	*nonsi*	bark
brown	*Acacia catechu*	*si siad*/cutch	wood
orange/gold	*Lawsonia inermis*	*thian king*/henna	leaves
orange	*Bixa orellana*	*khamsaed*/annatto	seedpods, leaves
blue	*Indigofera tinctoria*	*Khram*/indigo	stem, leaves

Insect Dyes

red	*Lakshadia chinensis*	*krang*/shellac	insect resin

A *teen jok* pattern referred to as 'flock of birds'.

Opposite:
Detail of the central panel of a *phasin* with silver supplementary weft in floral patterns. Nan province.

The Transmission of Design

There were prototype designs for weaving patterns, transmitted from generation to generation, and used throughout the inland states. Weavers made patterns and produced images based on the iconography of Buddhism, of spirit religion and of nature. Some designs are sufficiently realistic to make identification possible. The snake *(naga)*, the swan *(hong)*, ceremonial offering bowls *(kan kra hyong)*, flowers *(dork)* are good examples, although many of these designs are highly conventionalised. Some other designs bear no resemblance to the objects they are said to represent. They were probably transmitted from generation to generation and the original realistic treatment of the image has not endured. At some time in the past, there was a visual reference in the design, perhaps to a temple, or a Buddhist monument, or a mythical human or animal, or to some other natural form. The sources of design are particularly interesting in reference to the inland states because there was constant movement and resettlement of people. Discontinuous supplementary weft patterns named after the cities of Chiang Saen *(lai chiang saen)* and Lampang *(lai lakhon)* were produced by weavers living in the remote Mae Chaem valley, far from either city.[10] In Mae Chaem the weavers say the patterns were produced by resettled weavers who came from Chiang Saen and Lampang.[11] Local history backs up their claim and the Tai Yuan chronicle *(pongsawadan yonok)* records that in 1804 the Burmese destroyed Chiang Saen and the inhabitants fled to Chiang Mai and Lampang. Mae Chaem was at that time an outlying dependency of Chiang Mai and about 40 years later a Prince of Chiang Mai ordered the resettlement of people to Mae Chaem as part of a policy to stabilise the border regions. It is likely that among the settlers were weavers who had fled from Chiang Saen to Chiang Mai and others who fled initially to Lampang. The movement of weavers over the centuries has meant that, with dialectical variations, similar names for weaving patterns can be identified in the Shan States, in Laos and in Sipsong Pan Na.

There are also weaving designs based on abstract concepts of colour, harmony, rhythm and movement. Well known examples include the tapestry weave pattern 'running water' *(lai nam lai)* and the discontinuous supplementary weft pattern *'hang s'pao'* that resembles the movement of water in the wake of a boat. Some patterns that are picked by hand allow an element of freedom in the process. For example, 'flock of birds' *(nok)* and 'tortoiseshell' are produced in several forms and colours and the weavers say that they work freely and decide what the pattern should be called after it is finished.[12] This way of working is obviously restricted by the grid of warp and weft but the weaver can select yarns and create a sense of rhythm and symmetry by the way the yarn is introduced into the weft and the colours that are selected.

Designs created during the process of weaving were the work of talented and innovative women. In Bangkok, Princess Dararatsami of Chiang Mai had access to Burmese, Siamese and European designs that

Opposite:
A late 19th century design of continuous supplementary weft that is a fusion of Lan Na and Bangkok style.
(Darabhirom Museum, Chiang Mai)

A late 19th century continuous supplementary weft design which combines Lao and Bangkok styles. The design includes the flame (kranok) pattern, stylised flowers and pendants.
(Chao Dararatana Na Lamphun)

she adapted and incorporated with Tai Yuan weaving patterns. Several of her designs were influenced by the delicate patterns of European lace, particularly flowers and butterflies. Some became popular and prototypes in the form of samplers were sent to Lan Na workshops to be copied.[13]

The interpretation of Lan Na weaving patterns by foreign writers makes fascinating reading. Sir Ernst Satow was intrigued by the bird patterns woven in the hem borders of women's skirts and said they resembled the Chinese phoenix *(fung hwang)*.[14] Kamol also described the bird as a type of phoenix, a common symbol until the reign of the Chinese Emperor Wan-li (1573-1607) and a design that was popular in Siam during the Ayutthaya period (14th-18th century).[15] Fragments of Chinese textiles with swan motifs are attributed to the Tang Dynasty (618-907) and the Jin dynasty (1115-1234). Paired birds facing each other, also a common pattern on hem borders of Lan Na skirts, were said to have come to China from West Asia.[16] Lan Na weavers call the single bird 'bird' *(lai nok)* or swan *(lai hong)*, and call birds in pairs 'facing swans' *(lai hong ku)*.

Images of grotesque human figures and a lion (*singh*) are tattoed on a man's thigh. Mural painting, Wat Phumin, Nan.

U Aye Myint describes a similar bird that appears in Burmese design, describing it as a swan *(hamsa)* and stating that *hamsa* is a Pali term, translated in Hindi as duck or goose, thus referring its origin to India rather than China. This takes the discussion concerning the origin of design outside the arena of Lan Na and its female weavers into an India versus China argument that rests on the experience and personal bias of textile scholars. Lan Na weavers say that in Sinhalese Theravada Buddhist iconography the bird symbolises the end of suffering.[17]

In contrast to weaving patterns created by women, there are designs drawn and printed on cloth and paper by men. These include mystical symbolic diagrams *(yantra)* and letters and script recited as magical incantations *(gatha)*, Buddha images and grotesque human and animal forms. A spirit doctor selected the designs that were copied from sacred books either using a pen and black ink or by block printing. Some were hand coloured. The ferocity and grotesque images produced on some cloths suggests that they were selected to ward off extreme forms of evil. In contrast some designs were created in peacetime to bring good luck and prosperity.

Detail of a grotesque human figure, surrounded by *yantra*, drawn on a cotton cloth cut and sewn into a verst worn for protection.
(Oriental Collection, The British Library)

Designs were also created in the form of tattoos that were pricked into the skin using a stylus and a sharp serrated comb. The pigment was made from soot collected from burnt animal fat mixed with animal bile and water.[18] Tattoo artists travelled the country with prototype designs in pattern books or in manuscript form, passed down through generations of tattoo artists. There was an element of personal choice and designs were selected for their aesthetic appeal as well as for their potency.[19] Men selected the designs from mice *(noo)*, guardian beasts *(rachasee)*, lions *(singha)*, monkeys *(ling)*, tigers *(sua)*, elephants *(chang)*, bats *(kang kao)* and also birds *(nok)* that included peacocks, pigeons, storks and birds of prey. At the waist, wavy lines and pendant motifs provided borders.

Opposite:
Two young men with thigh tattoos, Wat Phra Singh, Chieng Mai.

Detail of discontinuous supplementary weft worked with facing birds (*lai hong ku*) set with diamond and hook pattern. (Darabhirom Museum, Chiang Mai)

Opposite:
A silk blanket. The design is worked in a supplementary weft pattern with repeat hooks and diamonds.
(Bank of Thailand Museum, Chiang Mai)

Weaving Techniques and Patterns

In Lan Na the names given to weaving patterns are expressed in a particular form. First the technique is specified, for example the term for continuous supplementary weft *(khit)* comes before the name of the pattern. Thus a small floral design *(dork picun)* produced in continuous supplementary weft is described as *khit dork picun*. The term *lai* (pattern) may also be included so that the term *khit lai dork picun* is used. The names given to patterns are not consistent and in some cases change from village to village. There are also dialectical differences. The names recorded in this chapter are in local dialect that has been translated literally into English.

Lan Na weavers use a loom described as a Burmese frame loom.[20] It has tongue and groove joints and can be easily dismantled and stored. This is particularly important in the villages where the loom occupies an area under the house that was also used to dry harvested crops and raise animals. The style of the loom and accompanying equipment for processing yarn are standard for village and court, although the wooden implements used as court, such as heddle pulleys and yarn spools were often delicately carved and painted. A loom provides tension for a warp while heddle shafts create space in a warp for interlacing the weft. The weaver passes the weft through the space created in the warp (called a shed) with the aid of a shuttle. After each row of weft the weaver beats the yarn in with a beater that is attached to the loom frame and contains a reed made with palm wood teeth. Reeds come in a variety of gauges.

A loom set up in a workshop in Lamphun.

A woman weaving discontinuous supplementary weft. The wrong side of the pattern is facing up.

Sets of loom heddles hanging from roof beams. Each set contains a complete supplementary weft pattern. They may be produced in single sets or repeats.

Fine silk thread requires a reed with teeth close together *(fuum kan)*, a requirement for weaving court dress, whereas for cotton the teeth are more widely spaced *(fuum saa)*. Weaving patterns are created by the use of three basic systems. The yarn is either dyed into patterns before weaving, a technique called ikat *(matmi)*, or the pattern is pre-set in the loom with the use of shed sticks, or the pattern is picked by hand.

Plain Weave

Plain weave is the simplest method of weaving; the weft thread passes over and under each warp thread, then under and over on the following line. Although the method is simple there are many variations that enable the weaver to create amazing textures and light variations. The warp may be a thicker ply than the weft, or the weft thicker than the warp, or the two may be the same ply, described as a balanced weave. Plain weave can produce monochrome fabric, or 'shot' silk, the warp one colour and the weft another colour. This creates tonal variations across the surface of the fabric that change according to the direction of light. Tonal qualities can be enhanced by plying (twisting) two yarns of different colours or tones together, either in the warp or in the weft, or in both warp and weft. This technique is known as *hang karok*.[21] The shimmering, marbled effect created in this way can be further enhanced by plying the yarns in an 'S' direction in the warp and a 'Z' direction in the weft, or vice versa.

A more complex application of this technique is employed in the production of plaid designs. Sets of coloured striped yarns in the warp are crossed with sets of colours in the weft to create a 'shot' effect in squares. This technique may include plying yarns in the warp and contrasting the ply (in a 'Z' or 'S' direction) in the weft. This technique creates squares of shot silk in a range of colours that when turned towards light produce a marbled effect. Plaid designs often include rows of white silk in the warp and weft, used to outline and enhance the squares.

It has been argued that Buddhist man wore plain weave without figurative designs as a statement of their religious committment. Throughout their lives men may choose to pass from secular society into a religious community as novices and monks. Patterns free from representations of nature and the natural world symbolise male proximity to the spiritual life, represented ultimately in the monochrome robes of the monks.[22]

Plain weave (balanced weave or weft faced) was used for women's skirts where horizontal stripes formed the main design. The plain weave might have a few rows of plied yarns *(hang karok)* set at intervals between the stripes. Lan Na Tai, Karen and Lawa skirts were woven in this way. Waistbands and the lower hem borders for skirts were also woven in plain weave.

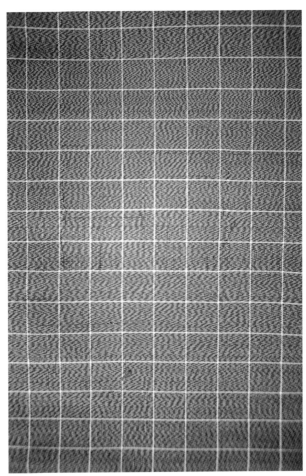

Continuous Supplementary Weft (khit or muk)

The simplest way of creating supplementary weft is to hand pick the patterns row by row using a wooden sword to create a shed for the intersection of the supplementary weft, woven from selvage to selvage. This was a common technique in the inland states although women also used a pre-determined system in which shed sticks were inserted in the warp to simplify and accelerate the process. Simple supplementary weft designs involve two to four rows of pattern set between rows of plain weave. Gold and silver metal threads were introduced in this way. Supplementary weft designs could be repeated continuously, or the patterns could be set at intervals. Star shaped flowers *(lai dork picun)*, 'pretty' flowers *(lai dork soey)*, zig zags *(lai khlun)* and diamonds patterns *(lai khao lam tat)* are examples of the supplementary weft patterns used for female court dress. Some supplementary weft designs are set in isolated motifs. They were probably introduced into Lan Na in the late 19th century and were based on designs produced in the southern Siamese provinces of Nakhon Si Thammarat, Surat Thani and Pattani.

Pha chong kraben in a simple plaid silk design. The squares contain twisted yarn *(hang karok)* that give tonal variations.

Left: A *pha chong kraben* of shot silk in two shades of green.

A silk *phasin* with horizontal stripes woven in plain weave.
(Bank of Thailand Museum, Chiang Mai)

Detail of a Tai Lao *phasin* woven in continuous supplementary weft. The vertical patterns from the central panel are stylised flowers and hooks. The horizontal hem border has similar designs.
(Chutinart Songwattana collection)

Opposite:
A red silk *pha chong kraben* with vertical
matmi patterns in green and black with
white stripes in the borders.
(Chutinart Songwattana collection)

A folded Lan Na *phasin* from Mae Chaem, with
a central panel of silk *matmi* and a
discontinuous supplementary weft pattern in
the hem border, c.1900.

Ikat (matmi)

The ikat technique involves tie-dyeing yarn into patterns before weaving.
The yarns that are tied resist the dye when immersed in a dye bath. The
yarn is re-tied and re-dipped if more than one colour is required. Lawa
and Tai groups, particularly the Tai Lao use this technique. The Lawa
produce skirts with narrow bands of ikat, usually around six rows set at
intervals between plain weave, while the Tai Yuan use ikat between rows
of plain weave and supplementary weft. The Tai Lao produce silk ikat for
male *chong kraben* and for *phasin*.[23]

Long, narrow ikat loin cloths *(yak rung)* were worn by soldiers who
twisted and tucked the fabric high on the hips to reveal thigh tattoos. The
designs include repeat geometric and stylised plant patterns, such as
'panicle of rice' *(lai phum khao bin)*, and water melon design *(lai taeng mo)*.
and diamonds *(lai khao lam tat)*, hooks *(lai kokrua)* and bamboo leaves
(pha hoi).

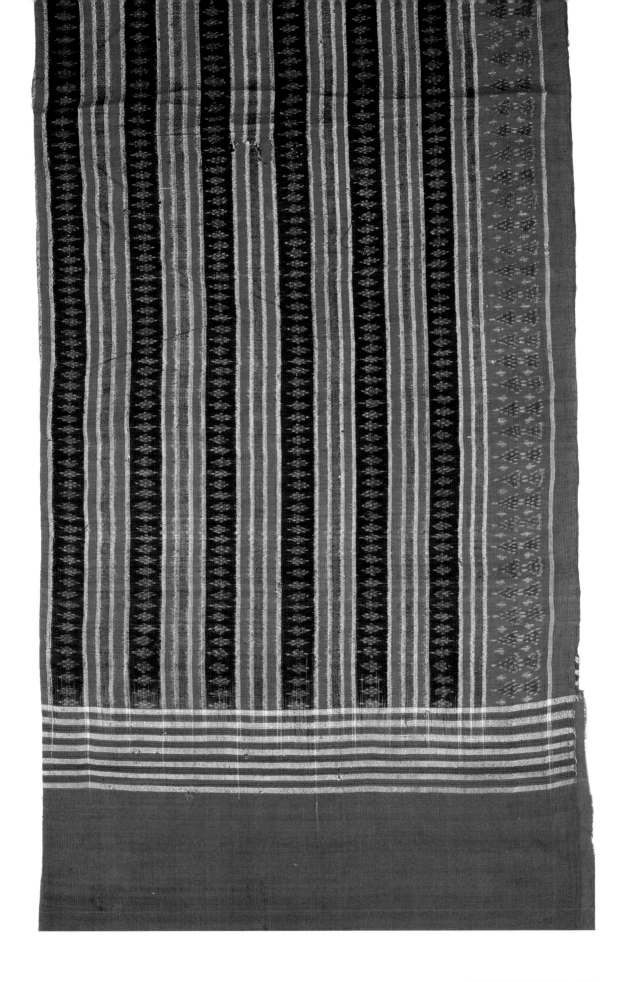

196

A red silk *pha chong kraben* with *matmi* patterns of stylised plant motifs in the central panel and geometric designs in the borders. (Chutinart Songwattana collection)

A red silk *phasin* with horizontal bands of *matmi* in the central panel set between bands of continuous supplementary weft. The hem border is discontinuous supplementary weft with diamonds and bird patterns. (Bank of Thailand Museum, Chiang Mai)

Opposite:
A *phasin* with two wide bands of tapestry weave set between horizonatal bands of plain weave, continuous supplementary weft and ikat.
(Chutinart Songwattana collection)

Tapestry Weave: ko and luntaya

Tapestry weave is a plain weave of discontinuous weft. The weaver keeps shuttles of yarn in front of her and creates isolated motifs of contrasting colours that together form the cloth structure. A more complex tapestry weave *(luntaya)* was imported from Burma. *Luntaya* tapestry weave is extremely intricate and is worked with up to 200 shuttles. The designs have been well documented and are based on landscapes, particularly mountains and rivers.[24] The designs involve undulating and interlocking wave-like forms intersected with stylised plants, flowers and birds.

Detail of the *phasin* shown at right.

A *phasin* with a central panel of continuous supplementary weft in triangle and hook patterns set above a wide band of tapestry weave.
(Chutinart Songwattana collection)

A *phasin* with three bands of tapestry weave set between multi-coloured horizontal bands of plain weave and supplementary weft.
(Chutinart Songwattana collection)

Silk *luntaya* in a wavy design with plant tendrils
worked in yellow, white and blue.
(Chutinart Songwattana collection)

A silk *phasin* with a *luntaya* design of multi-
coloured waves set between stylised flowers.
(Chaba Suwatmekin collection)

Detail of silk *luntaya* with a wave design interspersed with flowers,
described by U Aye Myunt (1993) as 'strings and flowers'.
(Chutinart Songwattana collection)

A complex silk *luntaya* pattern with twisted wave patterns interspersed with
silver metal thread and bordered by curling tendril designs.
(Chaba Suwatmekin collection)

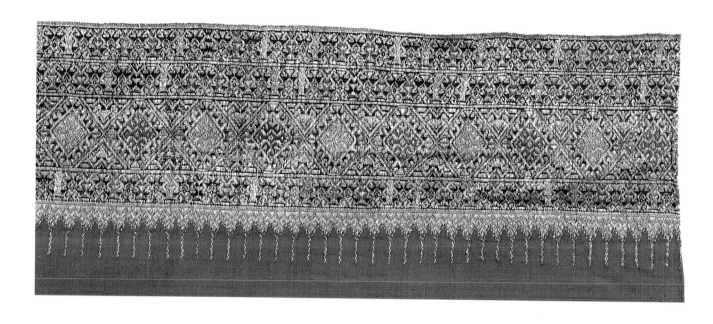

Two details of the hem of a *phasin* in discontinuous supplementary weft in multi-coloured silk and gold and metal thread with diamonds, flowers and hooks. The pendant pattern is known as *hang sapao*, and represents the ripples from the wake of a boat.
(Chaba Suwatmekin collection)

Discontinuous Supplementary weft (jok)

The most refined supplementary weft technique is called *jok* meaning 'to pick'. Patterns are formed by the use of multicoloured silk and gold and silver metal thread. They are introduced into a cotton ground weave as discontinuous supplementary weft. The reverse side of the work usually faces the weaver.[25] The patterns are picked using the fingers or with the aid of a porcupine quill, or needle, and a bow-shaped tool helps to keep the warp threads level and evenly spaced. This technique provides the greatest opportunity for creativity in design and is used in the hem borders *(teen jok)* of women's skirts. The work is extremely time consuming, one band 16-18 cms in length can take from six to eight weeks to produce.

The designs are laid out in a basic format. Narrow bands of repeat patterns are set in rows above and below a central design of repeat diamonds *(lai khao lam tat)* or hexagons, with smaller designs set inside and around the outside of each one. The designs include stylised roof gables *(chofa)*, monuments *(stupa)*, offering bowls *(kan kra hyong)*, water jugs *(nam ton)*, birds *(nok)*, swans *(hong* or *hongsa)*, climbing snakes or sea serpents *(ngu loi)*, jasmine flowers *(mali leuai* or *dork mali)*, non-specific floral patterns *(lai dork)*, diamonds *(lai khao lam tat)* and hooks *(lai ko krua)*.[26]

A common design found in the top and bottom border of *teen jok* is a bird *(nok)* or two birds of the same colour facing each other *(lai nok ku)*. The single birds and bird pairs, form a repeat, in varying colours. The birds may be referred to as swans *(hong)*, or paired swans *(lai hong ku)*, sleeping swans *(hong nawn)* or, if they are black *lai hong dum*. Some weavers say that if the birds are set inside the central design, usually a

diamond shape, they are just called 'swans' (hong or hongsa). Other border designs include hooks (lai ko krua) and small diamonds (lai khao lam tat), floral designs, triangles and zig zags, temple roof gables (chofa), and offering bowls (kan kra hyong). Some border designs are called 'Chiang Saen outside' while the inside designs are referred to as 'Lakhon [Lampang] inside. The Chiang Saen pattern included birds (nok), set in triangles, edged with hooks, while the Lampang pattern had a central design of paired black swans (lai hong dum), set in diamonds. All the designs for teen jok have a vertical pendant pattern interwoven across the lower hem. This design is known as hang sapao (hang s'pao) and is described as the line of ripples created on the water in the wake of a boat.

There are other teen jok designs that have one name for the whole pattern, for example 'tortoiseshell' and 'flock of birds'. There are also simple geometric designs worked with only gold and silver metal thread on a black cotton ground. As metal thread is more difficult to manipulate when used in such density the designs are relatively simple.

Detail of teen jok with diamond and hook pattern bordered by plant tendrils with a pendant pattern in black and white (hang sapao).
(Darabhirom Museum, Chiang Mai)

Top: Detail of teen jok in silk geometric patterns worked on black cotton.
(Chaba Suwatmekin collection)

Three *teen jok* with geometric designs worked in multi-coloured silk and silver and gold metal thread. The designs include diamonds, hooks, pairs of birds, flowers, temples roofs and offering bowls. The vertical lines at the bottom of each design represent the line of ripples created by a boat moving through water.

Embroidery

At the Lan Na courts women produced embroidered trimmings on clothing and slippers and on household furnishings and the covers of temple manuscripts. Silk, velvet and cotton fabrics were used as a ground and Chinese floss silk for the stitching. Metal sequins, mother-of-pearl sequins and gold and silver metal wire, were couched on the surface. Embroidery was not a major occupation at the Lan Na courts and was imported from China. Embroidery from Siam was also sent to Lan Na in the form of coats for male rulers. They were made in Bangkok by court embroiderers and seamstresses. The embroidery was worked on a backing of hand-knotted white net created by the technique used to make fishing and mosquito nets. A lining of thin cotton supported the netting. The embroidered designs, each formed from couched gold wire and gold fabric, were sewn onto a cotton fabric backing, and then attached individually to the netting to create a repeat pattern. The most common designs were flame *(kranok)* and curvilinear flowers and leaves *(lai kan yaeng)*.[27]

Triangular pillows with embroidered end panels of couched silver and gold metal wire and mother-of-pearl sequins.
(Duangchit Taweesri collection)

210

A silk coat trimmed with couched silver and gold metal wire set in floral, leaf and *kranok* patterns. (Paothong Thongchua collection)

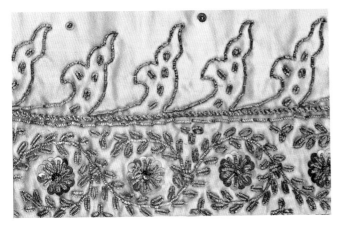

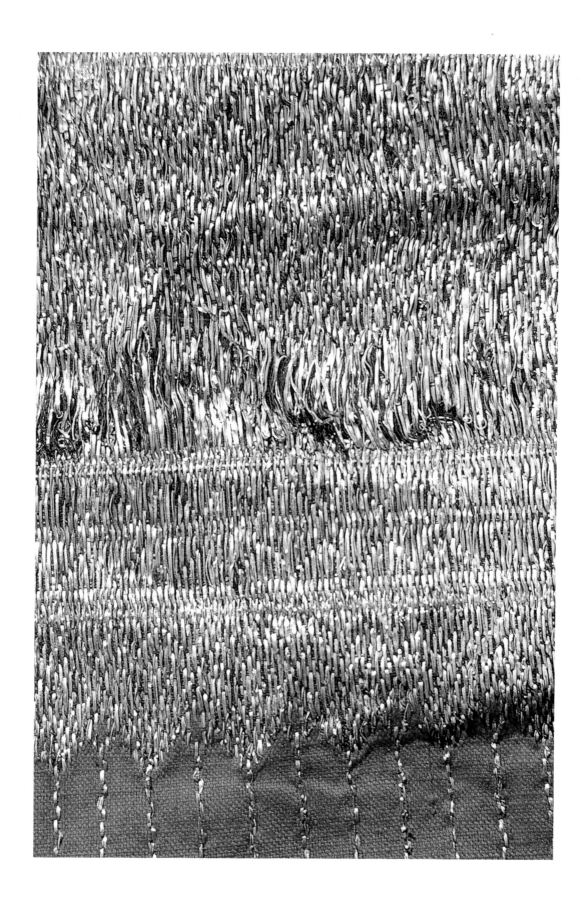

Conclusion

The preferred yarn for Lan Na court dress was Chinese silk, a symbol of prestige throughout inland Southeast Asian courts. The quality of the silk was particularly important for male court dress as the sheen and soft drape signalled prestige. This was in contrast to Hindu-Buddhist courts where hierarchical patterns were established through sumptuary laws. If weavers used indigenous silk, they discarded the coarse outer filament of the cocoons using only the inner filament as it was closest in texture and sheen to Chinese silk.

Although indigenous textiles worn at court were abstract in design, figurative images were present on textiles used as part of spirit religion practices. In the early 19th a stable Buddhist community did not exist due to a long period of war with Burma and the displacement of huge numbers of people. Princes, like their subjects, wore textiles, talismans and tattoos as armour to protect them against all forms of injury. The imagery was ferocious and grotesque, matching the chaos and violence that existed in everyday life at that time. In peacetime, spirit religion textiles did not require such aggressive imagery and tattoos were also selected as much for their decorative appearance as for protection. Buddhism and spirit religion were often represented on the same cloth, including images of the Buddha. Entwined scaly snakes appear on spirit cloths and in Buddhist art and architecture. The guardian beast (*rachasee*) is represented in stucco images that protect Buddhist temple gates and doorways, and are used as tattoo images to protect individuals. Grotesque animals and humans appear on spirit vests and are also represented in mural painting scenes of Buddhist Hell.

In contrast, women's dress was decorated with designs based on animals, plants, and architectural forms and there were no sumptuary laws governing patterns. One of the classic Lan Na designs was *teen jok* that involved a discontinuous supplementary weft technique. Although relatively unknown beyond inland Southeast Asia, *teen jok* was a complex patterning technique that required similar skills to the famed *luntaya* of the Burmese courts. *Jok* never gained the status and prestige value associated with *luntaya* because it was produced in the villages as well as at court workshops. There were no sumptuary laws to ensure its exclusivity for court society. The nature of cloth production in Lan Na has deprived court textiles of the status accorded to fabrics from courts such as Burma and Siam.

Weaving patterns were produced from prototypes, or were developed through an amalgamation of designs. Patterns produced in one technique were often reinterpreted in another. Lan Na textile designs are often viewed as images developed from Indian or Chinese prototypes, although given that Lan Na has an ancient indigenous weaving culture, designs could have developed independently or in parallel with those of other inland states. Although debate concerning the origin and history of patterns will continue it is clear that there were instances where

A Lan Na *teen jok* woven entirely in silver metal thread.

individuals added to the range of weaving designs. There were many talented weavers and designers who created new weaving patterns, but there are no records of their work.

The movement and resettlement of weavers in the late 19th and early 20th century led to an assimilation of weaving techniques and designs on cloth, although the tradition of resettlement, particularly of craft workers, is part of a much older tradition. The Tai chronicles record the forced movement of people from the time of King Mengrai of Lan Na (1259-1317) when victorious rulers resettled craft workers at their courts. Famine and disease also caused the movement of people from the time of the earliest Tai settlements. The problem for the textile historian is that no samples of cloth remain from before the 19th century as an indication of this complex process.

Opposite:
A Lan Na *phasin* with a white and black supplementary weft pattern set between multi-coloured horizontal stripes and plied yarns (*hang krarok*).
(Duangchit Taweesri collection)

1 Interview with Acharn Paothong Thongchua (Chiang Mai 1994). This attitude did not change until the present Queen Sirikit began to wear and promote indigenous silk in the 1960s.

2 Interviews with weavers in Lamphun and Chiang Mai (August 1993 and February 1996).

3 Interview with Ba Sangda Bansiddhi, Chom Thong, 1985.

4 Courtship poetry was translated into Central Thai from local dialect, by Acharn Jaruwan Thamawat (1980). Translation from Central Thai into English was by Acharn Surat, Khon Kaen 1983 (Conway 1992).

5 Interview with Ba Sangda Bansiddhi, Chom Thong 1985.

6 Interview with Chao Vilai na Chiang Tung , Chiang Mai, 1995.

7 Ferrars and Ferrars 1901.

8 Interview with Princess Vilai na Chiang Tung, Chiang Mai, August 1994.

9 Warington Smyth 1898.

10 Lampang is an ancient centre of Lan Na culture, with 15th century architecture and temple mural paintings. Chiang Saen was an important settlement from the 1th-14th century.

11 Interviews with weavers who produced the pattern called 'Chiang Saen', Mae Chaem, 1993.

12 This was discussed during interviews with Ba Sangda Bansiddhi of Chom Thong.

13 Prototypes were kept at the Lamphun workshops, interview with Chao Nid, Chiang Mai, 1995.

14 Brailey 1994.

15 Kamol 1976.

16 Wyatt and Wardwell 1998.

17 Woodtikarn 2000 n.p.

18 Bock 1884 repr. 1986: 171-173.

19 Interview with women villagers Khon Kaen Province, 1983.

20 Ling Roth 1918.

21 Gittinger and Lefferts (1992) use the translation *hang karok* (squirrel's tail).

22 Lefferts, 1992: 232.

23 Interview with Tai Lao weavers, Khon Kaen Province, 1986.

24 Htun Yi 1984, U Aye Myint 1993.

25 Weavers in Mae Chaem used a mirror to check the underneath (right side) of the pattern (personal observation Mae Chaem 1997).

26 The oldest samples of *teen jok* photographed for this research were dated early 19th century (interviews with Khun Nussura Tiangkhet and Mae Ueai, Mae Chaem, 1997).

27 U Aye Myint (1993) defines the patterns 'small flame' and 'single line flame' as Siamese.

Chapter Seven

19th Century Trade

This chapter looks at 19th century trade in Lan Na, particularly in relation to yarns, dyes, textiles and clothing imported for use at court. Because of its landlocked position, most trade involved overland routes that according to Chinese records have existed from at least the 8th century AD.[1] Caravans of ponies, bullocks and mules travelled throughout the inland states and some goods were distributed by riverboat. Human porters worked on routes across lowland areas and along river valleys. Elephants were used on difficult terrain although they were used mainly in moving logs. Some provincial trade was in the hands of villagers who sold their produce at local markets. They were restrained by mandatory corvée service that prevented them from trading too far from home because the princes could call on them for labour at any time.[2] Their tributary obligations to the princes, meant they received no payment for goods demanded by the courts. These restrictions kept long distance trade in the hands of the Yunnanese, Shan and Burmese merchants.

Trade and the Lan Na Rulers

The British official Richardson (1829-1835) noted that all the senior princes appeared to be traders. They strictly controlled the Yunnanese, Shan and Burmese merchants and taxed all their transactions. They received a regular income from timber concessions, from taxes levied on gambling houses and from bribes and presents taken from those seeking forest permits.[3] In the 1870s the Prince of Chiang Mai made an estimated ten to fifteen thousand rupees annually just from a tax on cloth.[4] Many

Traders and their ponies resting on the route
north from Lan Na.
(River Books collection)

A Chiang Mai market scene. Women handled most of local trade.
(White Lotus)

owned caravans of pack animals and they also used their slaves as porters. They made profits on the produce sold from their estates and from tribute goods that came in from villages throughout Lan Na and from outlying hill settlements. For example, the Karen-Lawa village of Maizaleen Tseetol, Mae Sariang, in the hills to the south west of Chiang Mai, sent two silver rupees, two blankets and forty viss (six kilos) of raw cotton annually to the Prince of Chiang Mai.[5]

Trade was not the monopoly of male members of the royal family. Princess Tipkesorn, wife of Prince Indra Witchayanon of Chiang Mai and her younger sister Princess Ubonwanna are mentioned in many expatriate records.[6] The latter held teak concessions and was able to issue concessions to others. She was also involved in money lending, in particular to Burmese and Shan traders. Holt Hallett was particularly impressed by her business skills:

> The princess was no ordinary person, and her life was a romance. Highly intelligent and a capital woman of business, a great trader, and the owner of large tracts of land, extensive teak forests and numerous elephants, serfs and slaves... She was one of the largest traders in the country.[7]

The Lan Na princesses also owned shops in the local markets and used their slaves to serve in them. In Chiang Mai there was a stall situated just outside the palace walls, and textiles featured prominently among the goods on sale.[8] There were bolts of imported muslin, calico, woollens, broadcloth, silk, velvet, buttons, needles and thread and silver jewellery.

International and Trans-regional Trade

According to British Foreign Office records there were five main trade routes to and from Lan Na running overland between Lan Na and Yunnan, between Lan Na and the Shan States, between the port of Moulmein and Lan Na and between Lan Na and Luang Prabang.[9] The fifth route between Lan Na and Bangkok went overland as far as Uttaradit where goods were transferred to riverboats. Some caravans made the journey to Thoen, a landing stage on the Ping River where the cargoes could also be transferred to the river. However, the overland routes were often impassable for periods in the monsoon season and many rivers were too shallow for boats during the dry season.

Even in the rainy season when rivers were navigable, journeys to and from Bangkok were arduous. The boats had to pass through rock pools and rapids that were fraught with danger and in some places totally impassable. The boats were then unloaded and the cargoes hauled along the banks with ropes until a place was reached where the river was negotiable again. This process alone could take several days. Going downstream the boats were lashed with bamboo poles along the gunwales to help prevent them from capsizing.[10]

Overland trade routes functioned in areas where there was good security, but were subject to banditry where there was a lack of policing. The route to Yunnan was unsafe in the mid-19th century, and bandits disrupted the Shan State routes in the same period. Traders relied on each other for information regarding safety and the physical condition of the passes. The British surveyor McCarthy (1895) encountered the leader of a Yunnanese caravan on his way from Muang Sing and the man asked him if his animals would be able to cross by the route McCarthy had taken. McCarthy informed him that one section would be difficult for laden ponies, and the trader decided he would leave it until the next season's trip.

On inter-state routes the taxes paid on goods in transit were regularised through trade treaties. The British-Siamese 'Treaty of Friendship and Commerce' of 1855, negotiated by Sir John Bowring, and usually referred to as 'The Bowring Treaty', limited the duty payable on goods imported by British subjects (who were mostly Burmese) and established the duties payable on exports from Lan Na. This treaty gave the Yunnanese caravans the option of continuing south from Chiang Mai to the port of Moulmein in Burma, although the danger from bandits and

The market on Tha Phae Road, Chiang Mai. Textiles can be seen hanging from the stalls. (Payap University Archive, Chiang Mai)

Female traders by the side of the road. (River Books collection)

A cargo boat on the Nan river, c.1900.
(Payap University Archive, Chiang Mai)

Elephants hauling logs in a Lan Na forest.
(River Books collection)

the poor state of the mountain passes made it a dangerous journey. In 1874 the second Bowring Treaty called on the Burmese to bring the banditry under control. Where this policy was enforced the caravans increased in number although their safety was never guaranteed.

Itinerant merchants were a regular feature of economic life in Lan Na and were allocated specific resting places at the city limits where they were permitted to camp, and feed and water their pack animals.[11] Carl Bock (1884) described the area outside the city wall of Chiang Mai where the Yunnanese caravans stayed, noting the packsaddles deposited at the roadside with fierce dogs guarding them.

Trade with Yunnan

In the 17th century the British explorer Ralph Fitch wrote:

> *Hither to Jamahay* [Chiang Mai] *come many merchants out of China and bring great store of muske, silver and many other things of China worke.*[12]

At that time trade with Lan Na was flourishing because the Chinese paid lower import duty on their goods than other traders in the region.[13] The Chiang Mai chronicle records that the rulers of Lan Na wore Chinese silk from the time of King Mengrai of Lan Na (1259-1317). In the 19th century, trade with China was in the hands of itinerant Yunnanese merchants domiciled mainly in the Dali [Tali] area of Yunnan. The majority were Chinese Muslims and had both Chinese and Muslim names.[14] They operated caravans from Dali via Simao to Chiang Rung, on to Muang Lem, Chiang Saen and Chiang Rai and then to Chiang Mai. Some continued south east to Lampang, others went east to Luang Prabang via Phrae. A few went west to the port of Moulmein when the paths were free of bandits.[15] W.J. Archer, the British Consul in Chiang Mai gave details of an extended route from Yunnan via Simao, Chiang Saen and Chiang Rai, to Phrae and Uttaradit, near the border with Siam. He noted that only a few caravans went as far south as Uttaradit and the majority went to Chiang Mai before going eastwards to Moulmein, if the route was safe. Uttaradit was a problem for traders because they had difficulty hiring boats for the southward journey to Bangkok.

The Yunannese were competitive traders on the overland routes because they used ponies and mules that were able to cross steep terrain and narrow mountain passes while many other traders relied on bullocks that were restricted to wider paths.[16] In the remote valleys of Lan Na, for example in the Mae Chaem valley, it was Yunnanese traders who made it over the passes into the villages.[17]

Princess Ubonwanna of Chiang Mai told Holt Hallett that between 700 and 1,000 laden mules and ponies came yearly from Yunnan to

Chiang Mai. The caravans were made up of 60 to 70 mules accompanied by ten to twelve men. An average caravan of 60 mules carried merchandise to the value of 12,000 to 15,000 dollars.[18] Near Muang Luang Puka, McCarthy (1900) met a Yunnanese caravan on the return journey to Yunnan. He counted 50 ponies, carrying raw cotton purchased in Lan Na.[19] On another occasion he passed a caravan of about 180 mules from Yunnan, carrying opium, wax, iron and iron dishes, felts and walnuts. Caravans appear to have varied in number from year to year. In 1893 the total number to Lan Na was estimated to be 15-50 animals in each caravan, their cargo valued at 3,000-3,500 rupees.[20]

The textile-related products carried from Yunnan included raw silk yarn, silk fabric, silk embroidery, silk embroidery thread, notions and trimmings, gold and silver metal thread and silk clothing.[21] Cities like Lampang had five or six caravans arriving annually, each caravan with 80-100 pack mules loaded with silk cloth, silk yarn, fur-lined coats, straw hats and other merchandise. If they risked the journey to Moulmein, they bought Burmese silk, cotton muslin, cambrics, printed calico, velvet and cotton piece goods that they sold on the homeward route. In Lan Na they bought raw cotton to take back to Dali.

The trade in Chinese silk yarn was particularly important because it was valued more highly than indigenous silk. Carl Bock wrote:

> *The cocoons of the wild silkworm are collected, and employed in the manufacture of native silk fabrics. The quality is coarse, and the supply insufficient for the home demand, considerable quantities of silk being bought from the Yunnan traders in exchange for the Lao* [Lan Na Tai] *cotton, of which far more than enough for local consumption is grown.*[22]

Chinese silk yarn was dyed and woven in the Lan Na court workshops, and imported Chinese silk and satin fabrics and trimmings were cut and sewn for shirts, blouses and jackets. The Yunnanese also served resettled immigrant communities and princesses who married into the Lan Na royal family, enabling them to buy the same yarn, notions and fabrics as were used in their original homelands. This was important in maintaining what was accepted as traditional dress.[23]

Trade with Burma and the Shan States

The unreliability of the routes to and from the port of Moulmein meant that many traders would not take the risk. There had been renewed hope of safer routes when the British defeated the Burmese in the First Anglo-Burmese War (1824-1826) and again following the Bowring Treaties. Some Lan Na princes were willing to negotiate with the British in Burma, but others distrusted them and their colonial ambitions. Relationships seem to have developed on a one-to-one basis. Prince Luang Phuttawong

Princess Tipkesorn, wife of Prince Indra Witchayanon of Chiang Mai, was a well-known trader.

Two grades of indigenous raw silk. The outer filament of the cocoon is particularly coarse.

Tai Shan in Muang Fang.
(White Lotus)

The throne of the Hsenwi Shan (*sawbwa*).
(The Green Centre for Non-Western Art at
the Royal Pavilion Art Gallery at The Royal
Pavilian and Museum, Brighton)

of Chiang Mai (ruled 1825-1846) sent a letter of friendship to the British in 1828 and they responded favourably. Prince Bunma of Lamphun established trade relations in 1829, but Prince Mahawong of Chiang Mai opposed treaties and remained fearful of British intentions in the region. In spite of this mixed reaction, in 1829 a British delegation led by Richardson, visited Chiang Mai and Lamphun. The party included a group of merchants from the port of Moulmein. Trade negotiations were amicable and as a result British subjects, mostly Burmese and Shan, established trade in cattle, forest products and teak.[24]

Princess Ubonwanna calculated that in the 1880s only 500-600 oxen made the journey annually from Chiang Mai to the port of Moulmein. It took approximately 17 days.[25] However, there were some Burmese traders who travelled to towns on the Mekong river via Sukhothai, Phitsanulok and Pichai. McCarthy encountered Burmese traders in all the major market town on this route.[26]

When they were available, imports from Moulmein sold well in the Chiang Mai markets, with high profit margins for those who were prepared to risk the journey. Gold leaf had a mark-up of 75 per cent, gold cloth 15 per cent, broad cloth 100 per cent and flannel between 32-50 per cent.[27] Although it is unclear which of these products actually came from Britain, as opposed to British factories in India, brass buttons with Queen Victoria's head stamped on them, Manchester calicoes, cotton velvet and sewing needles are listed as of British origin. It was recorded that the Burmese traders took Lan Na textiles back to Moulmein. There was one grade of embroidered silk with a mark-up of over 122 per cent and another grade marked up 100 per cent. Embroidered cotton cloth was marked up 150 per cent. The rates were probably accurate but not the

definitions of the cloth. Holt Hallett, who kept these records, confused embroidery with weaving and it is likely that the silks and cottons he described were woven using a supplementary weft technique. It is interesting that skirts worn in the Upper Irawaddy valley (Burma) were similar to Lan Na *phasin* in structure and were probably sold as part of this trade.

There was a sudden and rapid decline in the imports from Moulmein in the 1890s and by 1896 trade had reduced to one third of what it was in 1892. Between 1892-1896 exports from Lan Na to Burma also declined; the trade in raw silk fell by one half, the trade in woven silk fell by two thirds and piece goods trade ceased altogether (*see page 226*). In contrast the amount of textiles imported from Bangkok to Lan Na increased and in 1893 was calculated to be over four times the trade with Burma in the same year. The decline in trade was due to the physical deterioration of the caravan paths that were not maintained, while at the same time the cost of river transportation from Bangkok became more competitive.[28] The neglect of the paths from Moulmein anticipated the opening of the railway line between Bangkok and Chiang Mai in 1919.

Meanwhile trade with the Shan States thrived and by the 1880s Princess Ubonwanna estimated that between 7,000-8,000 laden mules and ponies travelled yearly to Chiang Mai from Chiang Tung, Chiang Hung, and other cities in the Shan States. The trip took about 15 days from Chiang Tung. About 35 caravans with 150 bullocks in each made the journey annually. Each bullock was loaded with 90-110 pounds and a caravan in total carried about 3,000 rupees worth of goods. Shan and hill tribe porters supplemented the bullock caravans, carrying loads of 50-70 pounds each, and received 15-20 rupees for each journey of 40 days.[29] Reports by British officials stated that Shan oxen caravans travelled regularly between Chiang Tung and Muang Pan through Muang Nai and Mokmai and on to the Burmese border.[30] Archer (1895) confirmed the importance of trade with the Shan States in a field trip report. He passed caravans on the route from Chiang Tung to Chiang Mai and he estimated that this was probably the most important thoroughfare in the whole region. In the course of one day he saw many caravans, some with a long file of over 100 bullocks. The greatest proportion of the traders were Shan (Ngios) domiciled in Chiang Tung. Archer noted that Lan Na Tai traders were not involved in the Chiang Tung trade, and he assumed that they were unable to compete. Holt Hallett gave a particularly colourful description of a typical Shan caravan:

> …*a party of Shans wearing blue trousers and jackets and great straw hats atop of the silk handkerchiefs which were twined round their top knots. All the oxen wore nosebags of rattan cane, to prevent them from browsing by the way; and the leaders wore a mask in front of their faces, fancifully worked with cowrie shells, and topped by a beautiful peacock's tail.*[31]

A Tai Shan woman.
(White Lotus)

Two porters one of whom carries a gong.
(White Lotus)

The Shan brought homespun silk yarn and silk cloth, earthenware, lacquerware, and iron tools to Lan Na and traded for cotton and salt. Among the Shan traders were some Tai Khoen, who provided textiles and trimmings, including decorative silver sequins to Tai Khoen immigrants in Lan Na.[32] The traders also carried silk from Inlay Lake and Burmese tapestry weave (*luntaya*).[33]

When the railway line opened to Lan Na from Bangkok in 1919, it had little affect on trade with the Shan States as Chiang Tung was not served by the line. Shan traders continued to arrive and trade actually increased at the turn of the century. A constant stream of pony and bullock caravans travelled the main route from Chiang Tung.[34]

Trade with Luang Prabang and the Lao states

Princess Ubonwanna told Holt Hallett that goods carried from Chiang Mai to Luang Prabang were transported by elephant as far as Chiang Saen and then shipped via the Mekong River to Vientiane, where they were transferred to pack animals for the overland journey north to Luang Prabang. They were then distributed to other towns in the region. This seems to be a most complicated route and may have been used by Ubonlawanna and other royal traders who had access to elephants. According to British Foreign Office reports many goods were transported south via Phrae and then on via the Nan valley to the Mekong River and across to Luang Prabang. Burmese, Shan and Yunnanese traders all used this route.

A porter with two panniers.
(Payap University Archive, Chiang Mai)

In Luang Prabang the traders loaded up with woven silk, raw silk, gum benjamin and giant catfish from the Mekong which they transported to Chiang Mai and other towns on the route. Silk sashes woven in Luang Prabang were popular in Chiang Mai, and were worn by members of the Lan Na royal family. By 1893 this trade had almost ceased and although the reason is not recorded it was probably the result of a new fashion for lighter sashes imported from Bangkok and worn over flimsy European-style blouses.

In Luang Prabang at the beginning of the 20th century, European goods were available in the markets. The French writer Marthe Bassenne noted that Burmese traders brought cottons, velvets, trimmings and notions, many of them with English and German factory labels. She bemoaned the fact that French products were not available and blamed the dangerous state of paths through the French Protectorates.[35]

A Shan ruler (*sawbwa*), his family and attendants.
(The Green Centre for non-Western Art Gallery at The Royal Pavilian and Museums, Brighton)

EXPORTS FROM BURMA TO LAN NA

(Adapted from Warington Smyth (1898) and Prasartset (1975).

Description	Year	Value (pounds sterling)
Cotton Manufactures		
	1890	15,998
	1892	13,310
	1893	9,632
	1894	12,045
	1895	5,567
	1896	5,881
Silk (type not stated)		
	1890	11,600
	1892	4,256
	1893	4,748
	1894	9,430
	1895	3,047
	1896	5,049

EXPORTS FROM LAN NA TO BURMA

Description	Year	Value (pounds sterling)
Raw Silk (Ibs)		
	1890	750
	1892	1,582
	1893	1,512
	1894	1,399
	1895	628
	1896	–
Silk (Manufactured)		
	1890	132
	1892	1,824
	1893	2,273
	1894	1,399
	1896	57
	1896	474
Piece Goods (yds)		
	1890	162
	1892	57
	1893	239
	1894	370
	1895	–
	1896	–
	1898-1902	–

There is a general reference to 'other commodities' of 5,559 pounds sterling that may include textiles.

Detail of a *phasin* hem border from Chiang Tung. Silver sequins were made in Chiang Tung and exported to Chiang Mai. The embroidery came from China and was sold in strips.

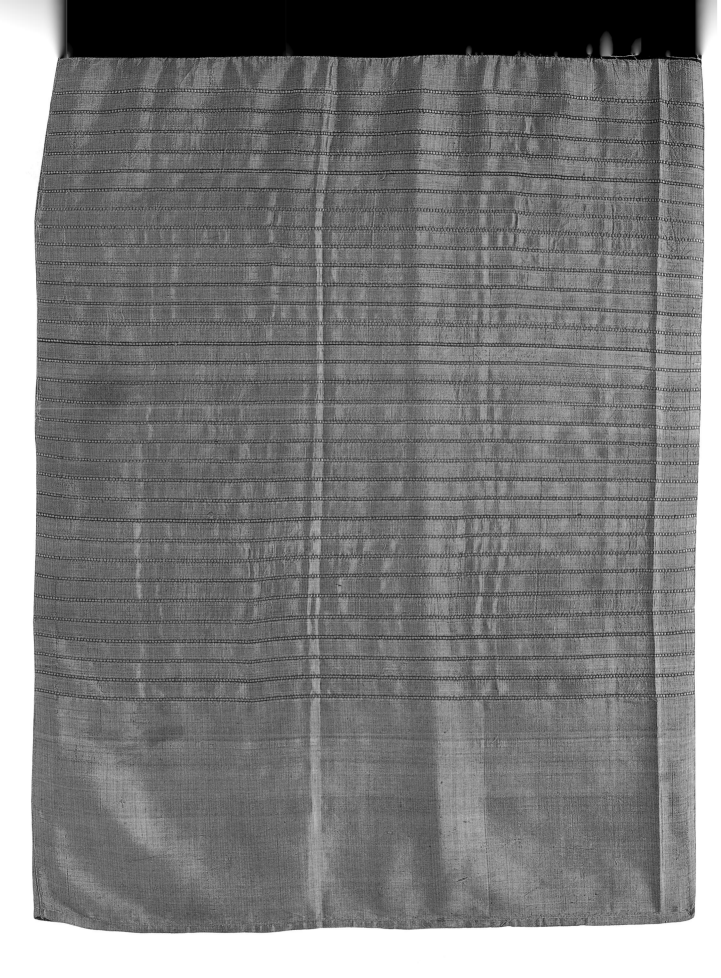

A section of the northern railway line passing through the mountains. (White Lotus)

Trade with Siam

Of all the 19th century trade routes, the one to and from Bangkok was the most difficult because of the problems navigating the Chao Phraya River and the difficult overland journey through mountains and tropical forest, and along river valleys prone to flooding. At night the traders kept fires burning to keep wild animals away. The route to Bangkok involved the caravans travelling overland journey and then transferring their goods to riverboats at Thoen or at Uttaradit. The river journey could only be undertaken in August and September following the monsoon rains when the upper reaches of the Chao Phraya River were navigable and boats reached Bangkok in November and December. The main products sent south to Bangkok were rice, salt, cotton, sappan wood, oil and teak. Teak logs were floated down on the current. Items coming specifically from Lan Na included stick lac, benjamin, ivory, beeswax, animal horns and hides, timber and cotton. Significantly, Sir John Crawfurd reported that in the 1820s the combined land and river route was extremely expensive to operate.[36] In consequence Bangkok did very little trade with Lan Na.

There was a slight improvement by the second half of the 19th century although the route remained difficult and many traders chose to avoid it and even in the 1900s it was quite common to hear of the problems of the journey. Foreigners were vocal on the issue. McCarthy did not complain of the discomfort of the journey but of the difficulties that arose on reaching the river port at Uttaradit, where goods had to be transferred to pack animals. He describes the long stretch of houses on

Opposite:
A silk *phasin* in the Lan Na style traded in the Shan States.
(Bank of Thailand Museum, Chiang Mai)

TRADE FROM BANGKOK TO CHIANG MAI		
(Adapted from Warington Smyth (1898) and Prasartset (1975).		
Description	**Year**	**Value (pounds sterling)**
Twist and yarns	1893	27,000
Cotton manufactures	"	26,000
Cotton shirtings	"	16,000
Silk manufactures	"	3,000
Coloured prints	"	3,000
Turkey red cloth	"	3,000
Aniline dyes		Amounts not recorded

the bank of the river that were inhabited by Chinese merchants who operated much of the trade but were taxed by the Lan Na rulers who owned many of the boats. On his downward journey to Bangkok McCarthy complained that because he had no influence it was almost impossible to secure boats at Uttaradit. He also noted that the journey down river was even more difficult than going upriver. He felt that these conditions made trading finacially hazardous and could see why some traders preferred to take the risk and travel west overland to Burma. The Siamese lost a great deal of trade as a result. Hallett estimated that goods valued at many thousands of pounds sterling went annually to Moulmein instead of going to Bangkok.

However, by the 1890s trade between Chiang Mai and Bangkok was beginning to improve and transport costs became competitive. The Ping River was dredged regularly, allowing boats and barges to replace animal caravans on certain sections of the journey north from Uttaradit. Godowns were constructed in Chiang Mai for the increased traffic on the Ping River.[37] The cost of transport to and from Bangkok fell by 400-500 percent in comparison with the cost of animal caravans from Burma to Chiang Mai. Imports from Bangkok to Chiang Mai in 1893 were listed as sewing thread (twists and yarns), white shirting, cotton manufactures, silk manufactures, cotton prints, Turkey red cloth and aniline dyes. Hallett confirms this list and described figured muslins, red muslins, bleached and unbleached muslins, cotton thread and green flannel. He noted that the cost of these goods in Chiang Mai was between 12.5-67 per cent higher than the prices paid in Bangkok.[38] Textile imports from Bangkok totalled 78,000 pounds sterling. In comparison imports from Burma to Lan Na were 14,380 pounds sterling. There are no figures for comparable Yunnanese trade.[39] Following the marriage of Princess Dararatsami of Chiang Mai in 1886, the courts of Chiang Mai and Lamphun added to the volume of exports by sending traditional Lan Na woven textiles, particularly *phasin* to the Bangkok court.

At the end of the 19th century King Rama V attempted to improve the quality of indigenous silk so that it could compete with Chinese silk that continued to dominate the markets. He established a Department of

Sericulture and hired a Japanese expert. Experimental nurseries were set up and modern Japanese methods of raising worms and reeling silk were introduced.[40] Although a great deal of time and effort went into trying to improve silk production, the preference for Chinese silk among the Lan Na royal family remained constant.

Trade and Tribute

Although the route to Bangkok was difficult and dangerous, the Lan Na princes were nevertheless obliged to make the journey once every three years to pay tribute to the King of Siam and report on affairs of state in the principalities. According to the Chiang Mai chronicle there were several occasions when a prince or a member of his entourage died on the journey. A sojourn in Bangkok meant an opportunity for the nobility to buy foreign goods that were not available in the markets of Lan Na. Bangkok was a major trading port and goods from the Malay states, Indonesia, Cambodia, India and Europe were available in the markets. The princes purchased household goods, clothing, furnishings and other luxury items that were fashionable in Bangkok and shipped them north. The American missionary Daniel McGilvary visited a Chiang Mai palace in 1877 and described some of the more unusual items that one of the princes had brought back from the Siamese capital:

The king of Muang Sing and his family, c.1890. Large cotton cloths provide a backdrop to the photograph. (White Lotus)

Two Siamese women traders portrayed in the murals of Wat Phra Singh. Unlike Lan Na women they wore *pha chong kraben*.

We were sitting in the new brick palace - the first ever built in the country. In the hall was a large pier glass with numerous other foreign articles, most of them bought in Bangkok and brought up as offerings at the coming dedication of the shrine.[41]

The princes and their families could afford such luxuries because they owned the boats and pack animals to transport them. This near monopoly changed when the railway line opened in 1919 and many more goods were transported north to Lan Na.

Trade with Britain

The Bowring treaties of 1855 and 1874 had led to a slight increase in trade between Lan Na and British Burma, mainly in cattle, teak and forest products. The British were keen to identify what manufactured goods they might sell in Lan Na, and in 1871 they sent Captain Lowndes, who was serving in Burma, to investigate. His report concluded that British textiles would not penetrate the Lan Na markets because all textiles sold locally were made by villagers and the market for imported attire was small.[42] This was a sound judgement, although the British continued to believe that if prosperity increased, markets could be created for their goods. Colquhoun thought that trade could be improved if a railway line was built to connect Siam, Burma, Lan Na and China. He wrote, in the spirit of Empire:

The enriching of Siam by the introduction of the railways means the opening up of an immense and yearly increasing market for manufactures. Every fresh acre of paddy land, every new mine, made possible in Siam by the construction of the iron way, will imply fresh hands in Manchester mills and growing activity on Liverpool wharves.[43]

His ambitions for the Manchester mills and Liverpool wharves were not realised, although some Manchester cotton was imported via Moulmein and transported by Yunnanese and Burmese traders.[44] According to a British Foreign Office report, the problem in marketing Manchester cloth was that the material and the dye could not withstand the constant laundering to which clothing in a hot climate is subjected.[45] Warington Smyth confirmed this when he described the response his men had to the imported flowery cloth he gave them as gifts. They told him that they did not like the colours and that the material would not stand wear and tear and frequent washing. Interior scenes in Buddhist temple mural paintings and in photographs indicate printed cotton, that might possibly be Manchester cloth was used as curtains and room dividers. Presumably the cloth was satisfactory for this purpose as it was not frequently laundered. Demand for British goods in Lan Na was always small. In 1889 a British

The Ping River at Chiang Mai. Regular dredging in the 1890s allowed boats and barges to navigate as far as Uttaradit.

merchant firm trading in Bangkok opened a branch in Chiang Mai but found that competition was too strong from Chinese merchants, and the market was too small to be profitable. In 1902 they closed down. Until the opening of the railway, most British goods available in the Lan Na markets were transported with other products, by Yunnanese, Burmese and Shan traders operating to and from Moulmein. The Germans successfully marketed aniline dyes, and although there is no indication of the amounts, dyes are listed by Warington Smyth in the import records for 1893 (*see page 230*). In the 1890s aniline dyes were available in the Lan Na markets and Pasqual (1926) claimed to have encountered the first German allowed to sell the dyes in Chiang Mai. As a result of this trade, the court workshops used aniline dyes as well as vegetable dyes on silk and cotton. The Lan Na princes brought British goods in Bangkok on their tributary visits, including furniture, glass and crockery to furnish their new palaces. However, this was only a small luxury goods market and the princes often bought only one or two items of furniture and then had them copied by their own craftsmen.

Trade with India

Some Indian cotton cloth was probably imported to Lan Na via Moulmein although there is no specific reference in the trade records. There are wall hangings and floor mats in court photographs that were possible of Indian origin. Prince Bunthawong is seated in front of a glazed cotton curtain that is similar to fabric made in India for the Siamese market.[46] However, glazed indigo cotton was also produced in Sipsong Pan Na and this could have been the source.[47] The cloth that provides a backdrop for the photograph of the Prince of Muang Sing could also be of Indian origin although similar cloth was also produced in Burma. We know that the Siamese kings included some Indian textiles in their gifts to the Lan Na courts. In terms of personal choice, the Lan Na courts preferred silk from China as did resettled royalty from the surrounding inland states.

The British had settled a number of their Indian subjects in Burma and some were merchants who benefited from the Bowring treaties.[48] By the end of the century the principal cloth dealer in Chiang Mai was a Sikh and there were Parsi gem dealers and other traders of Indian origin who frequented the Chiang Mai markets.[49] It has to be stressed that it does not follow automatically that Indian traders were trading Indian cloth. As they had come from Burma they had access to the same goods as other traders in the region.

Textile Outlets in Lan Na

In the Chiang Mai markets it was possible to buy umbrellas, fans, embroidery, English cotton piece goods, broadcloths, velvets, velveteens, satins, silks, muslins, Chinese silks and crepes, silk jackets and trousers, silk jackets lined with fur, German aniline dyes and needles, and finely woven silk shawls.[50] In the Lampang market, which was considered to be the most important trading centre after Chiang Mai, there was raw silk, silk goods, stick lac, Chinese silk piece goods, silk jackets and trousers, straw hats and printed cloth. Nan, situated in a relatively isolated valley, received only small amounts of imported goods, estimated in 1896 to amount to 36,000 rupees (about £1,800 pounds sterling). The usual route taken by the Yunnanese caravans passed far to the west of the town. What little trade existed was for the most part in the hands of British Burmese subjects and although imported yarn and cotton piece goods were on sale in the markets, the quantities were insignificant. Other main towns in Lan Na such as Lamphun, Phrae, Chiang Saen and Chiang Rai are also mentioned in trade reports although textiles are not listed. If one looks at the materials used for dress at the minor courts, it is evident that Chinese silk, silk fabrics and trimmings were available, probably carried by Yunnanese traders.

Indian printed cottons were traded in the Bangkok markets. Small quantities found their way north to Lan Na. (National Museum, Bangkok)

A Lan Na market scene.
(Payap University Archive, Chiang Mai)

Women ran the local markets, arriving in the early morning with agricultural and forest products. They included raw cotton, indigo and village textiles, pottery, rattan baskets and mats. Carl Bock described a typical market scene in Chiang Mai:

> . . . women do all the selling. They all sit on the ground with a basket on each side of them, sometimes with the contents emptied out and spread on a couple of plantain leaves. The principal articles offered for sale are provisions, fruits and vegetables; tobacco, betel nuts and lime; fish, dried, salted and stewed . . . buffalo meat . . . wax, cotton, earthenware pots, jars and jugs . . .[51]

Village women sold and bartered yarn and woven cloth with other villagers, described as primarily 'inter village' or 'kin and fellowship' related trade.[52] Goods were also sold on to itinerant merchants or to traders with permanent stalls in the local markets, as on the Tha Phae Road in Chiang Mai. The royal families depressed this trade by taking silk, cotton and vegetable dyes as tribute.

Men handled the trade that involved longer spells away from home. Journeys were undertaken at quiet times in the agricultural cycle, after the harvest and before planting the next season's rice crop. This trade was mainly in rice, tobacco and sugar, fermented tea leaves (*miang*) and betel nuts. The ability to reach distant markets was hampered by the princes who could call on villagers for corvée labour at any time. These obligations prevented local men from competing with the Burmese, Shan and Yunnanese traders.

Conclusion

Trade with China and the Shan States dominated the Lan Na markets for most of the 19th century. In contrast the sea trading coastal states of Siam, Indonesia and Malaysia imported court textiles and dress from India, considered to be a major influence on their textile designs.[53] Princesses who married into the Lan Na royal family, and female immigrants, relied on Yunnanese and Shan traders to bring them the same types of yarns, fabrics and notions as were used in their original homelands. There were also princesses who were important traders and their knowledge was invaluable to foreign officials seeking information on trans-regional and local trade.

English cotton piece goods, velvets and Manchester cloths were imported via the port of Moulmein although the trade was unreliable due to safety problems on the route. The British believed that they could import goods, including textiles, via India through the Shan states to the markets of Lan Na and Yunnan. British attempts to establish trading outlets in Lan Na were a failure because most people bought only limited amounts of ready-made cloth. This was not just a matter of taste and practicability but of cultural and social traditions.

Some Siamese and European goods were imported via Bangkok although profits were small due to the difficulty of the route and the high cost of transport. Wealthy Lan Na rulers could afford to have goods brought up from Bangkok and they imported luxury items to furnish their new palaces. Some rich merchants also obtained goods from Bangkok, if they had the necessary influence to secure boats and porters. However, it was not until the opening of the railway in 1919 that goods from Bangkok became readily available.

Proof of trade in Chinese silk and gold and metal silver thread in the satellite principalities of Lan Na counteracts the subsistence economy paradigm that is so often used to identify rural society as self sufficient.[54] Imported goods were beyond the reach of most villagers but there was a market among minor royalty and wealthy farmers and the Yunnanese traders travelled to meet demand. Surviving samples of 19th century textiles made with silk and gold and silver metal thread, kept as heirlooms by families whose ancestors lived in remote valleys, are confirmation of this luxury trade.

Women traders and their food stalls.
(River Books collection)

1   Maxwell Hill 1982.

2   Cohen 1981.

3   Prince Kamfan of Chiang Mai (1822-1825) was given the title Chao Luang Setthi (the very rich prince) as a result of his monopolies and trade deals (Sethakul 1989).

4   The value of the rupee can be roughly estimated by the wage rates paid in 1900. Villagers were paid about one eighth of a rupee per day for agricultural labour, wages for teak workers were paid around one quarter to one third of a rupee, and porters averaged one half a rupee a day (Bowie 1988).

5   Sethakul 1989.

6   Hallett 1890, Peoples 1890, and McGilvary 1912.

7   Hallett 1890 repr. 1988: 103.

8   Peoples 1890.

9   McCleod 1836, Lowndes 1871, Hildebrand 1875, Satow 1885-1886.

10 Warington Smyth 1898: 161.

11 Vatikiotis 1984.

12 Fitch 1587.

13 Smith 1977.

14 McCarthy met a trader called Suliman whose Chinese name was Ma Yueh Tcheng, and another called Suliman Maliki, whose Chinese name was Ma Chaw.

15 Archer 1886-1889.

16 Sethakul 1989.

17 Oral history interviews, Mae Chaem Valley 1996.

18 Cheek 1880.

19 McCarthy (1895) recorded the price of cotton in the Phrae market as 25 rupees for 133lbs.

20 Warington Smyth 1898.

21 Crawfurd 1828, Cheek 1880, Bock 1884, Hallett 1890, Warington-Smyth 1898, McCarthy 1895, Sethakul 1989.

22 Bock 1986: 324.

23 Moerman 1975: 157.

24 Sethakul 1989.

25 McCleod 1836.

26 McCarthy (1895)

27 Hallett 1890 repr. 1988: 296.

28 Sethakul 1989.

29 Warington Smyth, 1898: 288

30 Foreign Office report ZHC1/5466 no. 1089

31 Hallett, 1890, repr., 1988: 208

32 Interview with Khun Duangjit Taweesri, owner of a court textile collection in Chiang Mai (February 1990).

33 Shan caravans carrying woven silk were still operating in the 1980s in the border regions of Mae Hong Son (personal observation, Mae Hong Son border region, 1981).

34 Le May 1926.

35 Bassenne 1912 repr. 1995: 62.

36 Crawfurd 1828.

37 Sethakul 1989.

39 Warington Smyth 1898: 289.

40 Carter ed. 1904.

41 McGilvary 1912: 131.

42 Lowndes 1871.

43 Colquhoun 1885.

44 McCarthy 1895.

45 Foreign office Report F.O. 69/27/20.

46 Gittinger and Lefferts (1992: 149)

47 O'Connor 1994.

48 There are still Indian cloth traders operating in the Chiang Mai markets (personal observation 1983).

49 Le May 1926: 81.

50 Hallett 1988: 100-101.

51 Bock 1884 repr.1986: 229.

52 Sethakul 1989.

53 Gittinger 1982, Sheares 1983, Guy 1992, 1999.

54 Ingram 1971, Anuman 1988.

Opposite: A *phasin* with woven waistband and central panel and bands of imported cloth. (Bank of Thailand Museum, Chiang Mai)

Chapter Eight

Craft Workers at the Courts

Skilled craft workers were an essential component of the inland courts and their beautiful products gave status to ruling families. Powerful princes raided neighbouring states if they could not acquire by peaceful means the talent they needed. The Chiang Mai chronicle tells us that when King Mengrai (1259-1317) became ruler of Lan Na he travelled to Burma to ask the King of Ava for craftsmen. The response was favourable and Mengrai settled them throughout the country:

> *King Mengrai sent the goldsmiths to Chiang Tung, the bronzesmiths and their guardians to Chiang Saen and the jewelers and ironsmiths to Kum Kam. And so all the craftsmen were thenceforth in the land of Lan Na, to the present day.[1]*

The devastating war with Burma in the 18th century led to a mass exodus of people among them craft workers. Some were forcibly brought back when peace was restored. The British Vice Consul E.B. Gould who was stationed in Chiang Mai, wrote a report on their plight:

> *The captives were hurried mercilessly along, many weighted by burdens strapped to their backs, the men, who had no wives or children with them and were therefore capable of attempting escape, were tied together by a rope pursed through a sort of wooden collar. Those men who had their families with them were allowed the free use of their limbs. Great numbers died from sickness, starvation and exhaustion on the road. The sick when they became too weak to struggle on, were left behind. If a*

A Lan Na princess at her embroidery frame.
(White Lotus)

Howdah in gilded wood.
(Hariphunchai National Museum, Lamphun)

house happened to be near, the sick man or woman was left with the people in the house. If no house was at hand which must have been oftener the case in the wild country they were traversing, the sufferer was flung down to die miserably in the jungle. Any of his or her companions attempting to stop to assist the poor creatures were driven on with blows. . . . Fever and dysentery were still at work among them and many more will probably die. Already, I was told, more than half of the original 5,700 so treacherously seized are dead.[2]

Labourers of all kinds were needed in Lan Na and craft workers were required for building and restoration projects. Builders, carpenters, wood carvers, painters, silversmiths and goldsmiths, lacquer makers, jewellers, umbrella makers, weavers and embroiderers all contributed to the work of rebuilding, furnishing and decorating the palaces and temples. They also made products for the personal use of the prince rulers and their families including woven and embroidered textiles, ceremonial water bowls, vessels and umbrellas, teapots, betel trays and betel nut boxes that were symbols of rank. Silversmiths and goldsmiths also produced earrings, bangles, necklaces, bracelets and hairpins for female members of the royal families.[3]

Working for the princes was restricting. Many were overwhelmed with orders and paid little or nothing for their labour.[4] Prince Indra Witchayanon of Chiang Mai (ruled 1871-1897) kept craft workers in his service for many years and they were not permitted to work for anyone else unless he commanded them to do so.[5] The American Presbyterian missionary Hugh Taylor commented on conditions of employment:

There seemed to be no limit to the amount of manufactured goods or farm and garden produce a lord could demand of his serfs, and of their time, for that matter.[6]

Palace Communities (khum)

The Lan Na term for a palace is *khum,* meaning 'community'. The *khum* where senior princes lived were usually situated by a river, inside fortified city walls, in keeping with Lan Na spatial concepts of the *muang* and its princely courts. The prince and his senior consorts, their children and household staff lived in pleasant walled compounds with large shady gardens. In the major *khum* there was accommodation for the most highly skilled craft workers.[7] Female textile workers were housed in the quarters of the princes' consorts.[8]

The number of textile workers in a *khum* varied but accounts by foreigners who visited them personally imply that they were small concerns with 10-20 workers at most. They were made up of *khon muang* and immigrants, many Tai Lue who were excellent weavers and

Lan Na women plaiting bamboo to make lacquer bowls.
(White Lotus)

silversmiths. Other Tai groups worked at court and there were also Siamese weavers and Chinese tailors. Their duties were to provide textiles for the royal family, the household and the temple.

The larger *khum* provided extensive facilities for textile production. There were outbuildings for storing wood and charcoal that fuelled the dye baths and large ceramic jars for collecting rainwater. Raw fibres and dyestuffs were cleaned and processed, dye vats prepared and yarn dried in this area. Dyes, mordants and skeined yarn were kept away from direct sunlight and protected from moths and white ants. In the smaller *khum*, out-workers processed raw fibres, ginned cotton and reeled silk as part of the corvée labour system. The yarn was then sent to the palace.

An accomplished weaver had status in society and it was perfectly acceptable for female royalty to be employed in a palace workshop. Weaving, embroidery, flower arranging, lace making and cooking were all considered valuable occupations for women at court.[9] Female members of the royal family personally supervised their workers and many princesses were recognised for their individual artistry.[10]

> *Even a wealthy princess is not exempt from the necessity for making the silken garments which are the symbol of her rank, any more than the poorer women can do without weaving their cotton clothes.[11]*

The royal princesses were also responsible for the production of bed sheets, blankets and pillows for the royal household.

Silver and brass containers and ivory
weaving shuttles from northern
workshops.
(White Lotus)

Opposite:
Above: The musicians to the court of
Prince Suriyapong of Nan.
(Payap University Archive, Chiang Mai)

Below: Detail of blanket from Luang Prabang,
a fine example of court workmanship.
(Bank of Thailand Museum, Chiang Mai)

*Many of the "upper classes" are also skilled in embroidering the cushions
or pillows which take the place of chairs.[12]*

Princesses also supervised the production of dress for court performers.
Every palace of any size had its own dance and theatrical troupe.[13] The
Lan Na court workshops also produced textiles that were sent to other
inland courts and to Siam, as part of tributary gift exchange.[14]

Most significantly, female royalty had obligations to provide textiles
for the monasteries, a way to make merit for themselves and their
ancestors. At the time of Buddhist festivals, members of the royal family
donated robes, sheets, blankets and pillows for the personal use of the
monks. The also made temple banners and manuscript covers. Some have
survived because they were kept in temple repositories. Wat Phanom
Khon Muang, Chiang Mai, has a Buddha image on cloth, donated by
Prince Kawiloros of Chiang Mai (ruled 1856-1870) and Wat Phra Non
possesses a set of hand-woven banners presented by his wife, Princess
Usa.[15]

At courts where the royal families were involved in the commercial
market, they used their slaves as workers. The skilled weavers among
them fetched a good price. In the 1880s a female slave could be bought
for 50 rupees and this was considered a bargain as in one year her
weaving made at least a 100 rupees in profit for her owner.[16] Female
members of the elite contributed to the industry. The wife of the Lord
Chief Justice of Chiang Mai was an excellent weaver and could make a
silk *chong kraben* in five days. When multiplied over several months her
output was extremely profitable and she was recognised by her husband
as a great commercial asset. Female members of the royal family also
made large profits from the textiles produced by their female slaves. Their
returns were increased by tribute payment in kind from female citizens
(phrai) in the form of yarn, dyes and mordants. Women *phrai* could be
called on for free labour in the court workshops and many were expected
to provide finished textiles such as loincloths, blankets, sheets and
pillows.[17]

Regional Court Workshops: Outside the khum

Although some textiles for the commercial market were produced within
the *khum* most were made by workers living outside. Immigrants,
including weavers were resettled in communities beyond the main city
walls but inside the earthen ramparts that formed the outer defences of
the city. Some textiles were woven in the villages where immigrants lived
with Tai Yuan *(khon muang)* although they were not allowed to form large
groups.[18] Weaving centres existed in the vicinity of all the major cities. It
is rare to find records of the actual numbers working in the textile sector
but Hildebrand (1875) wrote that Prince Indra Witchayanon of Chiang

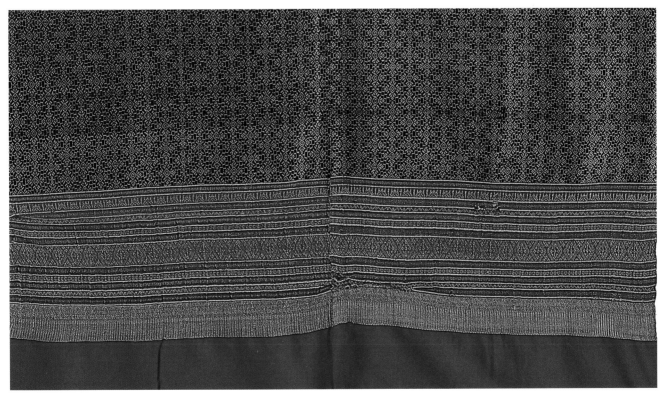

Princess Dararatsami with her family at a fancy dress party in honour of a visit by HRH Prince Bhanubhandhu in 1916. (River Books collection)

Lanna ladies in a procession to the temple, c. 1920. (River Books collection)

Mai made a good income from the weaving produced by several 100 slaves. As the princes held a monopoly on cloth production, they controlled all commercial enterprises in towns and villages throughout the *muang*.

Production in Chiang Mai

The senior princes of Chiang Mai lived in *khum* situated by the Ping River. Foreigners were frequent visitors and it is their records that explain the nature of cloth production. In 1876 Holt Hallett reported that Princess Ubonwanna, sister-in-law of Prince Indra Witchayanon of Chiang Mai, had a broad shady verandah where women sat embroidering triangular shaped pillow ends and weaving silk *phasin*. He praised their colour sense and the high standard of workmanship.[19] A few years later Carl Bock also called on the princess and noted that she and her ladies were working together at a number of looms while others were sewing. Bock made several visits to the large teak palace of the Second Prince of Chiang Mai (probably *uparat* Bunthawong) where he found the prince's wife busy making silk garments with her slaves working close by spinning silk.[20] The American missionaries were frequent callers at the Chiang Mai *khum* and Daniel McGilvary wrote that Princess Tipkesorn, wife of Prince Indra Witchayanon (1871-1897) was a highly skilled at weaving and embroidery. On one occasion he found her embroidering pillow ends while her attendants were weaving robes for the monks.[21] These accounts refer to work inside palace buildings but some compounds also contained purpose-built weaving workshops.

There was an increase in the production of hand-woven textiles when Princess Dararatsami of Chiang Mai (1873-1933) set a fashion for Lan Na *phasin*. Under the supervision of her mother Princess Tipkesorn, these textiles were sent to the Bangkok court. Extra weavers were taken on to help fill orders. Princess Dararatsami returned to Chiang Mai from Bangkok after the death of Rama V in 1910. A new residence was built for her in Mae Rim, to the north of Chiang Mai where she gathered together her elderly relatives and their retainers. They included some of the weavers who had worked for her mother, the now deceased Princess Tipkesorn.[22] They had come originally from a settlement around the temple of Wat Duangdi in Chiang Mai, a location renowned for skilled weaving. As the temple is situated inside the city wall it is likely that the weavers were *khon muang*.

In Chiang Mai, Mom Sae, a consort of Prince Kaew Nawarat of Chiang Mai (ruled 1911-1939) supervised textile production at court. Princesses from Chiang Mai and the surrounding inland states (married to members of the Chiang Mai royal family) acted as assistants to Mom Sae.[23] One of the best weavers called Khun Wandee came from the Wat Duangdi area where Princess Tipkesorn had recruited. There were two skilled brocade weavers, Khun Udon who came from Bangkok and Khun Bun Long from the southern provinces of Siam.[24] A Chinese male was in charge of dyeing the yarn.[25] There was a talented prince who designed costumes and sets for the dancers and theatrical performances. When there was a lot of work, tailors and seamstresses were brought in from outside to help. Fabrics, including Burmese *luntaya*, and trimmings were purchased in the Chiang Mai market while Lan Na style dance dress was provided by court weavers.

Princess Dararatsami (at left) holds Prince Pongkavil on her lap on the day when a *khwan* ceremony was being performed for him at the palace of Prince Kaew Nawarat in 1925. (River Books collection)

Princess Mok, daughter of Prince Burirat of Lampang.
(River Books collection)

Production in Lamphun

The city of Lamphun was evacuated during the war with Burma and only small numbers of *khon muang* remained in the surrounding countryside. Prince Bunma, brother of Prince Kawila of Chiang Mai, restored the city and began resettlement with *khon muang* from Lampang and Chiang Mai. In 1805 the ruler of Muang Yong, Sipsong Pan Na, with a group of his Tai Lue subjects, accepted land on the east bank of the river opposite the city of Lamphun. A Tai Yuan population inhabited the city and Tai Lue were settled in the countryside so that 80 per cent of the population in Lamphun Province is of Tai Lue origin.

When the Lamphun palace was restored in 1820 a weaving workshop was set up in the spacious grounds where *khon muang* and Tai Lue weavers were employed.[26] In 1880 the Prince of Lamphun built a new palace with a workshop in the grounds.[27] It was supervised by Princess Suanboon, wife of Prince Chakrakam Kajornsakdi, tenth ruler of Lamphun. The princess had been taught to weave under the supervision of Princess Dararatsami. Princess Suanboon's daughter-in-law, Princess Pongkaew of Chiang Mai also worked there following her marriage to Prince Pattana of Lamphun.[28] The quality of weaving produced there was acknowledged throughout Lan Na. The traveller Pasqual wrote of a journey he made from Bangkok to Lamphun around 1900:

> *Next comes Lampoon* [Lamphun] *where the famous Laos* [Lan Na] *silk sarongs are manufactured by women with hand looms.*[29]

There were about 20-30 looms in operation at the Lamphun workshop.[30] Imported silk yarn and gold and silver metal thread were brought to the court by itinerant Yunnanese merchants. When river transportation between Chiang Mai and Bangkok improved the workshop shifted its orders to Bangkok. Yarn, metal thread and dyes were brought up to Chiang Mai and woven textiles sent down to Bangkok.

Nan

According to the Nan chronicle, Nan suffered devastation during the war with Burma, and the population fled in advance of the Burmese army. The resettlement of Nan began in 1790 with Tai Lue groups, followed by a number of *khon muang* and twenty years later with more Tai Lue from Sipsong Pan Na. There were skilled weavers among them and they contributed to the reputation for fine textiles produced at the Nan court. Reginald Le May wrote:

> *Nan also produces in rivalry to Chiengmai* [Chiang Mai] *a large selection of beautiful silk and cotton skirts, by many considered the finest*

in Siam; and certainly the designs and colours chosen are in nearly every
case both bold and pleasing. The Nan silk sin *that I saw, which was*
made in the Palace, were of the finest quality. . . After a long inspection
I made a choice of three, the first with broad stripes of rose and saxe blue,
and a narrow band of silver between them; the second a very sumptuous
one, mainly of gold thread on a red background; and the third of blue
and red bands with a good deal of silver work.[31]

Although Le May tells us that the textiles were made in the palace, there
are no records of the workshops.

A seamstress working at the Vimanmek
Palace, Bangkok, c. 1900.
(National Archives, Bangkok)

A woman working with a sewing machine
at the Vimanmek Palace, Bangkok, c. 1900.
(National Archives, Bangkok)

Lampang

The city of Lampang·and its environs became a refuge for many Tai Yuan
people fleeing south away from the Burmese army. During the
resettlement period Tai Lue families were brought from Muang Yong to
live in villages to the south of Lampang. The city was an ancient seat of
Lan Na culture and significantly, Prince Kawila held a major victory
ceremony there. Although the city is rich in Buddhist architecture, its
Buddhist chronicles have not been translated into English and there is
little information to establish even a genealogy chart of the royal family.
Oral history confirms that there was weaving at the Lampang courts, but
provides no details of court workshops.

Bangkok Court Workshops

The Bangkok court workshops produced some woven and embroidered
textiles that were sent to the Lan Na princes as part of gift exchange. The
workshops were situated in the women's quarters of the palace
compound, isolated from the rest of the palace.

> *The domestic arts of the court ladies residing in the inner sanctum of the*
> *Grand Palace primarily served the king in his observances of the*
> *traditional rites . . . These ladies were proficient in culinary skills,*
> *perfumery and flower arranging, as well as sewing and embroidery . . .*
> *A delicate touch and an eye for pattern are the traditional skills of*
> *domestic crafts at court. The art of embroidery demands the same talents.*
> *Court embroiderers made intricate designs with patience and dexterity.*[32]

Although there were weavers at the Bangkok court, the emphasis on
embroidery is important because robes embroidered with gold thread
were sent to the Lan Na princes, initially as part of tributary exchange
gifts, later as part of mandatory court dress. They were expensive to

Opposite:
The reverse side of the scripture cover
on page 73, showing a deity
embroidered in gold thread.
(Hariphunchai National Museum, Lamphun)

produce because of the handwork involved and the cost of the gold thread.

Conclusion

Until 1908 Lan Na royalty controlled the manufacture and sale of cloth throughout the country. The end of the monopoly enabled entrepreneurs to enter the market without being subject to crippling taxes. Royalty also lost the right to own slaves, to corvée labour and to tribute in kind from the *phrai*. This stripped them of financial advantage. The Lamphun workshop survived the change in circumstances and still operates because there is continuing demand for high quality textiles. Today the workshop in the grounds of the Lamphun palace has four to six looms in operation. The weavers make silk textiles for Queen Sirikit of Thailand, for other female members of the royal family and the court. They also take orders from women in northern Thailand who take pride in wearing Lan Na style dress, particularly on public occasions.

Two members of the royal household
hand sewing lace at the Vimanmek Palace,
Bangkok. (National Archive, Bangkok)

250

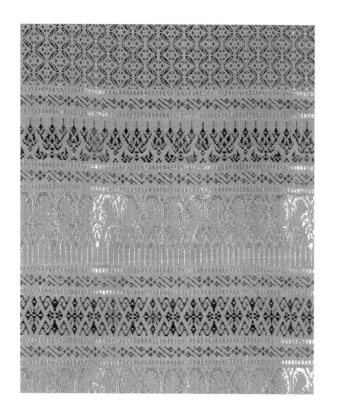

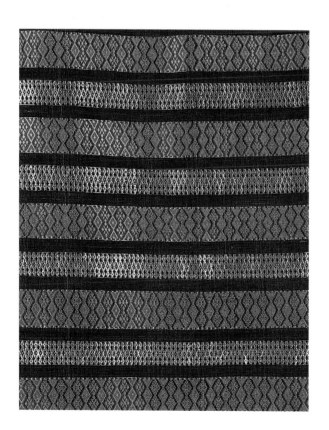

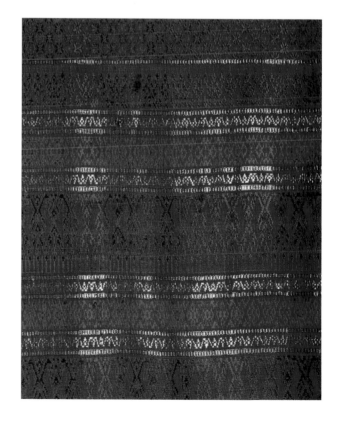

1   Wyatt and Aroonrut 1995: 37-38.

2   Gould, E.B. letter to Knox, 4.8.1876. (Foreign Office, London, Vol. 69 no. 64).

3   Hallett 1890.

4   Brailey 1994: 155.

5   Bock 1884.

6   Taylor 1888-1930: 166-167.

7   Interview with Dr. Roongruangsri, Chiang Mai University 1997.

8   Interview with Chao Ja Pa and Khun Na Sompan, Chiang Mai Feb. 1996.

9   Viravaidya 1994.

10   Kanchanajari 1990.

11   Bock 1884 repr. 1986: 322.

12   Bock 1986: 322.

13   Curtis Johnson 1903.

14   Correspondence of the Tributary State Rulers requisitioning paper and white cloth for use at the Royal Cremation, National Library Bangkok R2 C.S.1171/1.

15   Interview with Acharn Benjavan Thongsiri, Chiang Mai University (Chiang Mai, Feb. 1996).

16   Hallett 1890.

17   Lowndes 1871, McCleod 1875.

18   Grabowsky 1993: 24.

19   Hallett 1890.

20   Bock 1884 repr. 1986: 322, 366.

21   McGilvary 1912.

22   Kanchanajari 1990.

23   Interview with Chao Ja Pa and Khun na Sompan, dancers at the Chiang Mai court in the 1930s (interview Chiang Mai, February 1996).

24   According to Chao Ja Pa and Khun na Sompan, Khun Udon came from Bangkok 'because she always wore Bangkok style dress'.

25   This is interesting information because women are the traditional dyers of cloth in the villages (personal observation, Chiang Mai province 1983, Nan province 1989). The fact that the man was Chinese meant that he was not subject to Tai taboos.

26   Interview with Chao Nid (Dararatana na Lamphun), daughter of Prince Patana of Lamphun and Princess Pongkaew of Chiang Mai.

27   This is recorded in the diary of the British diplomat Sir Ernest Satow who visited in 1885 (Brailey 1994).

28   Based on the funeral book of Prince Pongthada (in Thai) n.d.

29   The Penang Gazette, Malaya n.d.

30   Interview with Chao Nid, Lamphun July 1995 and Prince Patpong na Lamphun, son of Princess Pongkaew (Lamphun Feb.1996).

31   Le May 1986: 168-169.

32   Vivavaidya 1994.

Opposite and below:
A selection of contemporary silk textiles from the Lamphun workshops, which continue to produce magnificent textiles to this day.
(Chao Dararatana Na Lamphun)

Chapter Nine

Conclusion

The princes and princesses of the inland states who look out at us from portraits and photographs account for only a small select group. Many lived anonymously leaving few clues except for perhaps a beautiful item of clothing in the possession of a descendent, faded photograph, or a passing mention by a foreign traveller. Although there is so much to learn, we are fortunate that there are enough 19th century records and documents to provide insight into life at the major courts.

It testifies to the strength of Lan Na culture that it survived at all following 200 years of occupation by the Burmese. There was a strong historical attachment to the monarchy and the *muang* system of government dating to before the 13th century. Following the long and disruptive war with Burma, the princes were restrained financially, lacked manpower and had no strong political base. In those early days they were unable to create elaborate hierarchical systems of court procedure and for some years lived precariously in humble surroundings on the edge of cities that had been destroyed or damaged by war. Craft workers, including textile makers, were scattered and it took time before they could be resettled and set to work building and furnishing new palaces.

The princes' power was based on the loyalty of the people of the

A silk and cotton *phasin* with gold metal thread
in the hem border.
(Bank of Thailand Museum, Chiang Mai)

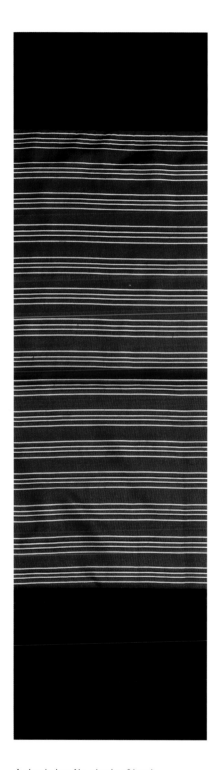

A simple Lan Na *phasin* of local cotton with the central panel woven with Chinese silk.
(Duangchit Taweesri collection)

muang. The Lan Na rulers had the sole right to perform ancient spirit religion rituals in which they mediated between their people and the highest guardian spirits of the *muang*. The princes were also defenders of Sinhalese Theravada Buddhism and had a duty to restore and rebuild Buddhist temples, create new sites and support religious communities.

The princes who ruled in the 19th century were not of royal descent but were elected to power because they were accomplished soldiers with the necessary attributes to uphold the Buddhist faith. They solved the problem of legitimate ancestry by commissioning historical fiction, recorded in new versions of the Buddhist chronicles. The princes were placed in a lineage that could be traced to the first Lan Na prince who descended from the Tavatimsa Heaven. He and his descendants were described wearing elaborate dress and regalia that defined them as *boddhisattva*.

The princes of the early 19th century were simply dressed in silk *chong kraben*, shirts, waist sashes and sometimes turbans, and they did not impose strict sumptuary laws on their courts. High quality Chinese yarn went into the production of their clothing. Complex weaving techniques were used to add shimmer and lustre to the fabric. On some occasions they wore brightly coloured Chinese silk fabrics decorated with floral patterns that placed them firmly in the world of luxury. Nevertheless, in comparison with the tiered crowns and gold and gem-encrusted dress worn by Burmese, Shan and Siamese princes, they were modestly dressed.

The authority of the Lan Na princes is conveyed to us by means of gold and silver water vessels and other containers displayed in portraits and photographs. As the princes were elected by a ruling council and anointed with water, the water vessel was particularly significant as a symbol of authority. Other containers were emblems of rank although it is not clear whether their distribution was highly regulated. The silver sword resting across the lap was a symbol of military prowess. It is more difficult to prove that they wore dress associated with spirit religion. They almost certainly used spirit cloths, vests and jackets for protection but as there were no hierarchical images it is not possible to identify surviving samples as belonging specifically to royalty. We know that the Lan Na princes were tattooed with designs and *yantra* symbols like their subjects, and this was in contrast to many societies where body markings were associated with rank.

The Lan Na princes received tributary exchange gifts from the court of Siam that included court dress and regalia, strictly graded according to a hierarchical system based on the sumptuary laws of the Bangkok court. The princes who showed outstanding loyalty to Siam, were rewarded with items that represented high rank. Princes whose loyalty was in doubt were given gifts that signified a lower rank. This system did not always match with seniority as acknowledged among the princes themselves. They displayed at court the dress and textiles presented to them.

Senior princesses had more authority than has been recognised. Unlike the consorts caricatured in Holly wood films like 'The King and I' and 'Anna and the King' they were not all kept in seclusion and treated as chattles. Many operated as effective businesswomen, their advice sought by informed expatriate civil servants and administrators. Although they were not taught formally to read and write, they controlled complex trading organisations that operated regionally and at inter-state level. Some princesses exerted influence among male members of the royal family through their power as spirit mediums. Political and economic decisions were taken on the strength of their pronouncements as to what would please or displease the spirits. The American missionaries went as far as to say that a princess could hold the reigns of government in her hands. The participation of female royalty in business and trade had its dark side and princesses were often as heavily involved in slavery as their male counterparts. The disapproving tone used by expatriate men to describe authoritative women working in 19th century Lan Na suggests that they were freer than most European women of a similar class. However, life was not always so liberated, their marriages were often arranged and they were sent to live at a foreign court where life was more restricting that at home.

The most complex weaving patterns, the greatest variety of yarns and a plethora of designs were reserved for female court dress. If she was sent to live abroad a Lan Na princess wore the dress of her homeland and she would probably find herself surrounded by consorts from other states wearing their distinctive dress. This was a way of visually communicating unity between states and was particularly significant in the 19th century. Britain and France had colonial ambitions in the region and the Lan Na princes, with other rulers in the region, were rapidly strengthening their alliances. Although female dress was used for political purposes, the princesses chose to wear their traditional dress even in the privacy of their apartments. On informal occasions they wore simple cotton *phasin* in the same designs as worn by village women at home.

The *phasin* is of great cultural significance to Lan Na women. It has matriarchal attributes that are ritualistic and symbolic and can act as a positive or negative force. As a symbol of the benevolent guardian spirit (*khwan*) the *phasin* can give protection, particularly for a son, but in other circumstances is capable of polluting and weakening men. *Phasin* are often kept as family heirlooms or are presented to the temple in honour of a deceased female relative. More recently they have become part of national and regional museum collections, their significance acknowledged by museum staff.

In terms of its structure and patterning, the *phasin* has evolved through centuries of intermarriage and resettlement that has resulted in the assimilation of designs. Generations of immigrants introduced new weaving techniques and ways of embellishing cloth. Female immigrants maintained their ethnic identity by keeping certain elements in their

A *phasin* with a cotton waistband and Chinese silk in the central panel. Both this and the previous example reflect a preference for Chinese silk yarn over the indigenous product.
(Daraphirom Museum, Chiang Mai)

A colourful Lan Na silk and cotton *phasin*. (Bank of Thailand Museum, Chiang Mai)

dress that could be identified with a particular homeland. In the 19th century this met with little opposition from the indigenous population because immigrants were welcome in a land that was under-populated and had a shortage of labour of all kinds. New settlers had no need to disguise their ethnic background for fear of political and religious oppression. The majority came from the extended cultural area and shared religious, cultural and linguistic traits with the existing inhabitants who often regarded them as distant cousins. Now that borders are open, the people of Sishuangbanna Autonomous Prefecture (Sipsong Pan Na) find they have much in common with those living in north Thailand (Lan Na). They recognise language and dialects, acknowledge common elements in their architecture, in Buddhist and spirit religion rites and in mythology and social customs. The weavers among them recognise shared weaving patterns and similar forms of dress that lead them to assume they are distantly related.

Away from Lan Na society, and in Bangkok in particular, the *phasin* became an object of fashion. Foreign princesses with little or no understanding of the cultural significance of the *phasin* ordered copies. Interestingly, senior Siamese consorts continued to wear the wrapped *pha chong kraben* that was their traditional court dress. Meanwhile Siamese women living in Lan Na also wore the *chong kraben* as an expression of their homeland although their younger daughters were often dressed in Lan Na *phasin*. The fashion for Lan Na dress in Bangkok may have reflected fashion in Europe at that time. The *phasin* bore some resemblance to the so-called 'hobble' skirt worn in Europe, and European women dressed their hair in a similar way to Lan Na women.

While recognising the cultural significance of the *phasin*, it was monk's robes that most clearly represented female religious obligations to Buddhism. To weave robes for the monks was a way of gaining merit for oneself and passing merit to ancestors. Lan Na female royalty also produced temple banners and manuscript covers and samples of their work have survived in temple repositories.

During the reign of Prince Indra Witchayanon of Chiang Mai there was a change in male court dress that reflected a major shift in political power. Fear of British and French colonial ambitions in Lan Na led King Rama V to impose Siamese authority. Power from Bangkok radiated outwards, absorbing former tributary states, including Lan Na while consolidating administrative control over them. Like Queen Victoria in her relationship with the princes of the Empire, Rama V lavished titles and honours, insignia and medals, on the princes of his tributary states while their real power was curbed. The princes were fitted into an administrative hierarchy that neutralised their role as independent Lan Na princes. Their uniforms were modelled on those issued to British Colonial officers and Consular officials. These uniforms were overlaid with traditional embroidered coats, as issued to senior Siamese officials. The fascinating outcome of Rama V's policy was that by adopting colonial methods and using them with great diplomatic skill, he prevented Siam, and by association Lan Na, from being colonised, as befell all other Southeast Asian states. While Gandhi and other freedom fighters were later to use indigenous cloth as a symbol of freedom from British rule, Rama V combined British colonial dress with elements of Siamese dress, as a symbol of his personal authority. In terms of dress history this was a unique response.

The transfer of power to Bangkok met with some resistance. The Lan Na princes had extraordinary authority as guardians of the *muang*, demonstrated in their sole right to conduct the annual appeasement ceremony at the city ancestor shrine. Rama V diminished this power by having ancestor shrines moved from city boundaries and incorporated with ancient Buddhist monuments. In this way the power of spirit religion was assimilated and controlled.

Until the 1880s the ability to resist interference from Siam lay in the remoteness of the principalities and most economic and cultural ties were with the surrounding inland states. The transition of power from Lan Na to Siam was assisted by improvements in communication to and from Bangkok. Once the railway line was completed in 1919 government officers could operate efficiently between regional headquarters and Bangkok. The improved transport system also affected trade. Until then goods were carried overland by itinerant Yunnanese, Shan and Burmese traders. When transport with Bangkok improved the cost of importing goods on that route fell by between 400-500 percent. Many other trade routes collapsed although pack animal caravans to and from the Shan States continued to be profitable. As part of colonial expansion, the British had drawn up plans to build a railway from Burma to Yunnan, believing that their goods, including mill-produced cloth, might be imported via India through Burma and the Shan States to markets in Lan Na and China. The extended railway line was never built and British attempts to establish trading outlets in Lan Na were not successful. Sales to the Lan Na courts were too small to be financially viable, most women wove cloth for themselves and their families, and competition with other traders was intense.

Research into Southeast Asian textile markets has usually focused on ocean trade, particularly with India and demonstrates the importance of Indian textiles to the courts of Southeast Asia. However there was no significant luxury trade in Indian textiles to Lan Na. Chinese, Burmese and Shan goods had a far greater impact on court dress and regalia. This applied to Lan Na and to other inland states. Indian textiles were sent to Lan Na as part of tributary gift exchange and they are listed in court records as printed and painted cottons, produced in India to Siamese specifications. Significantly, in Siam Indian printed textiles were worn according to sumptuary laws that restricted patterns by rank. As the Lan Na rulers were tributary to Siam, their allocation of textiles and dress fitted into a hierarchical system that they did not automatically accept.

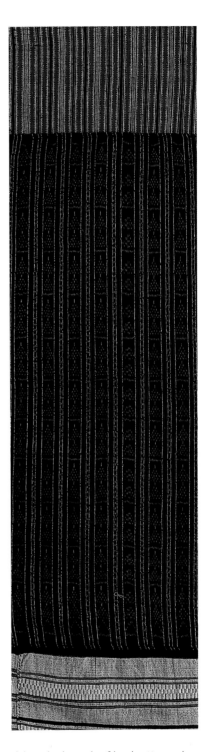

A Lao *phasin*. made of local cotton and silk with imported gold metal thread in the central panel.
(Bank of Thailand Museum, Chiang Mai)

Some high quality Indian cloth and Chinese silk brocades were donated to temple libraries for wrapping Buddhist manuscripts. Other pieces were used to protect and store court regalia. Larger pieces were laid as floor coverings or made into curtains and room dividers. Some traders operating on the Burma route carried cheap printed cottons to Lan Na, although amounts were small. In the past it has been assumed that silk brocades were of Indian origin although many were probably produced in the southern states of Siam or in Bangkok where there was a brocade weaving tradition that included immigrant Muslim communities.

Today in Chiang Mai and in other major urban centres, hand-woven silk and cotton textiles are on sale in shops and local markets and the consumer is spoilt for choice. They range from silk and cotton sold by the metre to ready-made *phasin* and other traditional Lan Na textiles and garments. A few weavers work only with hand-spun cotton and vegetable dyes, producing a range of subtle colours and textures that are particularly attractive to connoisseurs. While village weaving traditions have disappeared in many areas, they thrive in others, such as the Mae Chaem valley where an annual weaving festival is held and where there is a competition to judge the best *teen jok*. The surviving Lan Na royal workshop in Lamphun produces superb hand-woven silk for members of the Thai royal family and the court and for discerning women who choose to wear silk phasin on festive occasions. Recently a fantastic collection of Lan Na textiles has been saved for the nation by the Bank of Thailand Museum, Chiang Mai. This is a great source for scholars and students wishing to study Lan Na culture and in particular as a way of understanding the creativity of women.

Opposite:
A *phasin* with a hand-woven waistband and central panel, and imported Chinese satin for the hem.
(Paothong Thongchua Collection)

Detail of a *teen jok* border from a comtemporary silk textile from Lamphun workshops.
(Chao Dararatana na Lamphun)

Lamphun Royal Family

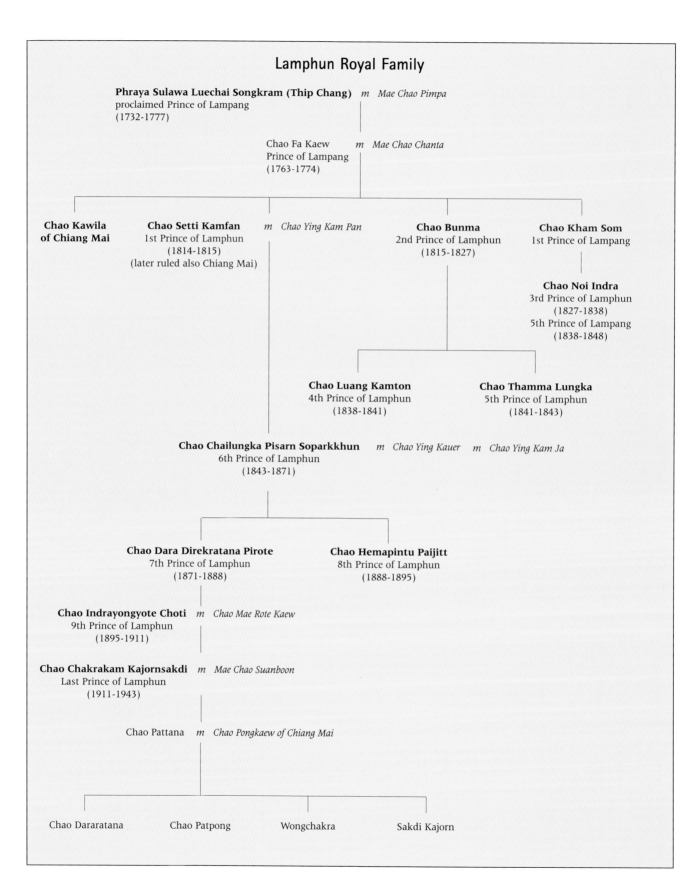

Phraya Sulawa Luechai Songkram (Thip Chang) *m* *Mae Chao Pimpa*
proclaimed Prince of Lampang
(1732-1777)

Chao Fa Kaew *m* *Mae Chao Chanta*
Prince of Lampang
(1763-1774)

Chao Kawila **Chao Setti Kamfan** *m* *Chao Ying Kam Pan* **Chao Bunma** **Chao Kham Som**
of Chiang Mai 1st Prince of Lamphun 2nd Prince of Lamphun 1st Prince of Lampang
(1814-1815) (1815-1827)
(later ruled also Chiang Mai)

Chao Noi Indra
3rd Prince of Lamphun
(1827-1838)
5th Prince of Lampang
(1838-1848)

Chao Luang Kamton **Chao Thamma Lungka**
4th Prince of Lamphun 5th Prince of Lamphun
(1838-1841) (1841-1843)

Chao Chailungka Pisarn Soparkkhun *m* *Chao Ying Kauer* *m* *Chao Ying Kam Ja*
6th Prince of Lamphun
(1843-1871)

Chao Dara Direkratana Pirote **Chao Hemapintu Paijitt**
7th Prince of Lamphun 8th Prince of Lamphun
(1871-1888) (1888-1895)

Chao Indrayongyote Choti *m* *Chao Mae Rote Kaew*
9th Prince of Lamphun
(1895-1911)

Chao Chakrakam Kajornsakdi *m* *Mae Chao Suanboon*
Last Prince of Lamphun
(1911-1943)

Chao Pattana *m* *Chao Pongkaew of Chiang Mai*

Chao Dararatana Chao Patpong Wongchakra Sakdi Kajorn

262

Lampang Royal Family

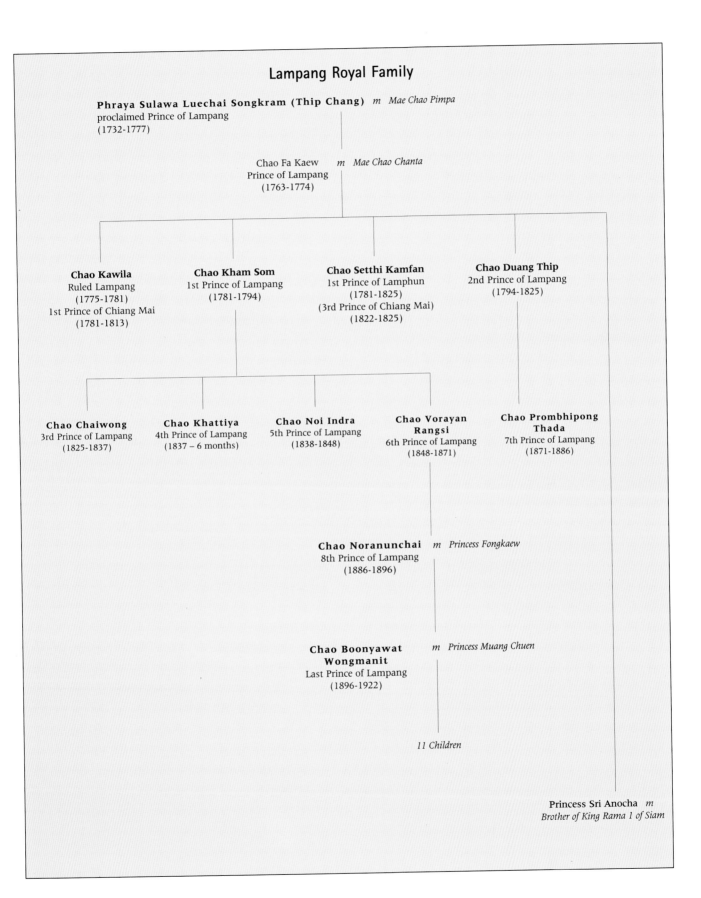

Phraya Sulawa Luechai Songkram (Thip Chang) *m* *Mae Chao Pimpa*
proclaimed Prince of Lampang
(1732-1777)

Chao Fa Kaew *m* *Mae Chao Chanta*
Prince of Lampang
(1763-1774)

Chao Kawila
Ruled Lampang
(1775-1781)
1st Prince of Chiang Mai
(1781-1813)

Chao Kham Som
1st Prince of Lampang
(1781-1794)

Chao Setthi Kamfan
1st Prince of Lamphun
(1781-1825)
(3rd Prince of Chiang Mai)
(1822-1825)

Chao Duang Thip
2nd Prince of Lampang
(1794-1825)

Chao Chaiwong
3rd Prince of Lampang
(1825-1837)

Chao Khattiya
4th Prince of Lampang
(1837 – 6 months)

Chao Noi Indra
5th Prince of Lampang
(1838-1848)

**Chao Vorayan
Rangsi**
6th Prince of Lampang
(1848-1871)

**Chao Prombhipong
Thada**
7th Prince of Lampang
(1871-1886)

Chao Noranunchai *m* *Princess Fongkaew*
8th Prince of Lampang
(1886-1896)

**Chao Boonyawat
Wongmanit**
Last Prince of Lampang
(1896-1922) *m* *Princess Muang Chuen*

11 Children

Princess Sri Anocha *m*
Brother of King Rama 1 of Siam

Nan Royal Family

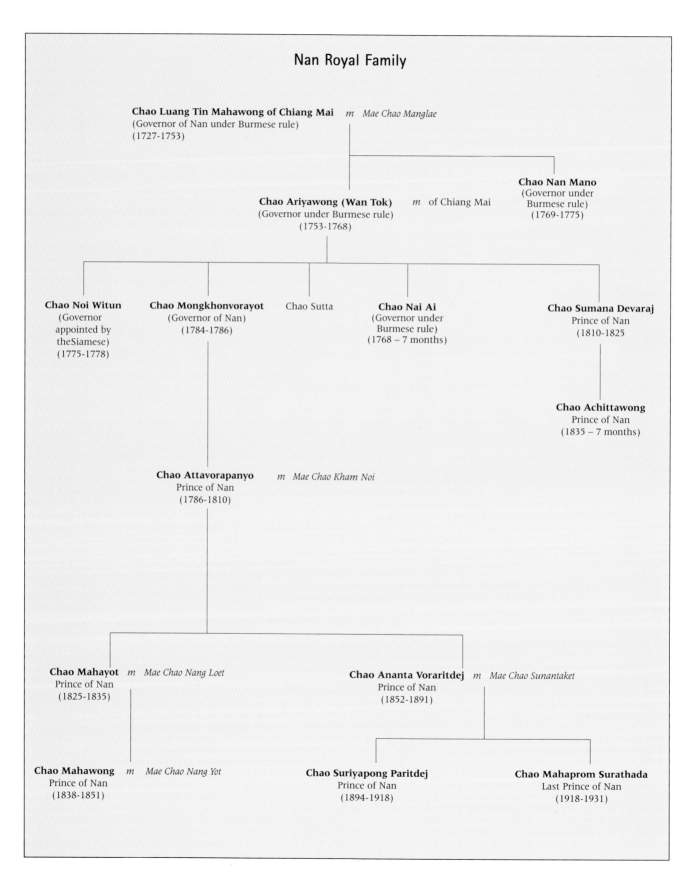

Chao Luang Tin Mahawong of Chiang Mai
(Governor of Nan under Burmese rule)
(1727-1753)   *m   Mae Chao Manglae*

Chao Ariyawong (Wan Tok)   *m   of Chiang Mai*
(Governor under Burmese rule)
(1753-1768)

Chao Nan Mano
(Governor under
Burmese rule)
(1769-1775)

Chao Noi Witun
(Governor
appointed by
theSiamese)
(1775-1778)

Chao Mongkhonvorayot
(Governor of Nan)
(1784-1786)

Chao Sutta

Chao Nai Ai
(Governor under
Burmese rule)
(1768 – 7 months)

Chao Sumana Devaraj
Prince of Nan
(1810-1825

Chao Achittawong
Prince of Nan
(1835 – 7 months)

Chao Attavorapanyo   *m   Mae Chao Kham Noi*
Prince of Nan
(1786-1810)

Chao Mahayot   *m   Mae Chao Nang Loet*
Prince of Nan
(1825-1835)

Chao Ananta Voraritdej   *m   Mae Chao Sunantaket*
Prince of Nan
(1852-1891)

Chao Mahawong   *m   Mae Chao Nang Yot*
Prince of Nan
(1838-1851)

Chao Suriyapong Paritdej
Prince of Nan
(1894-1918)

Chao Mahaprom Surathada
Last Prince of Nan
(1918-1931)

Chiang Mai Royal Family

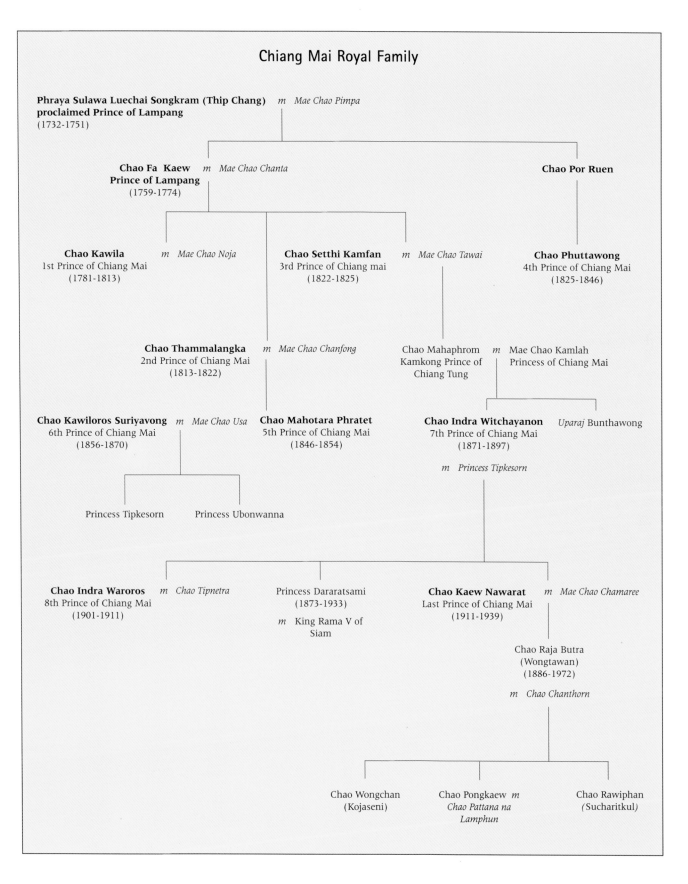

Phraya Sulawa Luechai Songkram (Thip Chang)
proclaimed Prince of Lampang
(1732-1751)   *m   Mae Chao Pimpa*

Chao Fa Kaew   *m   Mae Chao Chanta*
Prince of Lampang
(1759-1774)

Chao Por Ruen

Chao Kawila   *m   Mae Chao Noja*
1st Prince of Chiang Mai
(1781-1813)

Chao Setthi Kamfan   *m   Mae Chao Tawai*
3rd Prince of Chiang mai
(1822-1825)

Chao Phuttawong
4th Prince of Chiang Mai
(1825-1846)

Chao Thammalangka   *m   Mae Chao Chanfong*
2nd Prince of Chiang Mai
(1813-1822)

Chao Mahaphrom   *m*   Mae Chao Kamlah
Kamkong Prince of   Princess of Chiang Mai
Chiang Tung

Chao Kawiloros Suriyavong   *m   Mae Chao Usa*
6th Prince of Chiang Mai
(1856-1870)

Chao Mahotara Phratet
5th Prince of Chiang Mai
(1846-1854)

Chao Indra Witchayanon   *Uparaj* Bunthawong
7th Prince of Chiang Mai
(1871-1897)

m   Princess Tipkesorn

Princess Tipkesorn   Princess Ubonwanna

Chao Indra Waroros   *m   Chao Tipnetra*
8th Prince of Chiang Mai
(1901-1911)

Princess Dararatsami
(1873-1933)

m   King Rama V of
Siam

Chao Kaew Nawarat   *m   Mae Chao Chamaree*
Last Prince of Chiang Mai
(1911-1939)

Chao Raja Butra
(Wongtawan)
(1886-1972)

m   Chao Chanthorn

Chao Wongchan   Chao Pongkaew *m*   Chao Rawiphan
(Kojaseni)   *Chao Pattana na*   *(Sucharitkul)*
                     Lamphun

Acknowledgements

I would like to begin by acknowledging Professor Lou Taylor, Dr. Ruth Barnes and Dr Henry Ginsburg whose invaluable advice enabled me to complete this project. I would also like to acknowledge the James W. Thomson Foundation, Bangkok, for the grant that covered the fieldwork for this book and particularly Acharn William Klausner and Eric Booth for their support.

My thanks go to Acharn Choosri Sawasdisongkhram, Director, National Archives, Bangkok; Khun Kam Thorn Thep, Office of the Royal Household, National Private Museum, Khun Euayporn and staff of the Siam Society, and volunteers of the National Museum Volunteers Group, Bangkok. I would also like to acknowledge the help of the Director and staff of the Bank of Thailand Museum, Bangkok, and Khun Karen Chungyampin, curator of the Tilleke and Gibbins Collection, Bangkok. Thanks also to the staff of the National Museums of Nan, Ubon Ratchathani, Nakhon Si Thammarat and Surat Thani. Acharn Paothong Thongchua and Mom Luang Poomchai Chumbala kindly allowed me access to their private collections. I am grateful to Dr. Gary Suwannarat, Ms Sharon O'Toole, Khun Sisamorn, Khun Sunanthana, and Khun Wannee Vardhanabhuti for their help and advice.

In Chiang Mai, Khun Duangchit Taweesri and Khun Akadej Nakbunlang allowed me to photograph their textile collections. Thanks go to the staff of Chiang Mai National Museum, The Bank of Thailand Museum, Chiang Mai, Payap University Archive and Chiang Mai University Library. I would particularly like to acknowledge M.R. Rujaya Abhakorn, Dr Udom Roonruangsri, Acharn Saraswadee Ongskul, Dr Narin Tongsiri, Acharn Benjavan Tongsiri, Acharn Witthi Panichpant, Dr. Herbert Swanson and Dr Kanok and Dr Benjawan Rerkasem.

Thanks also go to Chao Ja Pa and Khun Sompan, former members of the royal household of Chiang Mai, for their detailed knowledge of court life. Acharn Benjawan Tongsiri, a descendant of the Chiang Mai royal family, accompanied me to the palace of Princess Dararatsami, and helped me to assemble the genealogy charts of the royal family. Khun Suchinder Heavener provided information on the royal palaces of Chiang Mai. Ba Sangda Bansiddhi, Khun Sawanee Chaisawong, Khun Payow and the weavers of Chom Ton and San Pathong, gave details of dyeing and weaving techniques, and local trade in textiles and raw materials in the Mae Ping River valley.

In Mae Chaem, Khun Nusura Tiangkhet and the villagers of Ban Rai and Ban Tong Fai allowed me to photograph their textiles. Interviews were also held in other villages in the Mae Chaem valley and I am particularly grateful to

Khun Naa, Mae Kham, Mae Euai Je, Khun Planee and Mae Euai Mai for their expertise and knowledge of local history. In Nan Province, I photographed the collection of Philip and Sawasdee Salmon and in particular wish to acknowledge the weavers of Ban Don Mun, Ban Lai Tung, Tambon Pon, Ban Nong Bua, Bua, Ban Dong Chai and Ban Pua.

Thanks go to Chao Nid and Chao Patpong of Lamphun who accompanied me to the palace of the Prince of Lamphun and allowed me to photograph the Lamphun court workshop and interview the weavers working there. Thanks also to descendants of weavers who had worked at the Lamphun palace in the 19th century.

Eleanor Gaudoin, a descendant of the royal family of the Shan State of Hsenwi, was particularly generous with knowledge of the Shan courts, and Chao Vilai na Chiang Tung gave information on the Chiang Tung court.

I also wish to acknowledge Buddhist communities in the temples of North and Northeast Thailand who allowed access to their temple repositories and manuscripts.

The Tai Lao weavers of Khon Kaen, Nong Khai, Roi Et and Sakhon Nakhon provinces provided an insight into Tai Lao weaving traditions. Acharn Suriya Smutkupt, Acharn Sukunya and Acharn Pairote Somasorn also provided information on Tai Lao culture and weaving traditions. Khun Patara Panichayakarn of Khon Kaen allowed me to photograph her textile collection. My thanks go to those who allowed me to photograph their Lan Na textiles, but wish to remain anonymous.

In the U.K., I am grateful to Dr Brian Durrans of The British Museum; and Dr. Deborah Swallow and Francis Franklin of the Victoria and Albert Museum, who allowed access to relevant textile material. In Oxford, my thanks go to Elizabeth Edwards of the Pitt Rivers Museum, in Liverpool to Louise Tythacott of the Merseyside Museum, and in Brighton to Dr Elizabeth Dell of the Green Centre for Non-western Art. Mr Revel Oddy, formerly assistant Keeper, Royal Scottish Museum, Edinburgh gave advice on the format of the Appendices.

I would like to thank Dr. Mattiebelle Gittinger for arranging access to the collections of the Textile Museum, Washington.

In conclusion, I am grateful to Khun Paisarn Piemmettawat for additiconal picture and genealogy research, and to my publisher M.R. Narisa Chakrabongse for her enthusiasm and vision in support of this publication.

Bibliography

Abhakorn, Rujaya, *Changes in the Administrative System of the Northern Thai States 1884-1908* (Chiang Mai: Chiang Mai University, 1984).

Anderson, Major J., 'Small Notes about the Karens,' *The Journal of the Siam Society,* Vol. XVII, Pt. 2, 1923.

Anonymous, *Textbook Thai Design* (Bangkok: Khanachang Press, n.d.) (in Thai).

Anonymous, 'The Helen K. Hunt Collection', *Burmese Art Newsletter*, Dept. of Visual Arts, Denison University, Ohio, Vol. I. no. 4, June 1969, pp. 1-8.

Anonymous, *Chao Luang Chiang Mai* (Chiang Mai: published privately, 1996), (in Thai).

Archer, W.J. Vice Consul, '*Report on a Journey to Chiang Mai 3rd April 1886*' , F.O. 69/109 1886, Public Records Office, Kew, London.

——————— 'Trade Report of Chiang Mai,' *Rangoon Gazette Weekly*, June 28th, 1895.

Aung Thwin, Michael, 'Kingship, the Sangha and Society in Pagan,' in K.R. Hall and J.K. Whitmore (eds.), *Explorations in Early Southeast Asian History: The Origins of Southeast Asian Statecraft* (De-Kalb: Center for Southeast Asian Studies, Northern Illinois University, 1976).

Backus, Mary (ed.), *Siam and Laos as Seen by Our American Missionaries* (Philadelphia Presbyterian Historical Society, 1884).

Barnes, Ruth, *The Ikat Textiles of Lamalera: A Study of an Eastern Indonesian Weaving Tradition* (Leiden: E.J. Brill, 1989).

——————— The Bridewealth Cloth of Lamalera, Lembata,' in M. Gittinger (ed.), *To Speak With Cloth: Studies in Indonesian Textiles* (Los Angeles: Uni. of Cal. Museum of Cultural History, 1989).

——————— 'Textile design in Southern Lembata: Tradition and Change,' in J. Coote and A. Shelton (eds.), *Anthropology, Art and Aesthetics* (Oxford: Clarendon Press, 1995).

Barnes, Ruth and Eicher, Joanne, *Dress and Gender: Making and Meaning in Cultural Contexts* (Oxford and New York: Berg, 1992).

Bassenne, Marthe, *Au Laos et Au Siam*, (Paris: 1912, reprinted as *In Laos and Siam* W. Tips trans., Bangkok: White Lotus, 1995).

Bayly, C.A., 'The Origins of Swadeshi (home industry): Cloth and Indian Society, 1700-1930,' in A. Appadurai (ed.), *The Social Life of Things: Commodities in Cultural Perspective* (Cambridge: Cambridge University Press, 1986).

Bean, Susan, 'Gandhi and Khadi, the Fabric of Indian Independence,' in A.Weiner and S.W. Schneider (eds.), *Cloth and Human Experience* (Washington D.C. and London: Smithsonian Institution Press, 1989).

Blundell, E. A. (ed.), 'An Account of Some of the Petty States Lying North of the Tenasserim Provinces (drawn from the journals and reports of D. Richardson Esq. Surgeon of Tenasserim Provinces)' *Journal of the Asiatic Society of Burma*, Vol. 58, 1836, pp. 601-625 and 628-707.

Bock, Carl, *Temples and Elephants:Travels in Siam 1881-1882* (London 1884). Reprinted Oxford: Oxford University Press, 1986).

Boisselier, Jean, *Thai Painting* (Tokyo: Kodansha International, 1976).

Boonserm, Satraphi and Sangeet, Chantanabho, *Lan Na in the Past* (Bangkok: Ruangsin, 1977).

Bowie, Katherine, 'Peasant Perspectives on the Political Economy of the Northern Thai Kingdom of Chiang Mai in the Nineteenth Century: Implications for the Understanding of Peasant Political Expression,' Ph.D. dissertation, Dept. of Anthropology, University of Chicago, Illinois, 1988.

——————— 'Unraveling the Myth of the Subsistence Economy: Textile Production in Nineteenth Century Northern Thailand,' *Journal of Asian Studies*, Vol. 51, Pt 4, 1992, pp. 797-823.

——————— 'Assessing the Early Observers: Cloth and the Fabric of Society in Nineteenth-century Northern Thai Kingdoms,' *American Ethnologist*, Vol. 20, Pt.1, 1993, pp. 138-158.

——————— 'Trade and Textiles in Northern Thailand: A Historical Perspective,' Anthropology Dept. University of Wisconsin, Madison, 1993.

Bowring, Sir John, *The Kingdom and People of Siam* (London 1857; reprinted AMS Press, Kuala Lumpur, 1975).

Brailey, Nigel, '*Chiangmai and the Inception of an Administrative Centralization Policy*' Southeast Asian Studies Vol. II, No. 3, 1973.

Brailey, Nigel (ed.), *Diplomat in Siam: The Diaries of Sir Ernst Satow 1885-1888,* Kiscadale Asia Research Series No. 4, (Gartmore: Kiscadale Ltd., 1994).

Briggs W.A., '*Woman's Work for Woman and Our Mission Field*,' Presbyterian Historical Society, Philadelphia, Vol. VIX, 1894, Microfilm collection, Payap University Archive, Chiang Mai).

Brown, Ian, 'Government Initiative and Peasant Response in the Siamese Silk Industry 1901-1913,' *Siam Society Journal*, Vol. 68, Pt. 2, 1980, pp. 34-47.

Bunnag, Tej, '*The Provincial Administration of Siam 1892-1915*,' Ph.D. dissertation Oxford University, 1977.

Calavan, Sharon Kay, 'Aristocrats and Commoners in Rural Northern Thailand,' Ph.D. dissertation, University of Illinois, Urbana-Champaign, 1974.

Carter, C. (ed.), *Report on Sericulture in Siam* (Bangkok: Siam Society Publ., 1904).

Cheek, Samuel, '*Correspondence 1880-1890*,' *The Presbyterian Historical Society, Philadelphia*. (Microfilm collection, Payap University, Chiang Mai).

Cheek, Samuel '*Siam Oriental Land of the Free*' *The Presbyterian Historical Society*, (Payap University Archive, n.d.).

Cheesman, Patricia, *Lao Textiles* (Bangkok: White Lotus, 1988).

Chongkul, Chira, 'Textiles and Costumes in Thailand,' *Arts of Asia*, Vol. 12, 1982, pp. 121-131.

Chumbala, Poomchai, 'The Textile Collections of Princess Boonchiradorn Chutajtut,' BA (hons.) dissertation, Winchester School of Art, Winchester, 1983.

Chutintaranond, Sunait and Tun, Than, *On Both Sides Of The Tenasserim Range: History of Siamese-Burmese Relations* (Bangkok: Institute of Asian Studies, Chulalongkorn University, 1995).

Coedès, Georges (trans.), *Chronicle of Chamadevi* (Paris: 1926).

Cohen, Paul T. and Wijeyewardene, Gehan, 'Introduction to Spirit Cults and the Position of Women in Northern Thailand,' *Mankind* Vol. 14, Pt. 4, 1984, pp. 249-262.

Cohn, Bernard, 'Representing Authority in Victorian India,' in E. Hobsbawm and T. Ranger (eds.), *The Invention of Tradition* (Cambridge: Cambridge University Press, 1983).

Cohn, Bernard 'Cloth, Clothes and Colonialism: India In the Nineteenth Century,' in A. Weiner and S.W. Schneider (eds.), *Cloth and Human Experience* (Washington D.C. and London: Smithsonian Institution Press, 1989).

Collis, Maurice, *Lords of the Sunset: A Tour in the Shan States* (London: Faber and Faber, 1938).

Colquhoun, Archibald Ross, *Amongst the Shans* (London: Field and Tuer, 1885).

Condominas, Georges, 'A Few Remarks about Thai Political Systems' in G.B. Milne (ed.), *Natural Symbols in South East Asia* (London: School of Oriental and African Studies, London Uni., 1977).

Condominas, Georges (ed.), *From Lawa to Mon, from Saa to Thai: Historical and Anthropological Aspects of Southeast Asian Social Spaces* (Trans. and ed. by Gehan Wijeyewardene. et al. from L'espace social apropos de l'Asie du Sud-Est, 1921-) (Canberra: Dept. Anthropology, Research School of Pacific Studies, The Australian National University, 1990).

Conway, Susan, 'The Temple Mural Paintings of North Thailand,' BA (hons.) dissertation, West Surrey College of Art and Design, Surrey University, 1981.

——————— *Thailand: Weaving and The Rice Cycle* (Farnham: West Surrey College of Art and Design, Surrey University, 1990).

——————— *Thai Textiles* (Bangkok: River Books, 2001).

——————— 'Bihar Quilting and North-East Thai Weaving: a Comparative Study of Status' *Textile History* Vol. 30 No. 1 Spring 1999 pp. 69-80.

Cordwell J.M. and Schwarz R.A. (eds), *The Fabrics of Culture: the Anthropology of Clothing and Adornment* (The Hague: Mouton Press, 1979).

Cort, Mary Lovina, *Siam: The Heart of Farther India* (New York: Anson, D.F. Randolph and Co. 1886).

——————— 'Woman's Work for Woman and Our Mission Field,' Vol. IV, No. 53, 1889, Presbyterian Historical Society, Philadelphia (Microfilm collection, Payap Uni. Archive, Chiang Mai).

——————— 'Women's Work for Women and Our Mission Field,' Vol. V. No. 54, 1889 Presbyterian Historical Society, Philadelphia (Microfilm collection, Payap Uni. Archive, Chiang Mai).

Crawfurd, Sir John, *Journal of an Embassy to the Courts of Siam and Cochin China* (London: Oxford University Press, 1828, reprinted, Kuala Lumpur, 1967).

Curtis, Lillian Johnson *The Laos of North Siam* (London: Fleming H Revell Co., 1903, rep. Bangkok: White Lotus, 1998).

Damrong, Rajanuphap, Prince, '*Prince Damrong's Personal Papers,*' The National Archives, Bangkok: Fifth Reign (R 5) 2.46/10, 1932.

——————— *Phraratchapongsawadan rattanakosin nai samai phrabatsomdet phrabutthalotlanphalai ratchakan thi 2* [The Royal Chronicles, 'Bangkok, Era of the Second Reign'] (Bangkok: Siam Society Publ.,1990).

Davis, Richard, 'Tolerance and Intolerance of Ambiguity in Northern Thai Myth and Ritual,' *Ethnology,* Vol. 13, 1974, pp. 7-24.

——————— 'Muang Matrifocality,' *Journal of the Siam Society* Vol. 61, Pt. 2, 1973, pp. 53-62 (reprint in *Mankind* Vol.14, Pt. 4, 1984, pp. 363-371).

Dhani, Nivat HH Prince, 'The Old Siamese Conception of Monarchy,' *Journal of the Siam Society,* Vol. XXXVI, Pt. 2, 1947, pp. 91-106.

——————— 'Traditional Dresses in Classic Dance of Siam,' *Journal of the Siam Society,* Vol. XL, Pt. 2, 1952, pp. 134-145.

Diskul, Subhadradis M.C. and Pisit, Charoenwongsa, *Archaeologia Mundi* (Geneva: Nagel, 1978).

Dobrenchuk, Anne, 'Thai Religious Architecture: Definition of Terms,' in *Sawaddi* (Special edition) (Bangkok: American Women's Club, 1986).

Dodd, William Clifton, *The Tai Race: Elder Brother of the Chinese* (Cedar Rapids: The Torch Press, 1923).

Dulyapach, Puengpit, 'The Role of Women in Agriculture,' Seminar on Research on the Role of Women in Agriculture in Thailand, (Bangkok: Institute of Farming Systems Research, Department of Agriculture; Kasetsart University, and Seattle: Oregon State Uni., 14-16 August 1985), (in Thai).

Duncan, H., 'Techniques of Traditional Thai Painting,' *Sawaddi* 1971, pp. 56-58.

Dunlap, K., 'The Development and Function of Clothing,' *Journal of General Psychology,* Vol. 1, 1928, pp. 64-78.

Dupaigne, Bernard, 'Jim Thompson and the Cham Weavers' Paper presented at the *James H.W. Thompson Foundation Symposium,* Bangkok, Aug., 1999, (n.p.).

Eicher, Joanne (ed.), *Dress and Ethnicity* (Oxford and Washington, D.C.: Berg, 1995).

Eicher, Joanne and Roach-Higgins M.E., 'Describing and Classifying Dress: Implications for the Study of Gender,' in R. Barnes and J.B. Eicher (eds.), *Dress and Gender: Making and Meaning in Cultural Contexts* (Oxford and New York: Berg, 1992).

Emery, Irene, *The Primary Structure of Fabrics* (Washington D.C.: The Textile Museum, 1966).

Erikson, Thomas Hylland, *Ethnicity and Nationalism: Anthropological Perspectives* (London: Pluto Press, 1993).

Esterik, Penny van (ed.), 'Women of Southeast Asia,' Occasional Paper No. 9, (DeKalb: Center for Southeast Asian Studies, Northern Illinois Uni., 1982.

Evans, Grant, 'Is Anyone Thai Roi Percent? The Sinicised Tai' in *Tai Culture,* Vol. II, No. 1, June 1997, (Berlin, SEACOM Edition). pp.16-29.

Feldstein Hilary, Sims and Poats, Susan (eds.), *Working Together: Gender Analysis in Agriculture* (West Hartford: Kumarian Press, 1989).

Ferrars, Max and Ferrars, Bertha, *Burma* (London and New York: Sampson Low, Marston and Co., 1901).

Fitch, Ralph, 'The Voyage of M. Ralph Fitch, Merchant of London,' in R. Hakluyt (ed.), *The Principal Navigations, Voyages, Traffiques and Discoveries of the English Nation 1599,* Vol. 5, pp. 465-505 (Glasgow: James MacLehose and Sons, 1903-1905).

Forbes, A., 'The "cin-ho" (Yunnanese Chinese) Caravan Trade with North Thailand During the Late Nineteenth and Early Twentieth Centuries,' *Asian History* Vol. 21, Pt. 2, 1987, pp. 1-47.

Foster B., 'Ethnic Identity of the Mons in Thailand,' *Journal of the Siam Society,* Vol. LXI, 1973, pp. 203-226.

Franklin, Frances and Swallow, Deborah, 'Identifying With The Gods,' *Hali Annual,* London, 1994, pp. 49-61.

Fraser-Lu, Sylvia, *Handwoven Textiles of South-east Asia* (Singapore: Oxford University Press, 1988).

Freeman, J. H., *An Oriental Land of the Free* (Philadelphia: Presbyterian Historical Society, 1910).

Gavin, Traude, *The Women's Warpath:Iban Ritual Fabrics from Borneo* (Los Angeles: UCLA Fowler Museum of Cultural History, 1996.

Gavin, Traude and Barnes, Ruth, 'Iban Prestige Textiles and the Trade in Indian Cloth: Inspiration and Perception,' *Textile History* Vol. 30, No. 1, 1999, pp.81-97.

Ganjanapan, Anan, 'The Partial Commercialization of Rice Production in Northern Thailand (1900-1981),' Ph.D. dissertation, Cornell University, Ithaca, New York, 1984.

Garnier, Francis, *Further Travels in Laos and in Yunnan: The Mekong Exploration Commission Report (1866-1868) Vol. 2*

(trans. W. Tips), ('Voyage d'Exploration en Indo Chine, Paris, 1885, rep. in trans., Bangkok: White Lotus Press, 1996).

Geertz, Clifford, *The Interpretation of Cultures* (New York: Basic Books Inc., 1973).

Gell, Alfred, *Wrapping in Images* (Oxford: Oxford University Press, 1993).

Gervaise, Nicholas, *The Natural and Political History of the Kingdom of Siam* (trans. and ed. J. Villiers), *(Histoire Naturelle et Politique du Royaume de Siam),* Paris: Claude Barbin, 1688, rep. in trans., Bangkok: White Lotus, 1989).

Ginsburg, Henry, *Thai Manuscript Painting* (London: The British Library, 1989).

Gittinger, Mattiebelle, *Splendid Symbols: Textiles and Traditions in Indonesia* (Washington D.C.: The Textile Museum, 1979).

——— *Master Dyers to the World* (Washington D.C.: The Textile Museum, 1982).

Gittinger, Matiebelle (ed.), *To Speak with Cloth: Studies in Indonesian Textiles* (Los Angeles: University of California Museum of Cultural History, 1989).

Gittinger, Matiebelle and Lefferts, Leedom, *Textiles and the Tai Experience in Southeast Asia* (Washington D.C.: Textile Museum, 1992).

Gittinger, Mattiebelle, Chungyampin, Karen Anderson and Saiyalard, Chanporn, 'Textiles and Textile Customs of the Tai Dam, Tai Daeng, and Their Neighbors in Northern Laos', *The Textile Museum Journal,* 1995-1996, pp. 93-112.

Goetz, H., *The Art of India: Five Thousand Years of Indian Art* (New York: Crown Publishers, 1959).

Gombrich, Ernst H., *The Sense of Order: a Study in the Psychology of Decorative Art* (London: Phaidon Press, 1979).

Gould, E.B. 'Letter to Knox', No. 4.8. (1876), Foreign Office, Vol. 69, no.64, Public Records Office, Kew, London.

Grabowsky, Volker, 'Forced Resettlement Campaigns in Northern Thailand During the Early Bangkok Period,' in *Fifth International Conference on*

Thai Studies, School of Oriental and African Studies, London, 1993.

Green, Colonel James H., 'The Tribes of Upper Burma north of 24 degrees Latitude and Their Classification', Rangoon, Burma, M.A. thesis, University of Cambridge, 1934).

Griswold A.B. and Prasert na Nagara, 'The Judgements of King Mengrai', Epigraphic and Historical Studies No. 17, *Journal of the Siam Society* Vol. 65, Pt. 1, 1977 pp. 153.

Guy, John, 'Indian Textiles for the Thai Market: A Royal Prerogative?' in *Textiles in Trade: Proceedings of the Textile Society of America Biennial Symposium,* Washington D.C., Sept. 14-16, 1990 pp. 82-96.

——— *Woven Cargoes: Indian Textiles in the East* (London: Thames and Hudson, 1999).

Haak, Feikje van der, 'Calling the Spirits: an observation of its practice,' *Journal of the Siam Society,* Vol. 75, 1987, 108-128.

Haddon, Alfred C. and Start, Laura, *Iban or Sea Dayak Fabrics and Their Patterns* (Cambridge University Press, 1936, reprinted Bedford: Ruth Bean, 1982).

Hall, D.G.E., *A History of South-East Asia* (London: Macmillan, 1964).

Hallett, Holt, 'My First Visit to Zimme,' *Blackwood's Magazine* Sept. 1889, pp.1-14.

——— *A Thousand Miles on an Elephant in the Shan States* (Edinburgh and London: Blackwood and Sons, 1890, reprinted Bangkok: White Lotus Co. Ltd., 1988).

Halliday, R., Siedenfaden, E, Smithies, M. Foster, B., *The Mons* (Bangkok: The Siam Society, 1986).

Hanks L.M, Hanks J.R. and Sharp L., 'Ethnographic Notes on Northern Thailand', Data paper No. 58, Southeast Asia Program, Dept. Asian Studies, Cornell Uni. Ithaca, New York, 1965.

Hardiman, J.P., 'Silk in Burma,' (Rangoon: Superintendant, Government Printing, 1901).

Harvey, G.E. and Barton, G.E., 'Mengmao Succession,' Burma Secretariat file, Imprint No. 99 H.P.D. 29.10.30, Rangoon, 1930.

Heine-Geldern, Robert, 'Conceptions of State and Kingship, *S. E. Asia Far Eastern Quarterly,* Vol. II, 1942, pp. 15-30.

Hildebrand, Mr, 'British Policy and the Shan States 1886-1942,' Foreign Office Report F.O. 69/65:16, 1875, Public Records Office, Kew, London.

——————— 'Report on a Special Mission to Chiengmai by Mr Hildebrand' (Hildebrand's Report) F.O. 628/10/157, 1875, Pub. Records Office, Kew, London.

Hill, Ann M., 'Familiar Strangers: The Yunnanese Chinese in Northern Thailand,' Ph.D. dissertation, University of Illinois, Illinois, 1982.

Hinton, E.M., 'The Dress of the Pwo Karen of North Thailand,' *The Journal of the Siam Society,* Vol. 62, Pt. 1, 1972, pp. 27-34.

Hobsbawm, Eric and Ranger, Terence, *The Invention of Tradition* (Cambridge: Cambridge University Press, 1983).

Hoskins, Janet, *Biographical Objects* (New York: Routledge, 1998).

Howard, Constance, *The Constance Howard Book of Stitches* (London: Batsford, 1979).

Howes, Michael, 'Thai Silk at the Crossroads,' *Investor Magazine,* October 1974, pp. 611-616.

Howes, David (ed.), *Cross-Cultural Consumption* (London and New York: Routledge, 1996).

Htun Yi, U *Nanthon Yin Paribhawga Hnint Wutsah-sinyinhmu [Vehicles, Furniture and Costumes of Royalty],* (Rangoon: Seinpanmying, 1984).

Hutchinson, E.W., 'The Lawa in Northern Siam,' *The Journal of the Siam Society,* Vol. XXVII, Pt 2, 1935, pp. 153-182.

Ibrahim bin Muhammed, 'A Persian Mission to Siam in the Reign of King Narai: The Ship of Sulaiman,' (John O'Kane, trans.), (New York: Columbia University and London: Routledge and Kegan Paul, 1972).

Ingram, James, *Economic Change in Thailand 1850-1970* (Stanford: Stanford University Press, 1971).

Innes, R.A., *Costumes of Upper Burma and the Shan States in the Collections of Bankside Museum* (Halifax: Bankside Museum, 1957).

——————— *Non European Looms* (Calderdale: Calderdale Museums, 1977).

Isan Anthropological Laboratory, *Isan Cloth from the Anthropological Dimension,* Dept. Sociology and Anthropology, Faculty of Humanities and Social Sciences, Khon Kaen University, 1989 (in Thai, unofficial translation).

Jain, Jyotindra, 'Textiles For Far-off Siam,' *The India Magazine,* Delhi, Oct. 1985, 54-69.

Jayawickrama, N.A. (trans.), *The Sheaf of Garlands of the Epochs of the Conqueror* (1528 AD) (Trans. of Jinakalamalipakaranam of Ratanapanna Thera), Translation Series 36, (London: The Pali Text Society, 1968).

Johnson Curtis, Lillian, *The Laos of North Siam* (London: Fleming H Revell Co., 1903, rep. Bangkok: White Lotus, 1998).

Jumsai, Manich, M.L., *King Mongkut and Sir John Bowring* (Bangkok: Chalermit, 1970).

Kamol, *Mural Paintings of the Ayudhya Period,* (trans. Intralib) (Bangkok: Muang Boran, 1976).

Kanchanajari, Nongyao, *Dararatsami* (Bangkok: 1990) (in Thai).

Kanokpongchai (ed.), *Wat Phra Singh* (Bangkok: Muang Boran Publising House, 1983).

Kaufmann, Howard, K., *Bangkhuad: A Community Study in Thailand,* Monograph no. 10, The Association of Asian Studies, New York, 1960.

Kerr, A., 'Ethnologic notes: The Lawa of the Baw Luang Plateau,' *Journal of the Siam Society,* Vol. XVIII, 1924, pp. 135-139.

Keyes, Charles, 'Kin Groups in a Thai-Lao Community,' in G. William Skinner and A. Thomas Kirsch (eds.), *Change and Persistence in Thai Society: Essays in Honor of Lauriston Sharp,* (Ithaca: Cornell University Press, 1975).

——————— 'Mother or Mistress but never a Monk' *American Anthropologist,* Vol. 11, Pt. 2, 1984, pp. 223-241.

Klausner, William, *Reflections on Thai Culture* (Bangkok: published privately, 1981).

Krairiksh, Piriya, 'Nature Symbols and Motifs in Thai Art' *Symposium of the Siam Society,* Bangkok, 1989, pp. 213-232.

Kundstater, Peter, 'Studies of the Lua Population of Northwestern Thailand,' *National Geographic Society Research Reports for 1963,* Washington D.C., 1963.

——————— 'Hill and Valley Populations in Northwestern Thailand,' in *Tribesmen and Peasants in North Thailand* (Chiang Mai: Tribal Research Center, 1969).

Leach, Edmund R., *Political Systems of Highland Burma,* (London: G.Bell, 1954).

Le Bar, Frank M., Hickey, Gerald C. and Musgrave, John, *Ethnic Groups of Mainland Southeast Asia* (New Haven: Human Relations Area Files Press, 1964).

Lefèvre, E., *Travels in Laos* (trans. W. Tips, *Un Voyage au Laos,* Paris: Plon, Nourrit et Cie, 1898) (rep. in translation, Bangkok: White Lotus Co., 1995).

Lefferts, Leedom 'A Collection of Northeast Thai Textiles: Contexts and Descriptions' unpublished manuscript 1980.

——————— 'Women, Men and Merit: The Household in Rural Thai Buddhism', unpublished manuscript, n.d.

——————— 'Textiles, Buddhism and Society in Northeast Thailand,' in *Cloth and the Organization of Human Experience,* Wenner-Gren Symposium, Washington D.C., 1983.

——————— 'The Kings as Gods: Textiles in the Thai State', in J. Vollmer (ed). *Proceedings of the First Symposium of the Textile Society of America,* Minneapolis Institute of Art, Minneapolis, Sept. 16-18,1988, pp. 78-85.

——————— 'Textile Exchange in T'ai Societies,' in Proceedings of the Fourth International Conference on Thai Studies, 11-13 May 1990, Vol I, Institute of Southeast Asian Studies, Kunming, China, pp. 363-371.

——————— 'Contexts and Meanings in Tai Textiles,' in M. Gittinger and L. Lefferts (eds.), *Textiles and the Tai*

Experience in Southeast Asia (Washington D.C.: Textile Museum, 1992).

——————— 'The Ritual Importance of the Mundane, ' *Expedition* Vol. 38, No. 1, 1996, pp. 37-49.

Le May, Reginald, *An Asian Arcady:The Land and Peoples of Siam* (Cambridge: W. Heffer and Sons Ltd., 1926, reprinted Bangkok: White Lotus, 1986).

Li, Li., 'China's Silk Trade: Traditional Industry in the Modern World 1842-1937,' Ph.D. dissertation, Harvard University, Boston, Mass., 1981.

Ling-Roth, H., *Studies in Primitive Looms* (Halifax: Bankfield Museum, 1918, reprinted Bedford: Ruth Bean, 1978).

Lowndes, Captain, 'British Burma Journal of Captain Lowndes whilst on a Mission to the Zimme Court,' [Lowndes Journal] Foreign Office Report 69/55, March 27- May 30 1871, Public Records Office, Kew, London.

Luce, Gordon, 'Rice and Religion: a study of Old Mon-Khmer evolution and culture,' *Journal of the Siam Society,* Vol. XXXVI, 1962, pp.139-152.

Mabbett, I. W., 'Introduction: The Comparative Study of Traditional Political Institutions,' in Mabbett, I. W. (ed.), *Patterns of Kingship and Authority in Traditional Asia* (Kent: University of Kent, 1985).

Malinowski, Bronislaw, *Magic, Science and Religion and Other Essays* (Boston: Beacon Press, 1948).

Mana, Thongsotsaeng, *Suksa silapa lai thai* [Study in Thai Design] (Bangkok: Ruamsan, 1979).

Mangrai, S. (trans.), 'The Padaeng Chronicle and the Jengtung State Chronicle,' in A. Becker, P. Hook, J. Musgrave and T. Trautman (eds.), *University of Michigan Papers on South and Southeast Asia* No. 19, University of Michigan, Ann Arbor, Mich., 1981.

Maxwell, Robyn, *Textiles of South-East Asia:Tradition, Trade and Transformation* (Canberra: Australian National Gallery/ Melbourne: Oxford Uni. Press, 1990).

Maxwell-Hill, A.,'Familiar Strangers: The Yunnanese Chinese in Northern Thailand,' Ph.D. dissertation, University of Illinois, Illinois, 1982.

McCarthy, James, *An Englishman's Siamese Journals 1890-1893* (London published privately 1895, rep. Bangkok: Siam Media International, n.d.).

——————— *Surveying and Exploring in Siam* (London: John Murray 1900, reprinted Bangkok: White Lotus 1994).

McCleod, Captain, 'A Journal kept by Captain W.C. McCleod, Assistant to the Commissioner in the Tenassarim Provinces, during his Mission to the Frontiers of China,' The British Library, India Record and Oriental Collections, Parliamentary Papers Vol. 50 (1867/ 1868), London.

McGilvary, Daniel, 'Letter Nov. 20 1877,' Presbyterian Historical Society, Philadelphia. (Microfilm collections, Payap University Archive, Chiang Mai).

——————— *A Half Century Among the Lao* (New York and London: Fleming H. Revell, 1912).

McGilvary, Emilie, 'Letter June 1877', in *Woman's Work for Woman and Our Mission Field,* Vol. II, 1877, Presbyterian Historical Society, Philadelphia. (Microfilm collection, Payap University Archive, Chiang Mai).

——————— 'Letter Nov. 16 1877', *Woman's Work for Woman and Our Mission Field,* Vol. II 1877, Presbyterian Historical Society, Philadelphia. (Microfilm collection, Payap University Archive, Chiang Mai).

——————— 'Letter May 5 1883,' in *Woman's Work for Woman and Our Mission Field* Vol XIII, 1883, Presbyterian Historical Society, Philadelphia (Microfilm collection, Payap University Archive, Chiang Mai).

Milne, Leslie and Cochrane, Wilbur, *Shans at Home* (London: John Murray, 1910, reprinted New York: Paragon Book Reprint. Corp., 1970).

Moerman, Michael, 'Who are the Lue: ethnic identification in a complex civilisation,' *American Anthropologist,* Vol. 67, 1965, pp. 1215-1229.

——————— 'Chiangkham's Trade in the "Old Days,"' in G. William Skinner and A. Thomas Kirsch (eds.), *Change and Persistence in Thai Society: Essays in Honor of Lauriston Sharp* (Ithaca: Cornell University Press, 1975).

Naenna, Patricia, 'The Classification of Tai Textiles,' Paper presented at 3rd International Conference on Tai Studies, Canberra, Australia, 1987.

——————— *Lao Textiles: Ancient Symbols-Living Art* (Bangkok: White Lotus, 1988).

Nai Bancha Phumasathan, 'Report of Nai Bancha Phumasathan,' in The National Library, Bangkok, files of Krom Mahatthai M65/2, trans. and ed. by Constance M. Wilson in *The Burma-Thailand Frontier Over Sixteen Decades* (Athens: Ohio University, 1985).

Nartsupha, Chatrathip and Prasartset, Suthy (eds.), *The Political Economy of Siam 1851-1910* (Bangkok: The Social Science Association of Thailand, 1978).

Nash, Manning, *The Cauldron of Ethnicity in the Modern World* (Chicago: University of Chicago, 1989).

Nathalang, Siraporn, 'Tai Creation Myths: reflections of Tai Relations and Tai Cultures,' in *Tai Culture* Vol. II. No.1, Berlin,1997, pp. 56-66).

Navigamule, Anake, *Costumes and Fashion of the Ratannakosin Period* (Bangkok: Muang Boran Publishing House, 1982).

Nimmanhaeminda, Kraisri, 'Putting Vegetables into Baskets and People into Towns' in L. M. Hanks and L. Sharp (eds.) *Ethnographic Notes on Northern Thailand,* Cornell data Paper No. 8, Cornell Uni., Ithaca, New York, 1965.

——————— 'An Inscribed Silver Plate Grant to the Lawa of Boh Luang,' in *Felicitation Volumes of Southeast Asian Studies Presented to Prince Dhaninivat on his Eightieth Birthday,*Vol. 2, pp. 233-240 (Bangkok: The Siam Society, 1965).

——————— 'The Irrigation Laws of King Mengrai,' in L.M. Hanks and L. Sharp (eds.). *Southeast Asia Program,* Paper no. 58, Cornell University, Ithaca, New York, 1966.

——————— 'The Lawa Guardian Spirits of Chiang Mai, ' *Journal of the Siam Society,* Vol. 55, 1967, pp. 185-225.

No na Paknam & Kanokpongchai, Sangaroon, *Wat Phumin and Wat Nong Bua* (Bangkok: Muang Boran Publ., 1986).

Notton, Camille (trans.), *Annales du Siam* Vol. 1 (Paris: Imprimeries Charles-Lavauzelle, 1926).

O'Connor, Deryn, *Miao Costumes from Guizhou Province South West China* (Farnham: James Hockey Gallery, West Surrey College of Art and Design, University of Surrey, 1994).

Ongskul, Saraswadi, *Prawatsat Lan Na* (Chiang Mai: Chang Kan Pim, 1986, BE 2529) (in Thai).

——————— (trans. and ed.), *Lakthan prawattisat lan na cak ekkasan khampi bailan la phapnangsa* [Documents on the History of Lan Na from Palm Leaf Manuscripts] (Chiang Mai: Chiang Mai University, 1993).

Panichpant, Vithi, *Wiang Ta Murals* (Bangkok, 1993).

Pannikar, K.N., 'The Great Shoe Question: Tradition, Legitimacy and Power in Colonial India,' *Studies in History* Vol. 14, No. 1, New Delhi: Sage Pub., 1998, pp.32-47.

Pasqual, J.C., *A Trip Through Siam* (Penang: Gazette Press, 1926).

Patcharee, Pokasamrithi, *Pha Thai* (Bangkok, n.d.) (in Thai).

Peetathawatchai, Vilmophan, *Esarn Cloth Design* (Khon Kaen: Faculty of Education, Khon Kaen University, 1973).

Penth, Hans, 'On the History of Chiang Mai,' *Journal of the Siam Society,* Vol. 77, Pt. 1, 1989, pp. 11-32.

——————— *A Brief History of Lan Na* (Chiang Mai: Silkworm Books, 1994).

——————— *Jinkalamali Index: An Annotated Index to the Thailand part of Ratanapanna's Chronicle Jinakalamali* (Oxford: The Pali Text Society, 1994).

Peoples, Mrs., 'Letter June 1885' in *Woman's Work for Woman and Our Mission Field,* Vol. XV, 1885, Presbyterian Historical Society, Philadelphia (Microfilm collection, Payap University Archive, Chiang Mai).

——————— 'Letter Sept. 1890' in *Woman's Work for Woman and Our Mission Field,* Vol. V, 1890, Presbyterian Historical Society, Philadelphia (Microfilm collection, Payap University Archive, Chiang Mai).

Perkins, S., 'Laos, Land and Life,' S. Schenectady (ed.), *Siam and Life* (Philadelphia: Presbyterian Board of Publication, 1884).

Phayre, Sir A, *History of Burma* (London: Susil Gupta,1883).

Pisit Charoenwongsa and Diskul, Subhadradis M.C., *Archaeologia Mundi* (Geneva: Nagel, 1978).

Phuaphansakun, Pathom, 'The Domestic Architecture of the Khon Tai in Mae Hong Son,' in *National Seminar on Oral Tradition* (Thailand), Sri Nakharinwirot Uni., Phitsanulok, 1-5 November, 1981.

Potter, Sulamith Heins, *Family Life in a Northern Thai Village* (Berkeley: University of California Press, 1977).

Prangwatthanakun, Songsak, 'Northern Thai Textiles,' in *Thai Textiles: Threads of Cultural Heritage* (Bangkok: National Identity Board, 1994).

Prangwattanakun, Songsak and Naenna, Patricia, 'Southern Thai Textiles,' in *Thai Textiles: Threads of Cultural Heritage* (Bangkok: National Identity Board, 1994).

Prangwattanakun, Songsak and Cheesman, Patricia, *Lan Na Textiles: Yuan Lue Lao* (Chiang Mai: Center for the Promotion of Arts and Culture, Chiang Mai University, 1987).

Prasert na Nakara, *Mengraisastra: The Laws of King Mengrai* (Bangkok: Liengsieng Charoen, 1977).

Prasartset, Suthy, *A Study of Production and Trade of Thailand* (Bangkok: Social Science Association of Thailand, 1975).

Premchit S. and Tuikheo P. (trans.), 'A List of Old Temples and Religious Sects in Chiang Mai,' Transliteration Series No. 7, Chiang Mai University, Chiang Mai, 1975 (in Thai).

Premchit, Sommai (trans.), *Tamnan Chiangmai,* Transliteration Series No. 10, Chiang Mai University, Chiang Mai, 1978 (in Thai).

Premchit, Sommai and Dore, Amphay, *The Lan Na Twelve Month Traditions* (Chiang Mai: So Sap Kan Pim, 1992).

Presbyterian Board of Publication, *Siam and Laos, As Seen by Our American Missionaries* (Philadelphia: Presbyterian Board of Publications, 1884).

Pritsana, Sirinam, 'Khwamsamphan Rawang Thai Lae Prathetsart Nai Huamuang Lan Na Thai Samai Rattanakosin Ton Son [The Relations between Thailand and the Tributary States in the North during the Early Bangkok Period] M.A. thesis, Chulalongkorn University, Bangkok, 1973.

——————— 'Khwamsamphan Rawang Thai lae Prathetsarat nai Huamuang Lan Na Thai Prown,' in D. Jules, *Mind in Matter: An Introduction to Material Culture Theory and Method,* Dept. of the History of Art, Yale University, Conn., 1982.

Quaritch Wales, H.G., *Siamese State Ceremonies* (London: Curzon Press,1931).

——————— *The Universe Around Them* (London: Curzon Press, 1977).

——————— *Divination in Thailand* (London: Curzon Press, 1983).

Rajadhon, Anuman, *Life and Ritual in Old Siam: Three Studies of Thai Life and Customs* (trans. and ed. W. Gedney), (New Haven: HRAF Press, 1961).

——————— *Some Traditions of the Thai and Other Translations of Phya Anuman Rajadhon's Articles on Thai Customs* (Bangkok: Thai Inter-religious Commissions for Development and Sathirakoses Nagapradipa Foundation, 1987).

Ramsay, J.A., 'The Development of a Bureaucratic Polity: The Case of Northern Siam,' Ph.D. Dissertation, Cornell University, 1971).

Ratanaporn, Sethakul, 'Political Relations Between Chiang Mai and Kengtung in the Ninteenth Century,' in Prakai Nontawasee (ed.), *Changes in Northern Thailand and the Shan States, 1886-1940* (Singapore: Institute of Southeast Asian Studies, 1988).

Ratanapanna, Thera, *Jinakalamali-pakaranam* [The Sheaf of Garlands of the Epochs of the Conqueror] Mss. Rattavanavihara Temple, Chiang Mai, 1516. (N.A. Jayawickrama, trans.) (reprinted London: The Pali Text Society, Translation Series 36, 1968).

Reid, Anthony, *Slavery, Bondage and Dependency in Southeast Asia* (St. Lucia: University of Queensland, 1983).

—————— *Southeast Asia in the Age of Commerce 1450-1680,* Vol. 1, *The Land Below the Winds* (New Haven: Yale University Press, 1988).

Rhum, Michael, 'The Cosmology of Power in Lanna, '*Journal of the Siam Society,* Vol. 75, 1987, pp. 91-107.

—————— *The Ancestral Lords,* Special Report No. 29, Monograph Series on Southeast Asia, DeKalb,: Center for Southeast Asian Studies, Northern Illinois University, 1994.

Richardson, David, 'Journal of Missions to the Shan States, Siam and Ava,' Manuscript no. 30.354, 1830-1836, British Library, Western Manuscript Dept. British Museum, London.

—————— 'Burma Siam Frontier,' India Office Political and Secret Dept. L/P &S/20 D/221/1-3 D222, India Office Library Collections, British Library, London.

Roach-Higgins, M.E., 'Fashion,' in G. Sproles (ed.), *Perspectives of Fashion* (Minneapolis: Burgess Publishing 1981).

Roach-Higgins, M.E. and Eicher, J.B., *Adornment and the Social Order* (New York: John Wiley and Sons, 1965).

Roach-Higgins, M.E. and Eicher, J.B., 'Dress and Identity' *Clothing and Textile Research Journal,* Vol. 10, No. 4, 1992, pp.1-10.

Rooney, Dawn F., *Betel Chewing Traditions in South-East Asia* (Kuala Lumpur: Oxford University Press, 1993).

Rosenfield, Clare and Mabry, Mary Connelly 'The Art of Teen Jok' *Sawasddi* Vol. 40 no. 2, 1994.

Ryder, Michael, L., 'Silk: a touch of luxury,' *Biologist* Vol. 42, No. 2, 1995, pp. 52-55.

Saraya, D.,'The Development of the Northern Tai States from the 12th- 15th Centuries,' Ph.D. dissertation, History Dept, University of Sydney, 1982.

Sarkar, Sumit, *The Swadeshi Movement in Bengal, 1903-1908* (New Delhi: Peoples Publishing House, 1973).

Satow, Ernst Sir, 'Letter from Satow to Gould,' Mss. F.O. 628/10/149, March 3 1885, Public Records Office, Kew, London.

—————— 'Journal of Sir Ernest Satow,' Mss 206: PRO 30/33/20/1, 21/1,1885-1886 Public Records Office, Kew, London.

Schenectady, S. (ed.), *Siam and Laos* (Philadelphia: Presbyterian Board of Publication, 1884).

Schneider, J. and Weiner, A., *Cloth and Human Experience* (Washington D.C. and London: Smithsonian Institution Press, 1989).

Schomburgk, R. H., 'A Visit to Xieng Mai, the Principal City of the Laos of the Shan States,' *Journal of the Royal Asiatic Society of Bengal,* Vol. 32, 1863, pp. 387-399.

Scott, J.G., *Burma and Beyond* (London: Grayson and Grayson, 1932).

Scott J.G. and Hardiman, J.P., *Gazeteer of Upper Burma and The Shan States,* Vol. 1 and Vol. II (Rangoon: Superintendent of Government Printing, 1900, 1901).

Seidenfaden, Erik, 'The Lawa: additional note', *Journal of the Siam Society,* Vol. XXVII, 1923, pp. 101-102.

—————— 'Siam Tribal Dresses,' *Journal of the Siam Society,* Vol. XXX, Pt. 3, 1938, pp.169-178.

—————— *Prebuddhistic Beliefs of the Peoples of Western and Central Indo-China* (Moscow: Oriental Literature Publishing House, 1958).

—————— *The Thai Peoples* (Bangkok: Siam Society, 1963).

Sethakul, Ratanaporn, 'Political, Social and Economic Changes in the Northern States of Thailand Resulting from the Chiang Mai Treaties 1874 and 1883,' Ph.D. dissertation, Dept. History, University of Illinois, Illinois, 1989.

Sheanakul, Nisa, 'Exhibition of Teen Jok Textiles,' *Siam Society Newsletter,* Vol. 2, No 2, 1986, pp. 9-10.

Sheares, Constance, 'The Ikat Technique of Textile Patterning in Southeast Asia,' *Heritage 4,* National Museum, Singapore, 1983, pp.33.

—————— 'Ikat Patterns from Kampuchea, Stylistic Influences,' *Heritage 7,* National Museum, Singapore, 1984, pp. 45-53.

Shils, E., *Tradition* (Chicago: University of Chicago Press, 1981).

Simatrang, Sone, *The Structure of Lan Na Mural Paintings,* Vol. 2 (Bangkok: Silpakorn University Press, 1983).

—————— (ed.), *Burmese Design Through Drawings* (Bangkok: The Toyota Foundation, 1993).

Singer, Noel, F., 'Palm Leaf Manuscripts of Myanmar,' *Arts of Asia,* Jan.-Feb. 1991, pp.133-140.

Sirinam, P., 'Relations between Siam and the Tributary States in Lan Na Thai during the Early Bangkok Period,' M.Ed. dissertation, College of Education, Chiang Mai, 1973.

Smith, M., 'Dutch East India Company of Ayutthaya 1604-1694' Ph.D. dissertation, Dept. of History, Northern Illinois University, Illinois, 1977.

Smutkupt, Suriya, 'Ways of Isan Weaver: The Development of Textile Production and Changing Roles of Women in Contemporary Isan Villages,' in *International Seminar Textiles: Common Heritage of Southeast Asia,* Thailand Cultural Centre, Sept. 16-17 1993.

Somasorn, Pairote, *E-Sarn Mural Paintings* (Bangkok: Amarin Publishing Group, 1989).

Sommai, Premchit (ed.), *Rai chu wat la nikai boran nai muang chiang mai* [List of Old Monasteries and Religious Sects in Chiang Mai], Transliteration series no.7, Chiang Mai University, 1975).

Steinberg, David J. (ed.), *In Search of Southeast Asia* (Honolulu: University of Hawaii Press, 1971, reprinted1987).

Steadman, Philip, *The Evolution of Designs* Cambridge University Press, 1979.

Stone, G., 'Appearance and the Self,' in A.M. Rose (ed.), *Human Behaviour and the Social Processes: An Interactionist Approach* (New York: Routledge and Kegan Paul, 1962).

Straub, Marianne, *The Significance of Yarn,* Lecture at the Royal College of Art, London, 1981 (n.p.).

Stringer, C.E.W. Acting Vice Consul, 'Trade Report of Chiang Mai, 1890,' *Rangoon Gazette Weekly Budget,* May 16, 1891.

————————— 'Report by Mr. C.E.W. Stringer of a Journey to the Lao State of Nan, Siam,' Parliament Papers by Command, C5321, London.

Sunait, Chutintaranond, and Than Tun, *On Both Sides of the Tenasserim Range: History of Siamese-Burmese Relations,* Asian Studies Monographs No. 050, Chulalongkorn University, Bangkok, 1995.

Swanson, Herbert, *Khrischak Muang Nua:* A Study in Northern Thai Church History, (Chuan Printing Press 1984).

————————— 'In Transition: Single Women, Women's Roles and Presbyterian Missions in Siam 1874-1885,' Office of History, Church of Christ in Thailand, Payap University, 1996.

Swearer, Donald K., 'The Northern Thai City as a Sacred Center,' in L. Bardwell Smith and Holly Baker Reynolds (eds.), *The City as a Sacred Center: Essays on Six Asian Contexts* (Leiden: E.J.Brill, 1987).

Swearer, Donald K. and Dokbuakaew, *Tamnan Ang Salang* [The Chronicle of the Water Basin], Chiang Mai (in the process of translation, n.p.).

Swift, Gay, *Embroidery Techniques* (New York: Larousse and Co., 1984).

Talbot-Kelly, R., *Burma* (London: A. and C. Black Ltd., 1905).

Tambiah, Stanley J., *Buddhism and The Spirit Cults in North-east Thailand* Cambridge University Press, 1970.

————————— *World Conqueror and World Renouncer* (Cambridge: Cambridge University Press, 1976).

Tan-kim-yong, Uraivan, 'Resource Mobilization in Traditional Irrigation Systems of Northern Thailand. A Comparison between the Lowland and the Upland Irrigation Communities' Ph.D. dissertation, Cornell University, Ithaca, New York, 1983.

Tannenbaum, Nicola, 'Power, Gender and Buddhism: Gender in Thailand Reconsidered,' typescript, n.d.

Tarling, Nicholas, *A Concise History of Southeast Asia* (New York: Praeger, 1966).

Taylor, Hugh, 'Autobiography of Hugh Taylor' Mss. 1888-1930:166-167, Payap University Archive, Chiang Mai.

Taylor, R., 'Change in Thailand and the Shan States 1886-1940,' School of Oriental and African Studies, London, 1997.

Thamawat, Jaruwan, *The Poetry of the Lay People* (Bangkok: Maha Sarakham University, 1980) (in Thai).

Thao Sittimongkhon, 'The Report Of Thao Sitthimongkhon On The Re-establishment Of Chiang Rai And Its Borders,' in Constance M. Wilson and Lucien M. Hanks, *'The Burma-Thailand Frontier Over Sixteen Decades: Three Descriptive Documents,'* Monograph in International Studies, Southeast Asia Series, No. 70, Uni. of Ohio, Athens, 1985.

Thongmitr, Wiyada, 'Preface,' in Kanokpongchai (ed.), *Wat Phra Singh* (Bangkok: Muang Boran Publishing House, 1983).

Thongthep, M. (ed.), *Ramakien: The Thai Ramayana* (Naga Books, 1993).

Thongchua, Paothong, 'The Original Design of Tai Yuan Fabrics,' *Silk Magazine* Vol. 2, No. 17, 1994, 104-114.

Turton, Andrew, 'Matrilineal Descent groups and Spirit Cults of the Thai-Yuan in Northern Thailand,' *Journal of the Siam Society,* Vol. 60, 1972, pp. 217-256.

————————— 'Northern Thai Peasant Society: A Case Study of Jural and Political Structures at the Village level and their Twentieth Century Transformations,' Ph. D. dissertation, School of Oriental and African Studies, University of London, 1975.

U Aye Myint (trans. U Thanoe), *Burmese Design Through Drawings* (Bangkok: Silpakorn University, 1993).

Udom, Roongruangsiri, *Tamnan Phun Muang Chiang Mai* [History of the Town of Chiang Mai: Chiang Mai Seven Hundred Years Anniversary], Center for the Promotion of Arts and Culture, Chiang Mai University, 1996.

U.K., 'U.K. Report for the Year 1891 on the Trade of Chiengmai' ZHC1/5466 #

1089 Public Records Office, Kew, London.

U.K., 'The Secretary to the Chief Commissioner Foreign Office Series no. 69/59, 17th July 1874', Public Records Office, Kew, London.

Van Vliet, *Description of the Kingdom of Siam* (Leyden: Frederik Haaring, 1692).

Vatikiotis, Michael, 'Ethnic Pluralism in the Northern Thai City of Chiang Mai,' Ph.D. dissertation, St. Catherine's College, University of Oxford, 1984.

Viravaidya, Putrie (Kritakara), M.R., 'Domestic Arts of the Grand Palace' in *1994 Festival of American Folklore* (Washington, Dc: Smithsonian Institution, 1994).

Warington Smyth, H., *Five Years in Siam,* Vol. I and Vol. II (London: John Murray, 1898).

Webb, J., 'Burma and Southeast Asia,' Lecture to the Royal Asiatic Society, London, 1983 (n.p.).

Weiner, A. and Schneider, J. (eds.), *Cloth and Human Experience* (Washington, DC: Smithsonian Institution Press, 1989).

White, J., *Ban Chiang: Discovery of a Lost Bronze Age* (Philadelphia: University of Philadelphia Press, 1982).

Wheatley, Paul, 'Urban Genesis in Mainland South East Asia, in Smith and Watson (eds.), *Early South East Asia* (London, 1979).

Wichiencharoen, Adul, 'The Buddhist Vision in Thai Art,' (Bangkok: *UNESCO Courier,* 1980), pp.25-41.

Wichienkaew, Aroonrut, 'An Analysis of Chiang Mai Society in the Rattakosin Period,' Ph.D. dissertation, Chulalongkorn University, Bangkok, 1977 (in Thai).

Wichienkhaew, Aroonrut, *Lan Na Suksa* [Thai Studies], Chiang Mai, 1981 (in Thai).

Wijeyewardene, Gehan, 'Northern Thai Succession and the Search for Matriliny' *Mankind* Vol. 14, No. 4, 1984, pp. 286-292.

————————— *Place and Emotion in Northern Thai ritual Behaviour* (Bangkok: Pandora, 1986).

————— (ed.), 'Thailand and the Tai Versions of Ethnic Identity,' in *Ethnic Groups Across National Boundaries in Southeast Asia*. (Singapore: Institute of Southeast Asian Studies, 1990.

Wilson, Constance, 'State and Society in the Reign of Mongkut 1851-1868: Thailand on the Eve of Modernisation,' Ph.D. dissertation, Cornell University, Ithaca, New York, 1970.

Wilson, Constance, M. and Hanks, Lucien, M., '*The Burma-Thailand Frontier Over Sixteen Decades: Three Descriptive Documents,*' Monograph in International Studies, Southeast Asia Series, No. 70, (Athens:University of Ohio, 1985).

Wilson, J., 'From Bangkok to Chiang Mai' in Schenectady, S. (ed.), *Siam and Laos* (Philadelphia: Presbyterian Board of Publication, 1884).

Wilson, Verity, *Chinese Dress* (London: Victoria and Albert Museum, 1986).

Wood, W.A.R., *A History of Siam* (London: 1926, reprinted Bangkok: Chalermit, 1959).

————— *Consul in Paradise* (London Souvenir Press, 1965, reprinted Chiang Mai: Trasvin Publ., 1991).

Woodward, Hiram, 'Indonesian Textile Patterns From a Historical Point of View,' in M. Gittinger (ed.), *Indonesian Textiles* (Washington DC: The Textile Museum, 1979).

Wray, E., Rosenfield, C., and Bailey D., *Ten Lives of the Buddha* (New York and Tokyo: Weatherhill, 1972).

Wyatt, David, 'The Chronology of Nan History, AD1320-1598,' *Journal of the Siam Society,* Vol. 64, 1976, pp. 202-206.

————— *Thailand: A Short History* (Yale: Yale University Press, 1982).

————— *Temple Murals as an Historical Source: The Case of Wat Phumin* (Bangkok: Nan Thai Studies Section, Faculty of Arts, Chulalongkorn University, 1993).

————— 'The Case for the Northern Thai Chronicles,' Paper for the Fifth International Conference on Thai Studies, School of Oriental and African Studies, London, July 1993.

————— (trans. and ed.), *The Nan Chronicle,* Studies on Southeast Asia No 16, Southeast Asia Program, (Ithaca: Cornell University, 1994).

Wyatt, David and Aroonrut, Wichienkaew (trans. and ed.), *The Chiang Mai Chronicle* (Silkworm Books, 1995).

Wyatt, James and Wardwell, Anne, *When Silk Was Gold: Central Asian and Chinese Textiles* (New York: The Metropolitian Museum of Art, 1997).

Young, George, *The Hill Tribes of Northern Thailand* (Bangkok: The Siam Society, 1962).

Yule, Henry, *A Narrative of the Governor General of India to the Court of Ava in 1855* (London: Smith Elder and Co., 1858, reprinted Kuala Lumpur: Oxford University Press, 1968).

Yunnan People's Publishing House, *The Folk Arts of Yunnan Ethnics* (Kunming: Yunnan People's Publishing House, n.d.) (in Chinese).

Zhu Liangwen, *The Dai* (Bangkok: D.D. Books and Kunming: The Science Technology Press, 1993).

TAI CHRONICLES

Chamadevivamsa (Chronicle of Chamadevi) (Georges Coedès, trans. 1926), (Paris: 1926).

Chronique de Xieng Mai (C. Notton, trans.), *Annales du Siam* Vol. 3. (Paris: Libraire Orientaliste Paul Geuthner, 1932).

The Jengtung State Chronicle (Sao Saimong Mangrai, trans.). Michigan Papers on South and Southeast Asia, University of Michigan, Ann Arbor, 1981.

The Nan Chronicle (P. Churatana, trans. and D. Wyatt, ed.), Data paper 59, Southeast Asia Program, Cornell University, Ithaca, 1966.

Tamnan Phuen Muang Lan Na Chiang Mai (Sommai Premchit ed. and The Palm Leaf Text Studies Project, trans.), Chiang Mai Social Research Institute, Chiang Mai University, 1981.

The Chiang Mai Chronicle (D. Wyatt and A. Wichienkaew trans. and ed.), (Chiang Mai: Silkworm Books, 1995).

ARCHIVES

Payap University Archive, Chiang Mai, Manuscript Division Record Group: Siam and Laos, Presbyterian Missions 1840-1910.

  McGilvary family papers 1849-1963.

  Papers of Dan Bradley 1906-1976.

  Violet Posayawat Photographic Collection

  Papers and Photographic Collection. of Dr. Samuel Craig Peoples, 1896-1917 RG 008/90.

National Library, Bangkok.

National Archives, Bangkok.

Photographic Archives, Chiang Mai National Museum, Chiang Mai.

Siam and Laos Missions 1840-1910, Presbyterian Historical Society, Philadelphia.

Photographic Archives, Asia, The Pitt Rivers Museum, Oxford.

The Green Centre for Non-Western Art at the Royal Pavilion Art Gallery and Museums, Brighton.

Public Records Office, Kew, London.

The Oriental and India Office Collections, The British Library, London.

The Asian Collections, National Museums and Galleries on Merseyside, Liverpool.

GLOSSARY

appliqué The sewing of one fabric on top another.

atwinwun Secretary of State, Mandalay.

bodhisattva a being on the way to Enlightenment.

bunbangfai a rain-making ceremony addressed to guardian spirits.

bun kathin Buddhist ceremony of merit making held between October and November.

bun khaw saak A ceremony to invoke the spirits of ancestors to guard the rice.

bun phrawes Buddhist ceremony of merit making held after the rice harvest.

chao prince.

chao burirat the third prince in the hierarchy.

chao chiwit title meaning Lord of Life.

chao luang the senior prince.

chao ratchabut a prince loyal to the *chao luang*.

chao ratchawong a prince loyal to the *chao luang*.

chao uparaj the second prince.

chedi a religious mound containing sacred relics. May also be called *stupa*.

chii a chaw single woven stripes in a Karen *phasin*.

chong kraben Silk trousers created by wrapping a large rectangle of silk around the waist, passing through the legs and secured with a belt.

corvee mandatory labour

couching yarn or wire stitched on the surface of cloth.

dam hua a ritual bathing ceremony.

deva Buddhist worshipping image.

discontinuous supplementary weft (jok) yarns are picked into a ground weave by hand.

ein gyi fitted blouse or jacket.

farang Caucasian.

floss silk silk used as embroidery thread.

fuum kan a reed with teeth set close together.

fuum saa a reed with teeth set further apart.

gatha numbers, letters and symbols read as magical incantations.

hang karok yarns twisted together before weaving.

hua head.

hta-mein a floor length Burmese or Shan skirt.

ikat Malay/Indonesian word for a resist dye process when the yarns are tied in selected areas to prevent penetration of the dye. The patterns form when the yarn is woven.

jok to pick or lift, also used to describe a discontinuous supplementary weft technique.

Kachin hill-residing group in the Shan States.

Karen hill-residing group in Lan Na.

kathin presentation of gifts and robes to the monks.

kee krang red dye obtained from the resinous secretions of insects.

kha slave.

khao sanam luang the ruling council of Lan Na that selected the prince ruler.

khaw phansa the beginning of Buddhist Lent.

khit continuous supplementary weft patterns.

khon muang people of this *muang* (city-state).

khum a palace and its compound.

khunnang name for an official or administrator.

khunying Lady.

khwan spirit.

ko tapestry weave.

kuad khaw phi offering made on the advice of a spirit medium.

kwaen a village or district leader.

lai pattern.

lai chang elephant.

lai chiang saen Chiang Saen.

lai chofa roof gable.

lai dork flower.

lai dork mali jasmine.

lai dork picun small flower.

lai dork soey pretty flower.

lai fung hwang Chinese phoenix.

lai hamsa Pali for swan, Hindi for goose.

lai hang s'pao ripples of water in the wake of a boat.

lai hong swan or goose.

lai hong dum black swan or goose.

lai hong ku pairs of swans or geese facing.

lai hong nawn swan or goose sleeping.

lai kan kra hyong offering bowls.

lai kanok flame.

lai kan yaeng leaves.

lai khao lam tat diamonds.

lai khlun zig zags.

lai ko krua hooks.

lai lakhon Lampang.

lai ling monkey.

lai mali leuai jasmine flowers.

lai tang mo water melon.

lai nam lai   running water.

lai nam ton   water jug.

lai ngu (noo) loi   mouse.

lai nok   bird.

lai pha hol   bamboo.

lai phum khao bin   pannicle of rice.

lai rachasee   guardian beast.

lai singha   lion.

lai stupa   Buddhist monument.

lai sua   tiger.

Lawa   people from the Mon Khmer linguistic group. Today they live mainly in Chom Thong, Mae Chaem and Mae Hong Son.

luntaya   Burmese tapestry weave.

matmi   *see* ikat.

maun   cushion or pillow.

Mon   a valley-residing group who speak a Mon-Khmer language.

muang Tai   city-state.

naga   snake.

ning a mea   an 'eye' or 'third eye' design.

ning a saa   black stripes on a *phasin*.

nirvana   a the extinction of suffering embodied in the cycle of birth and rebirth.

payar   courtship prose.

pha   cloth.

pha chet   small wiping cloth.

pha chong kraben (*pha nung*, *pha toi*) a rectangle of cloth worn tucked and draped below the waist.

pha kan yaeng   cloth with a flame pattern, for use at the Siamese court.

pha yearabab (*khimkhab*)   a type of brocade imported from India.

pha lop   bed sheet.

pha hom   blanket.

phansa   Buddhist Lent.

pha pok lai thong   fabric with Siamese patterns.

pha sabai   a rectangular sash.

pha sarong   a man's tubular loin cloth.

phasin   tubular skirt.

phaso   ankle length Burmese or Shan skirt.

pha tung   temple banner.

pha yok   silk brocade.

phrai   citizen.

pla buk   a type of fish caught in the Mekong river.

prathetsarat   a vassal state.

rachasee   guardian beast.

sawbwa   a Shan ruler.

suea   shirt or blouse.

seua kop long daeng   a lined jacket.

seua pat   a side-fastening blouse.

sin mai kam   a tubular skirt worn in the eastern Shan States.

sin man   irregularly-spaced horizontal stripes in a *phasin*.

sin pong   evenly-spaced stripes in a *phasin*.

songkran   Buddhist New Year rites when Buddha images are ceremonially bathed.

stupa   *see* chedi.

sumptuary laws   laws controlling precedence at court, including dress codes.

Tai   people inhabiting Assam, south China, the Shan States, Laos and Thailand, many sub-groups have been classified.

Tai Khoen   Tai inhabiting the Eastern Shan States and parts of Lan Na.

Tai Lao   Tai inhabiting Laos and North-east Thailand.

Tai Lue   Tai inhabiting Sipsong Pan Na and parts of Lan Na.

Tai Yai (Shan or Ngio)   Tai inhabiting the Shan States and parts of Lan Na.

Tai Yuan (Yon, Yun, Yonoka)   the original Tai inhabitants of Lan Na.

tapestry weave *(ko)*   a plain weave of discontinuous weft.

teen   the hem of a *phasin*.

teen jok   patterned section of the hem of a *phasin*.

Thai   the people of Thailand.

tham   a type of script.

thammasat   law.

thepanum   a worshipping angel.

wat   a temple complex.

yak rung   a narrow rectangular cloth tucked and draped below the waist.

yantra   mystical symbolic diagrams.

yin-zi   a rectangular Burmese or Shan breast cloth.

Index

alchemy 80
amulet 84
aniline dyes 180, 233, 235
anointment 138
appliqué 110, 116, 117
Archer, W. 144, 220, 223
architecture 66-70
atwinwun 91
Ayutthaya 51, 92, 136, 184

Bangkok 44-45, 50, 51, 126, 131, 132, 135,
    148, 155, 219, 223, 224, 229, 230, 237,
    247, 249-250
Ban Nang Eng 148
banners, temple (*pha tung*) 15, 66, 72,
    244, 251
Bassenne, M. 224
beads 161
bed sheets 88
beetle wings 92, 110, 161
betel 87, 236
betel box 86, 87, 145, 151
blankets 88, 189, 243, 245
block printing 81, 187
blouse 100, 110, 111, 116, 151-153, 151,
    152, 161, 168, 172
Bock, C. 49, 87, 148-149, 220, 221, 236,
    246
bodhisattva 39, 85, 86, 90, 96, 256
body decoration 23, 81-82
Bowring, Sir J. 45, 99, 219
Bowring Treaties 219, 220, 221, 232,
    235
Britain 11, 46, 47, 48, 51, 132, 134, 146,
    147, 152, 173-174, 221, 232, 236
British Consulate, Chiang Mai 48, 138
broderie anglaise 152
Buddha image 13, 23, 80, 83
Buddhist Lent (*phansa*) 57
bunbangfai 57
bun kathin 58
bun khaw saak 58
bun phrawes 14, 58
Boonphun Rajamitri (Singholaka),
    Khunying 155
Burma (Myanmar) 11, 29, 40, 45, 46,
    51, 104, 116, 124, 132, 133, 139, 148,
    152, 164, 174, 213, 223, 230, 232, 235,
    241, 248
Burmese 10, 25, 26, 32, 35, 42, 48, 68,
    85, 92, 116, 133, 182, 221
Burmese court dress 91, 92
Burmese traders 217, 218, 233, 236,
    259

calico 219
Cambodia 47
caravans, trade 216, 217, 221, 223, 259

carpets 144
Chao Burirat 44
chao chiwit 43
chao luang 43
Chao Ratchabut 44
Chao Ratchawong 44
Chao Uparaj 43
chandeliers 144
Chiang Hung 104, 22, 223
Chiang Kham 28
Chiang Khong 42, 43
Chiang Mai 8, 12, 20, 24, 25, 26, 28, 32,
    42, 43, 66, 78, 85, 86, 95, 99, 104, 116,
    120, 131, 140, 148, 164, 182, 218, 219,
    219, 220, 222, 230, 233, 235, 236, 241
Chiang Mai chronicle 18-19, 24, 36, 40,
    41, 42, 45, 66, 220, 231
Chiang Mai National Museum 68, 79, 142
Chiang Rai 25, 26, 220, 235
Chiang Rung 42, 70, 88, 95, 220
Chiang Saen 26, 39, 66, 92, 132, 182,
    220, 224, 235, 241
Chiang Tung 70, 88, 95, 116, 147, 164,
    223, 224, 241
chiffon 152
chii a chaw 97
China 11, 104, 146, 147, 174, 187, 236
Chinese dress 90, 147, 149, 222
Chinese phoenix 184
Chinese silk 93, 110, 136, 144, 161, 210,
    213, 221, 230, 235, 256, 260
Chinese silk yarn 100, 144, 150, 177-
    178, 221, 235, 237, 256
Chinese textile designs 139, 184
coats 136, 139, 140, 141, 142, 210, 211,
    259
Colquhoun, A. 95, 232
continuous supplementary weft (*khit* or
    muk) 111, 120, 183, 184, 185, 188,
    191-193, 193, 197, 200, 201, 214
corvée 30, 57, 217, 236
cotton 17, 55, 57, 95, 97, 110, 152, 210,
    218, 221, 224, 229, 230, 232, 236, 243
cotton netting 210
courtship prose (*payar*) 178
craft workers 66-70, 241-251
Crawfurd, Sir J. 229
crowns 136, 138
cushions (*maun*) 86, 88, 89

Dali 104, 220, 221
dam hua 50, 142
dancers 58, 132, 133, 140, 145
Delaporte 90
deva 21, 80, 83, 85, 96
discontinuous supplementary weft (*jok*)
    182, 206, 206, 207, 213
Dodd, W. 95, 161
dyes 180-181, 243

earlobes 140, 150
ear rings 150
ein gyi 124
elephants 132, 140, 145, 187, 220
embroidery 88, 89, 92, 110, 110, 116,
    117, 136, 140, 144, 158, 161, 164, 164,
    172, 210, 210, 221, 222, 227, 235, 240,
    242, 243
Emperor Fu Hsi 80
Emperor Wan-Li 184
ethnic dress and identity 23, 28, 65, 96-
    99, 126, 148, 156, 174

Fang 28, 132
farang 49
firearms 78, 134, 145
Fitch, R. 220
flannel 161, 222, 230
flock of birds pattern 182, 207
floor mats 139, 236
floral designs 182, 183, 188
floss silk 161
forest-dwelling monks 12, 23
foresters 48, 124
France 11, 46, 47, 48-49, 120, 132, 146,
    147, 152, 173-174
funeral chariot 86
furniture (palace) 144, 233
furniture (temple) 66, 67

Garnier, F. 90
gatha 14, 41, 81-83, 126, 133, 187
genealogy charts 262-265
Goetz, H 11
gold cloth 222
gold leaf 69, 86, 222
goldsmiths 66, 86-87, 242
gold thread 96, 100, 112, 116, 117, 120,
    151, 154, 168, 191, 206, 206, 221, 236,
    256, 257
gold wire 88, 110, 210
governors
    Aliyawong Wan Tok of Nan 37
    Nai Ai of Nan 37
    Noi Indra of Nan 15
    Nan Mano of Nan 37
    of Muang Lai 19
    Chao Phraya Luang Tin Mahawong of
    Nan 37
    Chao Mongkhonvaroyot of Nan 37
guerilla warfare 135

hair styles 78, 95, 99, 136, 140, 150,
    152, 156, 164, 172, 173
Hallett, H. 26, 64, 65, 144, 145, 146,
    148, 151, 152, 161, 172, 218, 220, 223 ,
    224, 230, 246
hamsa 187
Han Chinese 11, 37
hang karok 190, 191, 214

hang s'pao 182, 206
heddle pulleys 188
helmet 135, 136, 138
Hinduism 50, 51
Hinton, E. 96-97
Holland 47
hong 182
Hot 152
howdah 86, 86, 140, 141, 143, 145
hta-mein 124
hybrid dress 148, 156, 164, 172, 172

ikat (*matmi*) 120, 190, 194, 194, 195, 196, 197
India 10-11, 50, 139, 173, 184, 231, 235, 236, 257
Indian textiles 92, 94, 139, 234, 235
indigo 97, 236
Indonesia 47, 231, 236
intermarriage 163, 168
Inthakin pillar 24, 49, 142
Isaan 168
itinerant traders 96

jackets, for protection 82, 83
jackets 110, 110, 111, 116, 117, 118, 120, 120, 124, 124, 139, 151, 164, 172, 221, 235
jewellery 92, 95, 96, 96, 99, 150, 150, 152, 219
Jinakalamalipakarana 18, 84
Jin Dynasty 184
jok 100, 206

Kachin 18
kae ban 29
Kamol 184
kan kra hyong 182
kapok 88, 144
Karen 21-23, 26, 28-29, 28, 32, 96, 218
kathin 13
Kayah 26, 29
kha (slave) 29-31, 44, 65
khao sanam luang 26, 44, 87
Khmer 15, 50
khon muang 13, 23-25, 29, 242, 244, 248
Khun Borom 58
khunnang 44
khwan 83
kings
    Mengrai of Chiang 10, 24, 66, 215, 241
    Rama I of Siam 44, 45, 92, 136
    Rama III of Siam 44, 45
    Rama IV of Siam 45, 46
    Rama V of Siam 35, 39, 46, 48, 49, 91, 92 132, 134, 136, 139, 144, 146, 147, 152, 168, 173-174, 230, 247, 259
    Rama VI 134, 140, 142
    Rama VII 51, 141
    Sisawangwong of Luang Prabang 146

Zacharine of Luang Prabang 146, 147
kwaen 29

lace 152, 243, 250
lacquerware 66, 86-87, 224, 243
lai (pattern) 188
    chang 187
    chiang saen 182, 207
    chofa 206, 207
    dork 182
    dork mali 206
    dork picun 188, 193, 206
    dork soey 193
    fung hwang 184
    hamsa 187
    hang s'pao 182, 206, 207
    hong 182, 184, 206, 207
    hong dum 206, 207
    hong ku 184, 206
    hong nawn 206
    kan kra hyong 182, 206, 207
    kanok 184, 210
    kan yaeng 210
    khao lam tat 194, 206, 206, 207
    khlun 193
    ko krua 194, 206, 206, 207
    lakhon 182, 207
    ling 187
    mali leuai 206
    marg mo 194
    nam lai 115, 182
    nam ton 206, 206, 207
    ngu (noo) loi 187, 206
    nok 182, 184, 187, 206, 207
    pha hol 194
    phum khao bin 194
    rachasee 187, 213
    singha 187
    stupa 206
    sua 187
Lampang 8, 25, 28, 49, 66, 78, 94, 120, 132, 146, 148, 156, 177, 182, 220, 235, 248
Lamphun 8, 25, 12, 28, 66, 78, 94, 104, 132, 148, 156, 222, 230, 235, 248, 260
Lan Xang 70, 120
Laos 11, 25, 31, 41, 42, 45, 46, 47, 49, 146, 148, 152, 182
Lawa 18-22, 23, 24-29, 31, 96, 218
leggings 96, 98
Le May, R. 50, 138, 139, 155-156, 248
Lesser India 10
Lily Langtry 151
linen 152
logging 132
loom 57, 59, 59, 64, 188-190, 190, 246, 248
loom heddles 190
Lowndes, Capt. 232
Luang Prabang 10, 42, 43, 48, 88, 94,

102, 120, 146, 151, 168, 173, 224
luntaya 69, 92, 124, 124, 125, 153, 155, 157, 159, 160, 202, 203, 204, 205, 213, 224, 247

Mae Chaem 22, 156, 182, 194, 220, 260
Mae Hong Son 25, 28
Mae Sariang 28
Mahatma Gandhi 173
Malaysia 47, 236
Manchester 152, 232
Manchester cloth 222, 232, 236
Mandalay 116, 135, 147
manuscript cover 73, 244
marital alliances 8, 42-44, 65, 94-95, 104, 124, 126, 148, 152, 174
marriage customs 65
mathematical mysticism 80
mattress 88, 144
McCarthy, J. 39, 104, 219, 221, 222, 229, 230
McGilvary, D. 50, 86, 231, 246
McGilvary, E. 63, 64, 144, 151
Mekong River 132, 168, 222-224
merit 12, 50
military dress 78-84, 133-135
mirrors 144
missionaries 11, 29, 48, 61-65, 100
Mon 26, 28, 29, 32
money lenders 132
monopoly 132, 232, 246
Mon script 70
mordants 180, 243
Muang Sing 219, 231, 235
muang (Muang) 19, 23-24, 31, 35, 39, 42-45, 46, 49, 51, 52, 86, 88, 90, 100, 131, 132, 142, 146, 148, 174, 200, 219, 221, 223, 235246, 255-256
musicians 132, 133, 140, 145, 245
Moulmein 219, 220, 221, 222, 223, 230, 232, 233, 235, 236
muslin 219, 230, 235
mural painting 6, 16, 21, 22, 25, 26, 29, 30, 42, 45, 49, 56, 59, 61, 63, 67, 69-70, 79

naga 182
Nai Banchaphumasathan 133-134
Nakhon Si Thammarat 193
Nan 8, 25, 28, 40, 41, 43, 66, 78, 94, 104, 132, 148, 156, 235, 248
Nan Chronicle 18, 40, 42, 66, 92, 120, 248
needles 219
Nehru, J. 173
ning a mea 96
ning a saa 96
nirvana 12

offering bowl 182

ostrich feathers   139

Pa Kua   80
palaces (*khum*)   145, 144, 231-232, 242-
    250
palm leaf manuscripts   66, 69
parasol   93
Pa Sang   40
Pattani   193
Payap University Archive   99, 142, 150,
    173, 236
Penth, H.   18
Peoples, Mrs C.   63
petticoat   116, 117
pha (cloth)
    chet   88, 89
    chong kraben   31, 152, 172, 191, 195, 196
    kan yaeng   93
    khem khab   139
    pok rui thong   94
    sabai   99-100, 102-103, 120, 151
    yok   93
    phasin (skirt)
    Burmese (*phaso*)   158
    for protection   83
    Karen   28
    Lan Na   6, 46, 47, 53, 54, 65, 74, 76,
        88, 98, 127, 129, 144, 154, 161, 163,
        169, 214, 223, 228, 256, 257
    Lawa   97
    Nan   50, 62, 105, 108, 109, 112, 113,
        114, 115, 183
    Tai Khoen   116-119, 116, 117, 119, 162,
        163, 164, 165, 166, 167, 227
    Tai Lao   120-123, 121, 122, 123, 168,
        170, 171, 175, 193
    Tai Lue   104, 105, 161, 162, 166
    Tai Yai   124, 125, 157, 159, 160
    Tai Yuan   99, 99 151, 152, 155, 176
    tung   13
Phraya Prachachakrakornkit   141
Phayao   25, 28, 132, 156
Phraya Somtrai, wife and children   172
Phitsanulok   134, 222
Phra Amorawisai Soradet   134
Phrae   8, 25, 42, 43, 78, 94, 104, 120,
    145, 148, 156, 220, 224, 235
phrai (citizen)   29-31, 44, 65, 132, 244
Phra Maha Chakri Prasat   136, 138
Phu Sae   20
pillow (*maun*)   86, 88, 89, 144, 210, 210,
    243, 244, 246
Ping River   18, 19, 219, 230, 233, 246
plain weave   190-191
pollution   98, 178
polygamy   132
porters   217, 223, 224, 237
Prangwatthanakun   96
prathetsarat   48
princes (*chao*)
    Achittawong of Nan   37

Ariyawong Wan Tok   37
Anantayot of Nan   37, 42, 65, 92, 93
Attavorapanya of Nan   37, 40, 92, 93,
Bunma of Lamphun   38, 222, 246
Bunthawong of Chiang Mai   39, 78,
    78, 134, 144, 235, 246
Chai Kaew of Lampang   36
Chailungka Pisarn Soparkhun of
    Lamphun   38
Chai Worachakra   134
Chakraham Kajornsakdi of Lamphun
    38, 43, 64, 248
Chao Phraya Luang Tin Mahawong of
    Nan   37, 85
Dara Direkratana of Lamphun   38
Duang Thip of Lampang   38
Hemapintu Paijitt of Lamphun   38
Indra Waroros of Chiang Mai   37, 38,
    138-139
Indrayongyote Choti of Lamphun   38
Indra Witchayanon of Chiang Mai   21,
    22, 36, 37, 46, 49, 51, 77, 85, 131, 134,
    136, 139, 144, 218, 245
Intanon   94, 111, 164
Kaew Nawarat of Chiang Mai   37, 38,
    39, 131, 164, 247
Kawila of Chiang Mai   21, 22, 36, 37,
    38, 41, 42-43, 45, 65, 77, 85, 86, 104,
    116, 247
Kawiloros of Chiang Mai   31, 36, 37 ,
    45, 46, 51, 85, 86, 134, 141
Kham Som of Lampang   37, 38
Noranunchai of Lampang   38
Krom Luang Wongsa of Siam   99
Lawacangkara of the Tavatimsa
    Heaven   36, 85
Luang Kamton of Lamphun   38
Luang Thamma Lungka of Lamphun   38
Mahaprom of Chiang Tung   116
Maha Promsurathada 37, 43
Mahotara Phratet of Chiang Mai   37, 222
Mahayot of Nan   37
Mongkhonvaroyot   37
Noi Indra of Nan   15
Noi Indra of Lamphun   38
Pattana of Lamphun   248
Phichit Preechakorn of Siam   26, 140
Phuttawong of Chiang Mai   37, 78, 222
Promlue   31
Sakkarinrit   48
Setti Kamfan of Lamphun   37, 38, 116
Sirichai of Chiang Tung   116
Sulawa Leuchai Songkram (Thip
    Chang) of Lampang   36, 38, 86
Suriyapong Paritdej of Nan   cover, 34,
    38, 49, 136, 137, 138, 138-139, 138
Sumanadevaraj of Nan   37
Vajiravudh of Siam   143
princesses
    Alexandra of England   152
    Bua Kieuw   38

Bua Lai of Phrae   39
Chantima of Chiang Mai   116
Dararatsami of Chiang Mai   21, 49,
    130, 152-156, 153, 156, 174, 182, 230,
    246, 247, 247
Kam On of Luang Prabang   150
Ladakham   155, 161
Nang Wen Tip   95
Pongkaew of Chiang Mai   248
Sri Anocha of Chiang Mai   42, 45
Sukhantha of Chiang Tung   94, 116,
    164,
Tipkesorn of Chiang Mai   36, 63,
    151, 155, 218, 246, 247
Tipnetra of Chiang Mai   37
Ubonwanna of Chiang Mai   26, 63-
    64, 64, 65, 101, 124, 151, 152, 218,
    220, 222, 223, 224, 254
Suanboon of Lamphun   248
Prince of Chiang Rai   144
Prince of Chiang Rung   95
Prince of Lampang   44, 140, 144
Prince of Lamphun   93, 144, 145, 248
Prince of Luang Prabang   48
Prince of Nan   34, 40, 49, 132
Prince of Phrae   49, 145
Prince of Wales   151

Queen
    Chamdevi of Lamphun   84
    Chira Prapa   60
    Saowabha of Siam   152
    Sirikit of Thailand   250
    Victoria of England   139, 148, 172

railway   131, 142, 223, 224, 229, 232,
    237, 259
regalia   41, 86-87, 96, 136, 136, 138,
    145-146, 151, 173, 242, 256, 260
resettlement   26, 27, 132, 215, 244
ribbon   110, 172
rice cycle   17, 55-58
Richardson, D.   217, 222
rifles   134
ritual bathing   87
rubies   81, 150

satin   116, 161, 167, 221, 235
Satow, Sir E.   22, 49, 61, 134, 139, 145-
    146, 150, 177, 184
sawbwa   147, 149, 222, 225
Schomburgh, Sir R.   45
sequins   88, 92, 116, 117, 118, 119, 144,
    164, 210, 210, 224
sericulture   51, 57, 178, 231
seua kop long daeng   110, 111, 116, 161
seua pat   110, 111, 116, 161
Shan States   10-11, 18, 26, 28, 31, 41-
    42, 45, 69, 88, 94, 124, 133, 146, 147,
    152, 173, 178, 182, 223, 236
Shan traders   152, 217, 218, 223, 224,

280

233, 236, 259
shed sticks 191
shirts, for protection 41, 139, 146
Siam 10, 11, 13, 42, 43- 47, 49, 104,
    120, 142, 173, 220, 229-230, 232, 235,
    236, 244
Siamese 25, 28, 42, 44, 147
Siamese dress 50, 91-92, 172
Siamese High Commissioner 48-49,
    131, 132, 134, 140, 172
Siamese weaving 94, 243
silk cloth 221, 224, 235
silk filament 57, 178
silk, indigenous 17, 178, 221, 221, 231,
    236
silk, shot 190, 191
silk yarn 95, 100, 178, 221, 224, 235
silver foil 82, 84
silversmiths 66, 86-87, 242
silver thread 96, 100, 112, 116, 120,
    151, 168, 191, 206, 206, 208, 209, 212,
    221, 237, 248
Simao 220
Sinhalese Theravada Buddhism 12, 46,
    50, 126, 135, 187
sin mai kam 116
sin man 111
sin pong 111
Sipsong Pan Na 10, 26, 28, 31, 41, 42,
    43, 45, 69, 88, 94, 95, 104, 120, 146,
    148, 173, 182, 235
slaves (kha) 13, 22, 29-31, 44, 65, 132,
    218, 219, 244, 246
slippers 140
snake (naga) 182
songkran 57
Souei-Sa 91
spears 78, 145
spirit ceremonies 23, 84, 213
spirit doctor 13, 81
spirit religion 12, 19-20, 20, 23, 41, 46,
    80-81, 126, 135, 256
spittoons 145
stencilling 87
stick lac (shellac) 180, 229, 235
stockings 139, 172
stucco 87
stupa (monument) 10, 41, 66, 69, 182
sumptuary laws 126, 173, 213, 256, 260
Surat Thani 193
sword 79, 256

Tai 18, 21, 31
    Khoen 26-29, 31, 32, 43, 94, 95, 116,
        164, 224
    Lao 28-29, 31, 43, 94, 96, 168, 193
    Lue 26, 29, 31, 32, 43, 78, 94, 95,
        104, 110, 161, 164, 248
    Yuan 25-29, 31, 43, 65, 69, 78, 94, 96
Tai Yai (Shan) 26-29, 31, 32, 43, 68,
    78, 124, 222, 223, 248

Tak 25
talismans 41, 213
Tang Dynasty 184
tapestry weave (ko) see also luntaya 92,
    114, 115, 198, 198, 199, 200, 201
tattoos 81, 81, 186, 187, 187, 213, 256
Tavatimsa Heaven 35, 85, 86, 256
teak 48, 69, 132, 144, 217, 218, 229,
    232
teen jok 100, 104, 106, 107, 108, 120,
    155, 161, 179, 182, 188, 206, 206, 207,
    207, 208, 209, 212, 213, 227, 260
Thailand 10, 17, 25
tham (script) 70-71
thammasat 43
Thao Sittimongkhon 78
Thaton 28
Theravada Buddhism 12, 50, 51
Thoen 219, 229
thrones 86, 87, 136, 136, 145, 146
Tip Chang 86
traders 126, 132, 216-235
tribute 22, 44, 51, 65, 126, 139, 142,
    231, 244, 256, 259
tributary relations 88, 92, 217
trousers 81, 81, 136, 235
turban 84, 110, 116, 161, 256
tung yai 13

U Aye Myint 187, 204
umbrella, ceremonial 87, 145, 151, 235
USA 46
Uttaradit 25, 28, 219, 220, 229, 230

velvet 88, 100, 110, 144, 161, 210, 219,
    222, 224, 235
Vientiane 42, 43, 224
Vietnam 27, 47

Warington Smyth 232, 233
warp 190
wat (temple)
    Buak Khok Luang 16, 21, 42, 49, 79, 93
    Chamdevi 10
    Chedi Luang 49
    Ched Yot 85, 85
    Lai Hin 20, 56, 67, 85
    Phra That Lampang Luang 14, 30,
    56, 67, 68
    Lampang Rat Santan (Phayao) 10,
    24, 29
    Nong Bua 26, 61, 69, 98, 100
    Pa Daet 92, 98
    Phra Singh 25, 45, 60, 80, 135, 141,
    186, 232
    Phumin 15, 22, 45, 57, 59, 60, 79, 86,
    87, 95, 97, 187
    Pong Yang Kok 10, 56, 57
    Wiang Ta 8, 63
Water of Allegiance ceremony 45, 135,
    141, 173

weaving 58-60, 60, 243
weft 190
Wilson, Rev. 64
women
    as politicians 60, 257
    as polluters 84
    as professionals 60-61
    as protectors 83-84
    as slaves 65-66, 257
    as slave owners 63
    as spirit mediums 13, 60, 84, 257
    as traders, 60, 63-64, 99, 132, 218,
        219, 236, 237, 257
    as warriors 60
    education of, 64-65
    legal status of, 65
    male attitudes towards, 60-61
weaving designs 182-187
wood carving 66, 67, 70, 71, 87, 144
Wualai Road 78

Xieng Hong (Chiang Hong) 90

yak rung 81, 194
yantra 13, 14, 41, 71, 80-81, 81-83, 84,
    126, 133, 187, 187, 256
Ya Sae 20
yin-zi 124
Young, G. 96, 98
Yule, H. 44
Yunnanese traders 104, 110, 150, 152,
    177, 217, 220, 233, 235, 237, 259